Advance Praise for *Dearest S[...]*

"To read *Dearest Sister Wendy*...is to be touched by a depth of genuine communication and connection betw[...] Ellsberg is rare and exhilarating to behold. Yet, we are not simply left on the sidelines as admiring spectators. The Spirit animating the intimacy and scope of sharing between the two and bringing about challenge, healing, and enlightenment in the process also enfolds us into its transformative ambit. Page after page, I found myself moved and enriched in depths that I didn't even know existed. I am roundly convinced that it is impossible to overstate the blessedness and wonder of this remarkable book!" —**Michelle Jones, editor, *Ruth Burrows: Essential Writings***

"In their fascinating emails these two brilliant souls reflect one another, challenge one another, share dreams, disappointments, and hopes. Both Robert Ellsberg and Sister Wendy Beckett are brilliantly verbal so their reflections on almost any topic are provocative, touching, incisive, and frequently hilarious. But the chief delight of this wonderful book comes when all that brilliant conversation becomes something quite different, something far more fitting for a contemplative religious and a chronicler of saints. *Dearest Sister Wendy*...is—finally—a love story. We are privileged to watch in silent wonder as that love grows, ripens, and reaches its perfection as Sister Wendy's breath finally runs out. 'We have heaven already, we just can't see it,' she writes. Thanks to Robert Ellsberg and Sister Wendy we see it very clearly." —**Bill Cain, SJ, playwright, author, *The Diary of Jesus Christ***

"This book blew open the gates of my heart. What a quietly magnificent example of spiritual friendship! A blossoming mystic disguised as an American publisher of progressive Christian texts and a passionate art critic disguised as an English contemplative nun recognize each other, draw each other out, and lift each other up. By the end, I felt I knew and loved Sister Wendy almost as deeply as Robert did, and I wept when she died." —**Mirabai Starr, author, *God of Love* and *Wild Mercy***

"A *tour de force* which never loses momentum, *Dearest Sister Wendy*...is a riveting exchange between two correspondents of extraordinary intelligence and depth. If, at first, you feel you're eavesdropping on a private conversation between a nun and a publisher, you soon realize you're actually being drawn into a series of profound meditations on the spiritual life. Brimming with theological insights, humanity, and humor, this volume provides much material for prayer and reflection."
—**Michael Ford, author and former BBC religion producer**

"For the last three years of her life, Sister Wendy Beckett corresponded on almost a daily basis with her friend Robert Ellsberg. What followed is a rare treasure in the annals of spiritual literature—a moving, humorous, profound exchange about themes that mattered to them both: holiness, suffering, love, joy, and the things that make us human. This is a beautiful and profound book." —**James Martin, SJ, author, *Learning to Pray*.**

"This book surprises at every page. Beginning in wonderment as we witness the birth of an unlikely friendship, we grow to appreciate how necessary this friendship was for us all. An intimate look at the power of grace as it becomes real in the midst of our wounds, these letters of love will leave readers feeling grateful and awake. What a wondrous gift indeed." —**Cecilia González-Andrieu, PhD, Professor of Theology and Theological Aesthetics, Loyola Marymount University**

This book is deeply captivating, not only because you come to learn more about the lives of two interesting people, but also and especially because it is in the particularity of their friendship that you come to learn more about yourself, God, and the world. Once you pick up this book, you won't be able to put it down!" —**Daniel P. Horan, OFM, Professor of Philosophy, Religious Studies, and Theology at Saint Mary's College in Notre Dame**

"In this spiritual gem we are given privileged access into an extraordinary conversation between two remarkable pilgrims on the Christian journey. The one, a famous art historian and hermit who lived most of her life sheltered from the ordinary world of human engagement, and the other a writer and publisher who had the good fortune to engage some of the most distinguished figures in modern American Catholicism. In their remarkably frank and intimate exchanges, we are privileged interlopers in a conversation that both provokes and edifies." —**Richard Gaillardetz, Joseph Professor of Catholic Systematic Theology at Boston College**

"Reading these letters is like walking through the Louvre. Portal after portal into rich spiritual reflection is offered by the exchange between these friends long-devoted to the spiritual path. Relevant, penetrating, grounded, and rife with character, this spiritual exchange promises to intrigue, to challenge, and, like any good art exhibit, to draw the depth-hungry viewer (reader) back again and again. It is a much-needed spiritual conversation for our time. I expect my copy will swiftly become a tattered, dog-eared, well-loved tome." —**Melody Goetz, artist**

"This utterly captivating conversation in letters is a generous gift from two surprising friends and ever-curious spiritual pilgrims. Reading this book is like sharing a bottle of extraordinary wine. It will age well in the classics of Christian literature." —**Carolyn Whitney Brown, co-author (with Henri Nouwen) of *Flying, Falling, Catching: An Unlikely Story of Finding Freedom***

"'Perhaps all along we had been writing a book unawares,' Robert Ellsberg writes of the email conversation he shared with the late contemplative art critic Sister Wendy Beckett over a few short years before her death. At once mutually admiring, spiritually honest and grounded, *Dearest Sister Wendy...* invites us to imagine what waiting for heaven looks like." —**Rose Pacatte, FSP, DMin, award-winning film critic**

DEAREST SISTER WENDY...

DEAREST SISTER WENDY...

A Surprising Story of Faith and Friendship

Sister Wendy Beckett and Robert Ellsberg

ORBIS BOOKS

Maryknoll, New York 10545

Second Printing, December 2022

ORBIS BOOKS
Maryknoll, New York 10545

Fathers and Brothers
MARYKNOLL™

Founded in 1970, Orbis Books endeavors to publish works that enlighten the mind, nourish the spirit, and challenge the conscience. The publishing arm of the Maryknoll Fathers and Brothers, Orbis seeks to explore the global dimensions of the Christian faith and mission, to invite dialogue with diverse cultures and religious traditions, and to serve the cause of reconciliation and peace. The books published reflect the views of their authors and do not represent the official position of the Maryknoll Society. To learn more about Maryknoll and Orbis Books, please visit our website at www.orbisbooks.com.

Copyright © 2022 by Robert Ellsberg

Published by Orbis Books, Box 302, Maryknoll, NY 10545-0302.

All rights reserved.

A portion of the proceeds of this book will go to Sister Wendy's favorite charity: Aid to the Church in Need (https://acninternational.org/).

No part of this publication may be reproduced or transmitted in any form or by any means, electronic or mechanical, including photocopying, recording, or any information storage or retrieval system, without prior permission in writing from the publisher.

Queries regarding rights and permissions should be addressed to: Orbis Books, P.O. Box 302, Maryknoll, NY 10545-0302.

Manufactured in the United States of America

Library of Congress Cataloging-in-Publication Data

Names: Beckett, Wendy, author. | Ellsberg, Robert, 1955- author.
Title: Dearest Sister Wendy . . . : a surprising story of faith and
    friendship / Sister Wendy Beckett, Robert Ellsberg.
Description: Maryknoll, NY : Orbis Books, [2022] | Includes index. |
    Summary: "An intimate correspondence between Sister Wendy Beckett, an
    English hermit and famous "art nun" and Robert Ellsberg, an American
    Catholic writer and publisher about faith, holiness, suffering, and
    happiness"— Provided by publisher.
Identifiers: LCCN 2022003271 (print) | LCCN 2022003272 (ebook) | ISBN
    9781626984752 (trade paperback) | ISBN 9781608339372 (epub)
Subjects: LCSH: Beckett, Wendy—Correspondence. | Ellsberg, Robert,
    1955—-Correspondence. | Nuns—Great Britain—Correspondence. | Women
    art historians—Great Britain—Correspondence. | Catholic
    authors—Correspondence. | Catholics—United States—Correspondence.
Classification: LCC BX4705.B2675 A25 2022 (print) | LCC BX4705.B2675
    (ebook) | DDC 271/.971—dc23/eng/20220414
LC record available at https://lccn.loc.gov/2022003271
LC ebook record available at https://lccn.loc.gov/2022003272

To Sister Lesley Lockwood

"We carry our heaven within ourselves, because he who satisfies the saints with the light of vision gives himself to us in faith and in mystery. It's the same thing. I feel I have found heaven on earth, because heaven is God and God is in my soul. The day I understood this a light went on inside me, and I want to whisper this secret to all those I love."

—St. Elizabeth of the Trinity

"Each tiny act is an extraordinary event, in which heaven is given to us, in which we are able to give heaven to others. It makes no difference what we do . . . Whatever it is, it's just the outer shell of an amazing inner reality: the soul's encounter, renewed at each moment, in which the soul grows in grace and becomes ever more beautiful for her God."

—Madeline Dêlbrel

"All the way to Heaven is Heaven, because He said, 'I am the Way.'"

—St. Catherine of Siena

CONTENTS

FOREWORD

Sister Lesley Lockwood, OCD

In 1970, Sister Wendy Beckett received a papal dispensation from her vows as a member of the Sisters of Notre Dame de Namur, a teaching order she had entered in 1946 at the age of sixteen, and allowing her instead to become a consecrated virgin and hermit, living on the grounds of the Quidenham Carmelite Monastery in Norfolk, England. For many years she lived in a caravan (or trailer), attending Mass in the monastery but otherwise devoting herself to a life of prayer. Eventually, she also began to study and write about art.

In the 1990s she became known to the world through her television series and writings. During these years I was the Sister assigned by the community to bring her meals and attend to her other needs, and I continued in this role when her health eventually required her to move into a cell on the monastery grounds. My duties included conveying her to Mass each day, ordering books from the County Library's mobile van, and not least, helping with her correspondence.

Sister Wendy always replied to whoever wrote to her. Her responses were usually only a few sentences or a couple of paragraphs long, homing in on the core of the correspondent's message. She spoke to the heart with love, truth, appreciation, and encouragement, then took their concerns into prayer. I was surprised at how well she remembered each one. Much of her correspondence was with artists. She unfailingly saw the essence of their work and perceived the passion in their hearts. Sister Wendy delighted in how God was working through them to make Him visible in the world. Others wrote with spiritual concerns, anxious for insight into how to pray and how to live so as to please God, to know Him and love Him as radiantly as she did.

In general, however, she did not encourage protracted exchanges, feeling that much communication with the outside world was not consistent with her vocation to prayer and solitude. That practice makes the contents of this book all the more remarkable. In the last few years of her life, as I was privileged to witness, an exchange of letters with an American publisher—providentially occasioned by an Easter card gone astray—substantially changed Sister Wendy's life; it became the occasion for deep self-reflection and an unprecedented sharing of her inner life.

Robert Ellsberg, the editor-in-chief and publisher of Orbis Books, had published North American editions of several of Sister Wendy's books, and they had exchanged occasional notes over the years. As a young man Robert had worked closely with Dorothy Day, the holy and prophetic founder of the Catholic Worker movement, and he had edited several volumes of her writings, which Sister Wendy had read with enjoyment. She had also read several of his own books on saints and holiness, a subject of endless interest to Sister Wendy.

The exchanges that began in earnest in 2017 initially centered on these topics of common interest, as Robert sent copies of new books from the Orbis Modern Spiritual Masters Series, which Sister Wendy eagerly devoured. Yet the correspondence not only continued but grew increasingly deep and intimate. In her almost daily exchanges with Robert, which she dictated as I typed them on my laptop computer, Sister Wendy shared her thoughts and personal reflections in a way that was utterly unique. Through this experience I encountered a Sister Wendy I had never met before.

I was amazed at her candor. She spoke about herself! This was new. And she was eager to do it. As Robert shared deeply about his own spiritual journey, she not only listened attentively but responded in kind. Together they shared their dreams, they debated, and they told of the books and people that had shaped them. They reflected on what it means to be human, the nature of God, saints, suffering and happiness, and issues of faith and justice. They honored and rejoiced in the gift of friendships throughout their lives, expressed their deep gratitude for parents, mentors, for Robert's children and for his new partner, Monica. I'd thought I knew Sister Wendy pretty well, but now I marveled at encountering her afresh. I saw multi-faceted dimensions of her personality shining as through a cut-glass prism.

Sister Wendy and Robert were two gifted, passionate, and accomplished people who had concentrated their lives on bringing God's love and truth into the world, but by way of very different life experiences and temperaments: Robert as a social activist, inspired by his famous father, working for justice and peace, then as a publisher of books about holy people who had bravely given their lives for this cause; Sister Wendy as a pure contemplative, bringing God's transforming love into the world solely through prayer (with a detour into speaking and writing about art)—both striving toward the same goal, both delighting in the contrast and unity between them.

The energy of their conversations is alive in these pages. Sister Wendy rarely, and then very reluctantly, spoke of herself. But, as Robert noticed, there was an air of urgency, of providential purpose, surrounding the entire exchange. Sister Wendy sensed she was in the last months or perhaps year or two of her life. As you will see, she hadn't set out to write an autobiography (the thought repelled her), but the inspiration to speak in this way with Robert was irrepressible. I understand now that an autobiography by Sister Wendy could only happen in an easy reciprocal to and fro with someone whose heart and intellect she could dance with. She found that great gift in Robert Ellsberg.

As the amanuensis I felt I was in a liminal realm. At the end of some conversations, the joy and wonder of the experience, for both Sister Wendy and for me, often gave way to profound silence. Sometimes I think Sister Wendy herself was mystified by the powerful connection she shared with Robert. He opened a new place in her thinking and in her heart; he expanded her horizons. Mine, too. As I read through the pages of this manuscript I felt I was sitting again with Sister Wendy in her small room surrounded by icons and prints, shelves crammed with books, and small ceramics on every ledge. Sparkling colored glass objects sat on window sills or hung from string in front of the two small windows, sending prisms of rainbows into the room.

I could hear her lilting voice, its lightness, joy, acuity, and humor. I marveled again at her penetrating insight, concisely spoken in a few perfect words, the absolute authenticity of each utterance and gesture—completely and uniquely Sister Wendy. This was the Sister Wendy I knew.

I admit that at first I hesitated to begin reading this book, afraid it would be too painful to resurrect that most precious time with Sister Wendy. But that did not happen. The dynamic between Sister Wendy and Robert brought her voice alive; it evoked an intimate revelation of her thoughts, spiritual depth, and heart, never expressed before. I remember vividly sitting next to her, reading aloud Robert's messages and typing her replies, then the overpowering feeling that something enormously Spirit-filled was happening, and I was inside it.

It was Sister Wendy who first intuited that perhaps this correspondence was intended for a higher purpose and a wider audience. I am deeply grateful to Robert for pursuing this suggestion and, with his great editorial skills, rendering the book you hold in your hands. No doubt, Sister Wendy was a great mystic and spiritual master. Nowhere in all her writings and spoken words is that as evident as in these letters. But that is not to underestimate Robert's side of the conversation, which is exceptionally rich and deep, the fruit of a lifetime of spiritual searching, suffering, self-examination, and contact with holy people. Both Sister Wendy and Robert shared a sense of God's presence in their lives. In exploring that together, they also sensed that this was a message they ought to share with others.

It is truly providential that Robert and Sister Wendy found each other at exactly the right time. Here is an introduction to Sister Wendy that will delight and entrance you, whether you are meeting her for the first time or have loved her for years. But it is truly more than that. The exchange between these two friends is an invitation and guide to the topics that were closest to Sister Wendy's heart and the message she most wanted to share with the world: that, for all our sufferings and struggles, our lives and our world are enclosed in the love of God, and that in awakening to this reality we can discover, now, the meaning of Heaven.

INTRODUCTION

Like countless others, I first discovered Sister Wendy by accident. If someone had told me there was a program on public television featuring an English nun talking about art I might have skipped it, imagining something pious or didactic. Instead, I had the joy one evening of being taken by surprise, while scrolling through the television offerings, when I alighted on a small, medieval-looking nun with big eyeglasses, lively and intelligent features, and an English accent of indeterminate origin, who strolled about in a museum while reflecting aloud on what she saw. I couldn't look away. It turned out that this nun was the star of a television series: *Sister Wendy's Odyssey*, originally produced by the BBC in Britain but broadcast in the United States by PBS.

Though Sister Wendy had spent many decades as a member of a teaching order in her native South Africa, I learned that she was actually a "consecrated virgin," who lived as a hermit on the grounds of a Carmelite monastery in England. Somehow she had found the means to become an avid student of art history, and by some even more unlikely means she had

Sister Wendy Beckett

Copyright © BBC

been discovered by the BBC and given her own television series, thereby becoming an even more unlikely celebrity.

Sister Wendy was not exactly a figure out of "central casting": diminutive, slightly hunched in her old-fashioned black habit, with a bit of a speech impediment and teeth that had never seen braces. On the one hand she seemed not entirely of the modern world, as if she had walked onstage from a tale of Chaucer. Yet on the other hand she defied any stereotype of an otherworldly nun. She spoke appreciatively about all styles and forms of art—from cave paintings and Greek vases to Byzantine icons, Renaissance masters, French Impressionists, and abstract modern paintings. Whatever the subject, she spoke, unscripted, not only with authority and learning but with *compassion* and insight into the human condition. Invariably, reviews of her show singled out remarks that showed her lack of prudery in discussing the human form—thereby revealing more about the reviewers' own assumptions regarding the supposed innocence of a habited nun. Sister Wendy found this perplexing; God made the body, and there was nothing "dirty" or ridiculous about it.

I was a fan of Sister Wendy's show long before I had any notion that we might one day become friends. The initiative in our first interaction came from her. I had been working for many years as editorial director of Orbis Books, a publishing house owned by the Maryknoll Fathers and Brothers, a Catholic missionary society based in New York. Orbis had a reputation for publishing works on liberation theology from Latin America and other works by theologians that kept officials at the Vatican awake at night. But we had also published the English edition of an authoritative multi-volume history of the Second Vatican Council.

One day I received a handwritten note—very difficult to decipher—asking on behalf of the Quidenham Carmelite Monastery in England if we might have a damaged set of these expensive volumes to donate to their library. The letter came from Sister Wendy! I responded at once, assuring her that I would happily donate these books to the sisters. And that is how I came to know the famous "art nun." Over many years I received scores of short notes from Sister Wendy, sometimes on picture postcards, but often (in a testament to her frugality) written on the backs of envelopes, or on hotel stationery filched during her travels. At first these caused excitement in my office, as my colleagues eagerly vied to decipher Sister Wendy's virtually impenetrable script. Sometimes they would photocopy and enlarge her notes, attempting to crack her elusive code word by word. Over time, I found their enthusiasm for this sport dwindling, and messages from Sister Wendy were received with mixed emotions.

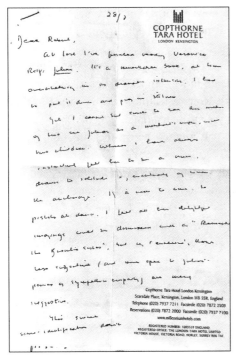

Sister Wendy's "indecipherable script"

These were not chatty letters, but mostly gracious thank you notes for gifts or news related to her own Orbis publications. For yes, I came to publish four books by Sister Wendy, the first two describing her discovery and exploration of the earliest Byzantine icons of Mary and Jesus. Aside from Sister Wendy's television fame she was also a noted author, having written several major books on art history, as well as short books featuring spiritual meditations on favorite works of art. As these books made clear, for Sister Wendy art was a vehicle for talking about the things of highest importance. Her response to art was not a digression from her contemplative life but an expression of it. Reflecting on beauty was for her an entry to reflection on the source of Beauty. And as she later wrote me, her work as a guide to art history was actually a kind of ministry—a way of talking about God to an audience who might otherwise be uncomfortable with religious language.

Eventually this public apostolate faded, and she was happy to return to the hidden life of solitude and prayer to which she had dedicated herself since 1970. Most of her fans knew very little about this side of Sister Wendy. Amidst all her writing and speaking, she purposely said very little about her inner life, and she vehemently resisted invitations from journalists or publishers to delve into such matters.

Apart from my professional work as an editor, I also had writing projects of my own. Early in life I had dropped out of college to work in New York City with Dorothy Day, founder of the Catholic Worker. Day, a convert to Catholicism, had spent her early life as a writer and activist engaged in the radical social movements of her day. After becoming a Catholic, she prayed for some way of combining her faith with her commitment to the poor and social justice. In 1933, after meeting a Frenchman named Peter

Maurin, she was inspired to start a newspaper and a movement devoted to living out and calling attention to the radical social implications of the gospel.

I worked with Dorothy Day for the last five years of her life, returning to college just months before her death in November 1980, and shortly after I myself had decided to become a Roman Catholic. Some years earlier Dorothy had named me as (a very young) managing editor of *The Catholic Worker* newspaper, an assignment that pointed me in the direction of my life's work—not just as an editor, but also as *her* editor. After her death I edited her *Selected Writings*, and also, many years later, her diaries and her selected letters. Sister Wendy, who adored Dorothy Day, became a great fan of these volumes, even including Dorothy's diaries, *The Duty of Delight*, on a list of five favorite books for a BBC program.

From my years at the Catholic Worker I had also come away with a fascination with saints and holy lives. In a series of books beginning with *All Saints* (1997), I had written about an eclectic range of "saints, prophets, and witnesses," combining traditional Catholic saints with writers, activists, modern mystics, and others who seemed to speak to the spiritual questions of our time. I had elaborated on some of these lessons in my book *The Saints' Guide to Happiness* (2003). Over the years Sister Wendy had appreciated many of these books, and for several of them provided generous endorsements.

Nevertheless, I would not have pretended that we were close friends. We shared a mutual esteem, and certainly a set of passionate interests and values. But Sister Wendy never crossed the boundary of true intimacy, and I respected that limitation. It was clear that her communications were functional, motivated by courtesy, business, or a combination of the two.

These boundaries were even more in place after she completely retired from public life and was forced by declining health to abandon her "caravan" on the monastery grounds and move into a room within the monastery cloister. In a letter of 2013, which seemed to be closing the door, she wrote me: "I like communicating with you . . . but if I'm to live a life of silence, communication without a real purpose has got to be sacrificed. Of course sometimes there is a real purpose, which I accept with joy. My life is full of joy and Our Lord seems so close that I laugh to recall to myself that I am only seeing Him in a glass darkly. How can we contain the happiness of what that face to face will mean? So rejoice with me, dear Robert."

But three years later the door was surprisingly opened. Evidently, communication had found its "true purpose."

It began in the spring of 2016 when an Easter card from Sister Wendy apparently went astray. Sister Wendy was now attended once a day by an American nun, Sister Lesley Lockwood, who delivered her frugal provisions and helped with correspondence. Sister Lesley would read aloud the day's emails, and Sister Wendy would dictate a reply, which Sister Lesley transcribed on her laptop computer—or what Sister Wendy called "her machine." Among other things, this meant that Sister Wendy's words were suddenly and magically rendered legible! At first the messages were from Sister Lesley, conveying Sister Wendy's intentions. But before long Sister Wendy herself had stepped from behind the veil. To my surprise, my emails were immediately answered, as one long email letter followed another, and then another. Before very long, we were exchanging letters on an almost daily basis.

In the beginning these letters focused on our common interest in saints and the general subject of holiness. Sister Wendy was fascinated by a series I had inaugurated on "Modern Spiritual Masters." She was a voracious reader, and in supplying her with fresh volumes from this series I could barely keep up with her insightful reviews. Before long, however, our exchanges extended to wider reflections on the spiritual life. I encouraged Sister Wendy to share more personal reflections on this subject. At first she scoffed at this idea. But as our exchanges grew deeper and more personal, she reflected that perhaps the book I had in mind was actually here in our correspondence.

I found that the best way to elicit personal reflections from Sister Wendy was to write about my own spiritual journey and experiences. Had she ever felt or experienced anything like that? Sister Wendy had a great aversion to self-examination. Yet gradually she began to open up, recounting aspects of her story, sharing with remarkable candor an assessment of her own character, and opening up an extraordinary window on her soul.

But as our correspondence continued I quickly dispensed with any pretense of "ulterior motive." Sometimes I wondered at the miracle that was unfolding. Sister Wendy had revealed that she was suffering from a terminal condition of her lungs. I imagined that her time was very limited, and these letters were written with her limited breath. Toward the end of her life, had I been chosen to receive this most precious gift of herself?

I found myself also emerging under Sister Wendy's gracious gaze, reviewing my own life as a kind of spiritual story, beginning with the circumstances of my unusual childhood, marked by my parents' divorce and the very diverse influence of their respective personalities. My father, Daniel Ellsberg, had become famous as the whistleblower who leaked the Pentagon Papers, a top-secret history of the Vietnam War, resulting in his arrest and prosecution by the Nixon administration. From him I had inherited a sense of purpose, a commitment to find my own way to serve the cause of peace and a better world. My mother, an ardent Episcopalian, had raised me to value honesty, modesty, and kindness. In different ways they had shaped my path, including my decision to join Dorothy Day at the Catholic Worker, when I was nineteen; to pursue an interest in writing about heroes of the moral and spiritual life; and eventually to become the publisher of books that would promote a spirit of faithful engagement with the needs of the world. Sister Wendy had deliberately avoided the realms of politics and social struggle, and my connection to these themes opened for her a window on a wider world.

But I was also passing through a time of transition, following the failure of a long marriage, the beginning of a new and hopeful chapter in my life, and the questions this posed about how to make sense of all this in terms of my identity as a Catholic. Sister Wendy encouraged me to see all of it as part of a spiritual journey in which God was present along the way—not just in moments of light, but also in darkness. She received it all: my work, the stories of my friends, accounts of my travels, my response to politics and tensions within the church, the developing relationship with my fiancée, Monica, whom I had first met when I was seventeen, and even my densely symbolic dreams. She took all of this, placed it on the altar of her heart, and returned it with her blessing

What all this meant to Sister Wendy I can only determine from her words, her extraordinary generosity, and from the evident affection that poured from her. She never tried to steer the conversation toward more "spiritual" topics. Life itself, with all that it revealed about the capacity for love, suffering, and joy, was itself a work of art whose meaning unfolded before her contemplative eye. And as with her appreciation of the human body, she accepted everything as part of God's creation, and she embraced it all in love.

Nevertheless, as she several times observed, this exchange was quite out of character, and actually unique in her experience. As much by temperament as by vocation Sister Wendy was a true solitary. She was happy to meet people during her forays into the world, traveling to museums with a film crew, meeting with producers and publishers and curators. She had a natural charm and an interest in people, but she was anything but an extrovert, and she had developed careful strategies for maintaining boundaries and discouraging trespassers.

And yet, in the course of our correspondence I could detect something changing; evidently there was a deeper story below the surface of our back and forth. This was reflected curiously in a subtle drama played out in her obsession with the famous Trappist monk and writer Thomas Merton. I later perceived this clearly only after several readings of our correspondence. Sister Wendy was constantly reading and rereading Merton's books, admiring his genius as a writer, but always accusing him of a kind of falseness in his pretense of living a contemplative life. I generally pushed back, arguing that Merton represented a kind of spiritual bridge between different conceptions of the religious life, and that his ongoing search and effort to go deeper into the heart of his vocation, even when it seemed he was leaving something behind, was part of his significance and attraction to other spiritual seekers. At times this became a subject of disagreement between us. Yet she would not drop the subject.

Then, toward the end of our second year of correspondence, a light went on. She determined that she had completely misjudged Merton, and that this reflected her own narrowness and rigidity. Her epiphany seemed almost to parallel an incident in Merton's own life, a famous experience he described after some years in the monastery when he felt himself suddenly awakening "from a dream of separateness," from a kind of self-isolation and "spurious holiness," that allowed him to enter into a more compassionate relationship with the world and his fellow humans.

Readers can judge whether I am reading too much into this. But as she entered into her final year, as breathing became increasingly difficult, and as she prepared for the long-awaited reunion with her Beloved, it seemed that Sister Wendy was still growing, still emerging from a kind of self-enclosure into a wider, freer, and more loving world.

Many other events occurred along the way, including an opportunity finally to meet face to face, when I was invited in 2017, with Monica accompanying me, to lead a retreat for the community at Quidenham. She keenly followed my work in promoting the canonization of Dorothy Day, read my stream of talks, books, and articles, including my letters of appreciation to our shared hero, Pope Francis. She followed with bated breath the exhausting but deeply rewarding service of helping my father write his memoir, a prophetic warning against the perils of nuclear doomsday. All this was transmitted in several hundred letters, from which this volume has been drastically edited and abridged.

Sister Wendy died on December 26, 2018, at the age of eighty-eight. She is still remembered fondly by many people as the famous "art nun," whether from her broadcasts or from her published commentaries and reflections which live after her. Anyone who has watched her programs or read her reflections knows of her brilliant powers of observation and empathy, and her ability to see in works of art a window connecting the everyday human world and deeper spiritual realities. She brought that same deeply intuitive power to her encounters with people, as I was privileged to learn. I was always astonished that on the basis of some very brief reference to someone she would seem to know and understand them completely. It was thus with my first mention of Monica, or my children, or anyone who came into her field of view. Many viewers and readers probably felt that she knew and loved them as well.

But perhaps those who read these letters will discover someone they never knew: a modern mystic, a genius of the spiritual life, a person of far-seeing sensitivities, a great lover of God whose capacity for love she was still discovering and exploring at the end of her life. Deep within what St. Teresa of Avila would have called her "interior castle," in her small room, within the walls of an enclosed monastery, there burned an intense, though secret fire. For a brief while I was privileged to warm myself at that flame. I hope others may now do the same.

————

A note on this volume, which is drawn from a correspondence of more than 350,000 words. I have divided the text into three parts, corresponding to the three years it covers, 2016–2018, beginning with a short prologue that intro-duces the real jumping-off point, and an epilogue following Sister Wendy's death. Naturally, I have omitted much that was of a personal nature, as well as long accounts of books read, news of the world, travels, and biographies of friends, authors, and family.

I would have been happy to leave myself out of the whole thing, as I had originally intended. But as it became clear, Sister Wendy and I shared an exchange of gifts, and my own part in this was an essential aspect of the underlying story.

I have added notes to explain references to many of the saints and fig-ures we discussed. Some of these figures, including Thomas Merton and Dorothy Day, seemed to require a longer notation, and thus appear in a bio-graphical glossary at the end.

PROLOGUE

In a note sent in April 2011, Sister Wendy let me know she had selected my edition of Dorothy Day's diaries, The Duty of Delight,[1] *as one of her five choices for a BBC program on "My Favorite Books." She said she had been torn between choosing Dorothy's Letters[2] and the Diaries: "Both speak of what it means to love Our Lord in the real world with a passion and conviction that one can find nowhere else. Well, perhaps one finds it in Therese of Lisieux,[3] that most saintly of the saints." And she added: "Perhaps we will meet someday, who knows?"*

In contrast to her usual, handwritten (and thus, frankly inscrutable) notes, this letter had been typed by a priest who served the Quidenham Carmelite community. In reply, I noted, "It is a very difficult tradeoff between the excitement of receiving a letter in your own hand and the exquisite pleasure of being able to decipher EVERY word (as opposed to the usual 75%)! Thank you so much for writing, and as long as your amanuensis is willing I hope you will write often."

I mentioned in passing my hope that she might one day write a personal account of her life. To this, she replied:

My Dear Robert,

Congratulations on being able to read 75% of my writing! Few of my friends are as successful. My sister tells me it is a great comfort to be able actually to read my letters, but this way something is lost.

---

1. *The Duty of Delight: The Diaries of Dorothy Day*, ed. Robert Ellsberg (New York: Image/Random House: 2008, 2011).

2. *All the Way to Heaven: Selected Letters of Dorothy Day*, ed. Robert Ellsberg (New York: Image/Random House, 2010).

3. St. Therese of Lisieux (1873–1897) was a French Carmelite nun who died at age 24. After her death, with the publication of her spiritual autobiography, *The Story of a Soul*, she became one of the most popular saints of modern times. She called her spirituality "the Little Way," a path to holiness that lay in attention to God and a spirit of love in all our everyday encounters and duties. She was canonized as a saint in 1925, and later declared a Doctor of the Church.

1

Unlike Dorothy Day, or Thomas Merton for that matter, I am not a letter writer, so you are missing very little.[4]

As for myself the very last thing I would want to write is any autobiography. I think I may be doing something on Biblical painting but I will keep you informed. You know dear Robert I am a reluctant writer and since I am dependent on dictating to Fr. Steve, and he may not always be available, the time of my deliverance may be at hand. But I would never want my desires, which are selfish, to stand in the way of any work that would help people to see the beauty of God.

Two years later, in 2013, I wrote Sister Wendy to describe the pleasure of visiting the Norton Simon Museum in Pasadena, California, and finding displayed there a short film of her leading a personal tour of the museum. I also made a passing reference to the Trappist monk, Thomas Merton, and would discover that on this subject Sister Wendy possessed surprisingly complex opinions—a source of ongoing debate in our later correspondence.

Her reply this time came through a young American Carmelite from the Quidenham community, Sister Lesley Lockwood, who would serve, among other duties, as Sister Wendy's scribe and portal to the outside world in her final years.

Dear Robert,

I am replying for Sister Wendy to let you know about her health. She has been diagnosed with idiopathic pulmonary fibrosis, a disease which causes a toughening of the tissues in the lungs. It is incurable and the prognosis is uncertain; it could be a number of months or several years. At present Sister Wendy is getting along quite well, though she hasn't much energy or stamina. She uses oxygen periodically throughout the day, but is able to stay in her caravan, drive her scooter up to the house for Mass, and continue in her prayer and life as a hermit. She wanted me to tell you that this is the happiest period of her life; a golden time.

---

4. Dorothy Day (1897–1980), was a radical journalist and activist who became a Roman Catholic and founded the Catholic Worker movement, an effort to promote the radical social message of the Gospels. Thomas Merton (1915–1968), also a convert to Catholicism, achieved fame from the publication of his autobiography, *The Seven Storey Mountain*, which culminated in his entry into an austere Trappist monastery. For more about both Day and Merton see the Biographical Glossary at the end of this book.

She also said she has the "tenderest memories of Pasadena." Concerning Thomas Merton, she said, "When Merton is writing about himself, for example, his autobiography, diaries, even his letters which are personal, I feel he's supremely interesting. He is an unrivaled master of style—a genius in his own way. It's when he speaks objectively about God and prayer that my heart sinks."

Thank you Robert for your love and your kindness toward her and especially for your prayers.

With all best wishes,
Sister Lesley for Sister Wendy

Replying at once, I thanked Sister Lesley for her kindness in sharing this information. I assumed, I wrote, that Sister Wendy would prefer not to receive lugubrious messages of condolence, and added: "I do pray that she continues to have enough energy for all the things that bring her delight. I have so enjoyed the luxury of legible communication with her via your gracious services, and I hope I have not imposed on her or you. She is always so punctual and thoughtful in her replies, and I don't want to make excessive demands on her energy. But communicating with her is one of the things that brings me delight, as I hope you will tell her."

Sister Lesley replied: "I will tell her, Robert. It is a delight for her too."

Two days later, a reply came directly from Sister Wendy:

September 13, 2013

Dear Robert,

That was a lovely email you sent. I like communicating with you too, but if I'm to live a life of silence, communication without a real purpose has got to be sacrificed. Of course sometimes there is a real purpose which I accept with joy. My life is full of joy and Our Lord seems so close that I laugh to recall to myself that I am only seeing Him in a glass darkly. How can we contain the happiness of what that face to face will mean? So rejoice with me, dear Robert.

Lovingly,
Sister Wendy

Seven months passed before I received a grateful note from Sister Wendy,
acknowledging her receipt of a recently published book about Julian of Nor-
wich,[5] *the fourteenth-century English anchoress and mystic, whom I could*
not help but associate with Sister Wendy—not only in her solitary life, but in
her broadly open conception of Christian faith. She mentioned that she had
recently passed her eighty-fourth birthday. I mentioned, in return, that my
father, who was eighty-three at the time, was in excellent health, swimming
in the frigid Pacific Ocean.

She replied on April 23, 2014:

My Dear Robert,

I've sent you an Easter card today but this is to thank you for your
email. But dear Robert never feel you have to write to me. I'm rather sorry
you told me about your heroic father. I am the antithesis of heroic—weak,
wobbling, breathless; on the other hand I am blissfully happy.

Very much love,
Sister Wendy

I replied: "I never feel I have to write you—and I know it is I who should be
offering you this assurance. Though it always thrills me to hear from you, I
don't want to intrude on your contemplative peace."

I assumed, with this exchange, that my relationship with Sister
Wendy—at least through correspondence—would diminish. She had gently
asserted the boundaries of her contemplative vocation, and with her health
in evident decline I respected her desire to sacrifice communication that
lacked "a real purpose." And so it was, for almost two years.

---

5. Veronica Rolf, *Julian's Gospel: Illuminating the Life and Revelations of Julian of*
Norwich (Maryknoll, NY: Orbis Books, 2013). Julian was a fourteenth-century English
mystic who spent much of her life as an "anchoress," enclosed in a cell attached to a
church in Norwich. There she wrote an account of a series of revelations she had received about Christ's passion and God's love for creation. She was one of Sister Wendy's
favorite saints. For more, see the Biographical Glossary.

PART ONE

THE ART OF SEEING

Each Easter and Christmas Sister Wendy personally selected a card that she liked to send to her personal circle of contacts. On April 12, 2016, Sister Lesley wrote to let me know that an Easter card from Sister Wendy had been returned with the notice "address undeliverable"—the result of a change in my office post office box. Providentially, this small incident of a card gone astray became the opening to a correspondence that would deepen our relationship and truly change our lives.

By this time, as I would later come to understand, Sister Wendy's declining health had forced a change in her circumstances. No longer able to live in her "caravan" on the monastery grounds, she had moved to a room inside the monastery enclosure. There she maintained her solitary life, was wheeled out to attend Mass, and was visited once a day by Sister Lesley, who brought her single meal of the day and who otherwise, by means of what Sister Wendy called her "machine," assisted with her correspondence.

In providing my correct address, I happened to mention my plan at Orbis to publish a book of letters by Vincent Van Gogh in our Modern Spiritual Masters Series, an eclectic series highlighting stories and essential writings of modern spiritual teachers. Evidently this piqued Sister Wendy's interest. She replied on April 14, in the first of hundreds of emails that she dictated to Sister Lesley.

Thursday, April 14, 2016

Dear Robert,

I hope my card does reach you because it's an extremely beautiful Brueghel the Younger, "Noli Me Tangere,"[1] and I know your prayerful heart will like my little commentary.

---

1. *Noli me tangere* ("touch me not"), the Latin rendering of the words that Jesus spoke to Mary Magdalene after she recognized him in the garden on Easter morning (John 20:17).

I'm intrigued by your counting Van Gogh among the spiritual authorities and look forward very much to reading it. Of course I'm hoping you could afford some color illustrations, but I shall have to wait and see.

Very much love and gratitude,
Sister Wendy

While I was delighted to hear from Sister Wendy, I assumed, following a polite exchange, that she would revert to the Great Silence. But that did not happen. My reply was followed by her response, and so it continued until her death two and a half years later.

April 14, 2016

Dear Sister Wendy,

I first proposed the book to a woman named Carol Berry, who has been leading retreats on Van Gogh. We had a tremendous quest to obtain rights to the English translation of Van Gogh's letters. (Among other things, the English publisher expressed incredulity at the idea that Van Gogh should be considered "a spiritual master"!) Fortunately, Carol is fluent in Dutch and French and she ultimately decided to prepare the translation herself. It is a beautiful and very moving book—however, alas, no color art, except on the cover; just his drawings inside.

I am so glad to hear from you. All is well here. There has been great interest in Dorothy Day and Thomas Merton since Pope Francis singled them out in his speech before Congress last year.[2]

I hope you are well. I had a dream about you—probably prompted, unconsciously, by your card, which was trying to reach me. I look forward to seeing it.

---

2. In a speech before a joint session of Congress on September 24, 2015, Pope Francis organized his talk around four "great Americans": Abraham Lincoln, Martin Luther King Jr., Thomas Merton, and Dorothy Day. He concluded: "A nation can be considered great when it defends liberty as Lincoln did, when it fosters a culture which enables people to 'dream' of full rights for all their brothers and sisters, as Martin Luther King sought to do; when it strives for justice and the cause of the oppressed, as Dorothy Day did by her tireless work, the fruit of a faith which becomes dialogue and sows peace in the contemplative style of Thomas Merton."

April 17, 2016

My dear Robert,

I'm so very happy about Dorothy Day. How far along is her cause [for canonization[3]]? I wouldn't have thought there'd ever be a movement to canonize dear Thomas Merton and hope I am right here. Dorothy was to my mind the essential saint. Merton was a man of enormous brilliance. I think he loved God as much as he could, but his capacity was as flawed as hers was complete.

Let me know if you don't get your card. And if we meet in dreams again, give me your blessing.

With much love,
Sister Wendy

Dorothy Day

Dorothy Day's cause for canonization was in fact something I knew quite a bit about. I had been part of a group of people who had known Day, and whom Cardinal John O'Connor, archbishop of New York, had consulted before recommending her cause to Rome. She was subsequently deemed a "Servant of God," the first step in the process of being named a saint. Later, I was one of the founders of the "Dorothy Day Guild," established to promote her canonization, and later still I would have a more official role.

---

3. A "cause for canonization" in the Roman Catholic Church is the process by which a man or woman is recognized as a saint. It begins with a petition from a local bishop or religious order regarding a person's reputation for holiness. If the cause is accepted by the Vatican, the person is declared a Servant of God. A long process of investigation follows; upon confirmation of the Servant's heroic holiness, he or she is declared Venerable. After that, a confirmed miracle is required for the person to be beatified, or declared Blessed. A second miracle is required for the person to be canonized or declared a saint. In the case of a martyr, the first miracle is waived.

April 18, 2016

Dear Sister Wendy,

I know you don't want to be pestered by too much mail—but since you did ask a question about Dorothy Day, let me say that her cause has definitely picked up steam in the last year. For years nothing really happened, but then things started to move. The archdiocese of New York has hired staff. They have lined up canon lawyers and theologians to study her writings, and this week will begin at last the process of interviewing witnesses (including me). Unfortunately, given that this is thirty-six years after her death, many of those who knew her are no longer available.

As for Merton—I am quite sure you are right, that he is unlikely to be canonized. I taught a course on Merton last year and gave a lecture wherein I described him as a "spiritual explorer." I don't know if that is quite the same as a saint, but it is a role that is particularly important in our time, I think, when there are so many people who don't feel that any particular religious structure fits them. Those who identify with Merton, in his searching, may make more progress in the end than those who venerate saints but are not inspired to imitate them. So I think.

I am very moved by Pope Francis's words about a "journey faith"[4]—a faith that emerges and unfolds on a journey, which may have twists and turns, stumbling and uncertainty—rather than a "lab faith" in which everything is clear cut and neatly defined.

I will let you know when my card arrives. And if we meet in a dream I will not let you go until you bless me!

———

April 20, 2016

Dear Robert,

Everything about Dorothy is of interest to me. Thank you for the information about her cause. (I might have known you were intimately connected with it.) She epitomizes for me the importance of canonization. It enables the church to spotlight her and give us both the warm encourage-

---

4. Pope Francis's distinction between a "journey faith" and a "lab—or laboratory—faith" occurred in an interview published in the Jesuit magazine, *America*, on September 30, 2013. "There is always the lurking danger of living in a laboratory. Ours is not a 'lab faith,' but a 'journey faith,' a historical faith. God has revealed himself as history, not as a compendium of abstract truths."

ment of seeing her holiness as well as the actual practical example. She gave herself to God in such countless small ways: a St. Therese for our times.

Merton fascinates me. I think I've read everything he wrote. Some of it more than once. He seems to me a genius and, as you say, he opens out the countless ways in which people can venture deeper into their faith. So I suppose intellectually he's an example, but morally a fascinating conundrum. The problem to me is that he did not want the discipline of religious life, but he did want the security and the uninvolvement, or rather involvement at choice that it brings. He certainly charges one's imagination with the fascinations of divine possibilities.

With love and prayer and mutual blessings,
Sister Wendy

––––––––––

It was initially the Modern Spiritual Masters Series that provided the common ground of our correspondence, but gradually that widened to encompass the world of saints, the meaning of holiness, and the spiritual life in general—topics of particular interest to Sister Wendy. And, over time, that would eventually widen to encompass everything.

April 29, 2016

Dear Robert,

I have just finished your Van Gogh book,[5] full of admiration for him and also for the editor, Carol Berry. She writes with such loving objectivity and her quotations are moving and apposite. It's a lovely book.

I've been looking at the list of books in the [Modern Spiritual Masters] series and thinking how much I would like all of them, but I know we can't afford this and I'm trying to decide which I would most like.

I was thinking that there are three aspects to being a spiritual master: personality, action, and message. Some, like Mother Teresa and St. Therese, have all three. Some like Thomas Merton have two, but don't work as far as actions go. I feel Van Gogh has one, because, despite all his earnest endeav-

––––––––––

5. *Vincent van Gogh: His Spiritual Vision in Life and Art*, selected with original translations by Carol Berry (Maryknoll, NY: Orbis Books, 2015).

ors as a person and in his actions, he was a failure. But his message is so overwhelmingly beautiful that one needs nothing more. I congratulate you on thinking of such a series.

Lovingly,
Sister Wendy

———

April 29, 2016

Dear Sister Wendy,

I am very moved by your thoughtful reflections on the meaning of spiritual masters. For me, such people are distinguished not just by their work or teachings—but the way they embody those teachings. Their life story is also their teaching.

In any case I am so glad you enjoyed the Van Gogh volume. He was, no doubt, a "failure" on the level of personality and action. But I would add another criterion to your qualifications for spiritual master: VISION.

In Pope Francis's marvelous speech before the US Congress—where he held up four "great Americans"—Lincoln, King, Dorothy Day, and Thomas Merton (!)—he said such persons help us "see and interpret reality" in a new way.

I think there are people like Van Gogh who were complete disasters in their personal lives—nobody should aspire to live like them! They are definitely not saints in action. But are they perhaps "saints in vision"? People who truly awaken our capacity for compassion, our capacity to recognize the sacred depths of reality? On that basis, I included people like him and Dostoevsky and William Blake in my book *All Saints*.[6]

I am so interested in the gospel story that is written through people's lives. I wish you had found the interest to write more about your own journey.

I am hoping that your recent correspondence means you are feeling somewhat better than you were last year. I pray this is so. I had a painful excursion to the hospital yesterday for kidney stones—a most unpleasant intimation of mortality!

---

6. *All Saints: Daily Reflections on Saints, Prophets, and Witnesses for Our Time* (New York: Crossroad, 1997). My first book on saints offered 365 short essays on a very wide personal selection of figures, ranging from traditional saints and likely candidates for canonization, to writers and artists, philosophers, mystics, and social activists, along with others whose spiritual vision or moral witness, I thought, speaks to the challenges of today.

In case you are wondering, I have not yet acknowledged the card you sent me, because it has not arrived.

————

May 1, 2016

My dear Robert,

I'm distressed to hear about the kidney stones, which I know can be agonizing. As for me, I've nothing like as dreadful as kidney stones, thank God. But my lung disease is terminal, and I won't be getting better; in fact, energy slowly ebbs and the struggle to keep going becomes harder. But this is a time of great happiness; this is truly something to give Our Blessed Lord to use for His Church. It always seems to me that, since our baptism enables us to live in Him, we have heaven already, we just can't see it.

When I spoke of the third strand in mastership, the teaching or the doctrine, I intended to include vision. I think with someone like Van Gogh, who did the best he could with a damaged temperament and a psychic imbalance, holiness is in his desire, not his achievements. I am quite happy to think of him as a saint, though as you say, not one who gives us example.

Hearing that you gave the testimony for Dorothy Day gives me a wonderful feeling of having my finger on the very pulse of the church. You have such an extraordinary and beautiful vocation. I rejoice in it for you, dear Robert.

Last year, to my horror, a very nice young publisher started to pressure me to write about myself. When I told him it was the very last thing I would want to do, he then came up with an eager biographer. Truly, Robert, I can't think of anything to say. The external course of my life has been remarkably undramatic and my relationship with Our Blessed Lord is so overwhelmingly real that I could never objectify it enough to speak about it. Fortunately I am now too weak to write anything, so I don't have to feel guilty.

Thank you for a lovely and stimulating message.

Gratefully and affectionately,
Sister Wendy

————

May 1, 2016

Dear Sister Wendy,

Thank you for sharing the information about your health. Though I am naturally pained by the thought of your suffering, I must try not to allow my own selfishness to disturb your beautiful equanimity.

I don't know which quality of spiritual master you might aspire to, but if it were up to me I would certainly point to your vision, your capacity to see into heaven, and to enable others to do the same.

The last chapter of my book *The Saints' Guide to Happiness*[7] is called "Learning to See." I quote St. Augustine: "Our whole business in this life is to restore to health the eyes of the heart, whereby God may be seen."

And St. John Vianney: "The eyes of the world see no further than this life, as mine see no farther than this wall when the church door is shut. The eyes of the Christian see deep into eternity."

I can well understand that you have had no interest in writing about the events of your life. The external story may be unremarkable. But I'm sure your adventures in "seeing" would fill many volumes.

Yesterday I lost one of my great friends and mentors, Father Daniel Berrigan, the famous Jesuit priest, poet, and peacemaker.[8] Probably you are familiar with his reputation. He was just weeks shy of 95. I had known him well for over forty years. He was famous for his courageous work for peace. But he was essentially an artist, a poet—with all the sensitivity, imbalance, and complexity that goes along with that. Like his friend Merton in some respects. He had a prophetic vision —so sensitive to violence and catastrophe that his message could be hard to hear. But he certainly had a heart of flesh, and he suffered deeply over the suffering of the innocent.

Daniel Berrigan in 2011

---

7. *The Saints' Guide to Happiness* (New York: North Point Press, 2003). I tried in this book, with reference to many saints and spiritual teachers, to relate the happiness we all desire to the holiness to which we all are called. This was outlined in a series of "lessons"—"Learning to Be Alive," "to Let Go," "to Work," Love, Suffer, Die, and so forth.

8. Daniel Berrigan, SJ (1921–2016), became famous for his part in the Catonsville 9, a group of Catholics who burned draft cards in protest of the Vietnam War. For more, see the Biographical Glossary.

Today is also the anniversary of the death of my mother—who continues to watch over me.

———————

May 2, 2016

My dear Robert,

Thank you for another beautiful message, one that comes from the heart, very open to the Spirit of Jesus. I only know Fr. Berrigan through Merton's letters and diaries. I know that he has been one of the prophets sent to America and to the world as well, warning us to look at God and not at anything less, such as our own foolish selves.

I, too, have the grace of a mother who I know watches over me, and father, too.

Oh Robert, what a great stock of beautiful quotations you have. How much you've read, how much you've remembered, how deep an influence these words of the saints have had on you. I'm ashamed to tell you I have very few quotations, but one I always love comes from St. John Vianney. Some ladies were enthusing about his holiness, which, as you can imagine, annoyed him. "It's nothing to do with holiness, I just take trouble." I think this taking of trouble, really attending and longing and doing what you see is called for, is what distinguishes the saints. It's how they act, isn't it, not what they say or how charismatic they are. And of course what we do is never us, it's only us-in-Jesus. We haven't a separate identity, which is such an enormous comfort.

I did read your *All Saints* when you sent it, but I was foolish and read right through. Now that Sister Lesley and I are reading the Saint of the Day, all the power and fragrance of the holy life is released. As I've aged and am forced to read more slowly, anyhow, I see how Lectio Divina[9] is the only true way of reading anything of value.

Don't feel sorry for me, because I really suffer very little compared with others, and suffering is a joy in itself, weirdly, in that we are taken up into the redemptive passion of Our Blessed Lord. We really are in a win/win situation, aren't we?

————————

9. Lectio Divina ("Divine Reading") is a monastic discipline of slow, contemplative reading of a text (especially scripture), to discover the author's deeper meaning and to discern how God is speaking to the reader through this particular text.

I'll be watching the post eagerly for what you will send and feel very, very grateful for this contact. I don't want you ever to feel you should write, but your letters are precious.

Very much love and prayer,
Sister Wendy

P.S. I notice that sixteen years ago you had three children, I hope you still have and that perhaps you may have children's children.

————

Over the years, I had not imposed on Sister Wendy with details of my personal life. With this postscript, she was definitely opening a new door in our correspondence. But I wondered how frank to be, and whether she would be disappointed to learn that I was divorced, and now recently engaged, and thus perhaps not the ideal Catholic she might have supposed. I had previously sent her notes for a retreat I had given for the Maryknoll Sisters about Pope Francis's idea of a "journey faith," and I referenced that here.

May 2, 2016

Dear Sister Wendy,

Today, by coincidence, I received at last your lovely card! It is very meaningful to me. After my friend Henri Nouwen[10] died I had a dream in which he said, "Don't cling to me." Of course this put me in mind of Jesus' words to Mary Magdalene, *Noli me tangere*—the very theme of your card. And this helped me understand what perhaps Our Lord meant: not to be attached to his bodily manifestation, which was here for a moment, but to trust in his Spirit, which is with us always.

We feel that impulse with everyone who is dear to us—our parents, our children, our

Henri Nouwen

————

10. Henri Nouwen (1932–1996), a Dutch-born priest and popular spiritual writer, taught at a number of American universities before becoming chaplain of a L'Arche community in Ontario. I knew and worked with him for twenty years before his death. See Biographical Glossary.

dear friends. And when I got your note the other day, mentioning your terminal illness, the same impulse came to me, an occasion to remember those words: *Noli me tangere*. Was that message deliberate in your card? How ironic that the faulty address on the card allowed me to renew our contact.

Since you ask: I still have three children, though now much older. My son Nicholas is nearly 30—married, though with no children. He is a film editor. I have two daughters, Christina 21 and Catherine 23, who are both graduating from college next month. The youngest has studied medical anthropology and in her spare time she fills her dorm room with her own beautiful icons and pictures of Jesus. My middle daughter has just written a thesis on French documentaries on the Holocaust. I wonder what will happen to them after graduation.

I had no thought to share such personal information with you—but: I got divorced two years ago, after several years of separation from my wife of many years. You can imagine that this was not something undertaken casually. And in this light perhaps you will understand more of what I meant in the retreat notes I sent you about a "journey faith"—a story that is not only marked by moments of grace and insight, but also by the experience of brokenness, failure, uncertainty. Pope Francis has helped renew my faith that God is present in this story, despite all its complexities.

But there is a new chapter. I am now engaged: a story for another time.

I loved your line from St. John Vianney: "*It's nothing to do with holiness. I just take the trouble.*" That describes Dorothy, to be sure. I have not had the consolation of knowing she would have approved of all my decisions. But I know she played a critical role in the direction of my life and everything that has followed.

I echo your words: don't ever feel you should write, but your letters are precious.

————

I wondered how my revelations would affect our correspondence. Her response was deeply reassuring.

May 5, 2016

My dear Robert,

First I must thank you for the retreat notes, which are beautiful, deep, and practical—three qualities not always found in spiritual writing.

I'm very sorry about the divorce, but as you say, life's journey has unexpected twists and turns. We don't plot the journey, but we can respond to it as Our Lord wants at every new surprise. It's allowing Him to be alive in us that matters, not what seems to be happening, but what He knows is happening.

I agree, it's part of God's lovely weaving of our tapestry of life that made your Easter card go astray and led to this correspondence.

With love and joy and hope,
Sister Wendy

————

May 10, 2016

Dear Sister Wendy,

This weekend I attended the funeral for Fr. Daniel Berrigan, SJ. It was a grand event, attended by at least a thousand people, including many old friends. I first met Dan in 1972, when I was 16. I could not have imagined that he would become my friend, and that I would have the privilege of working with him on so many books, the last published just the week of his death.[11] Asked to speak at his wake, I described his impact on so many young people like myself. Like the disciples who tagged after Jesus and asked him "Where are you staying?" (Their clumsy way of asking: What is the meaning of life?) And he answered, "Come and see."

————

Picking up on her cue, I had sent Sister Wendy a selection of volumes from the Modern Spiritual Masters Series.

May 16, 2016

My dear Robert,

Your books have arrived. Thank you so very much. I've arranged them in order of preference, with the one I want most to read on the bottom. Guess which? Thomas Merton. He has an enormous fascination for me.

I once was at the private Mass of St. John Paul II, nothing special, just his quick private interview. At the time I wasn't a great fan, but when I actu-

---

11. *The Berrigan Letters: Personal Correspondence between Daniel and Philip Berrigan*, ed. Daniel Cosacchi and Eric Martin (Maryknoll, NY: Orbis Books, 2016).

ally met him, I was bowled over by the depth of surrender to God that I saw in him. So to be anywhere near a saint must change us.

I'll be soon reading your books and you know that I will be appreciating them.

Love and gratitude,
Sister Wendy

————————

May 16, 2016

Dear Sister Wendy,

I have the terrible feeling that I am bombarding you with reading material, and thus interfering with your contemplative priorities! I do think about whether "to be anywhere near a saint must change us." On the other hand I think about all those people who encountered Jesus yet walked sadly (or angrily) away. Or who nailed him to a cross.

When I was interviewed by the tribunal for Dorothy's canonization they asked me, "Did people around her think of her as a saint?" I said she would have been very disturbed if people had treated her with special reverence or piety. As for myself, I thought of her as one of those great women in scripture who followed Jesus and waited on him—and had been faithful to that witness for her entire life. She certainly changed me!

————————

May 17, 2016

My dear Robert,

I can't help but feel that you are what you are because of Dorothy. But I also believe that being close to a saint, or an icon for that matter, can't change us unless we want God. Those people in Our Lord's life who sought God found Him in Him. Think of the Good Thief, crucified beside Him. Those, on the other hand, who rejected Him did not want God, though I find it very hard to imagine that state of mind.

As for the books, how can they disturb prayer? They speak of Him so clearly that they only deepen prayer. I'm convinced that real prayer is the air we breathe, a way of being, not just something we stop off our real life to do.

You have opened for me a great and beautiful sea in which I am swimming, or rather floating, with immense joy.

Much love and gratitude (gratitude for what you write and for what you are),

Sister Wendy

In my reply, I noted that her encouragement had lifted my spirits. I mentioned that Orbis Books, like many other religious publishers, was going through a difficult time with changes in the marketplace, the evaporation of retail bookstores, and changing reading habits.

May 18, 2016

My dear Robert,

Of course, I'm distressed for your sake and for the sake of the Church that a publishing house so completely to the Mind of the Lord—His voice speaking plainly and strongly—should be in such difficulties. For the plight of Orbis one can only pray and leave it to the Lord. But for your personal plight, there is surely great grace in its denudations.

She was particularly moved by a volume on Mother Maria Skobtsova,[12] a Russian Orthodox saint who combined her monastic discipline with the works of mercy and who ultimately died in a Nazi concentration camp as a result of her protection of Jews during the occupation of Paris. Sister Wendy had noted her spiritual kinship with Dorothy Day.

One of the beautiful things about Mother Maria, as of course overwhelmingly for DD, is the knowledge that one can only look at God and relate to Him. Whatever else happens, the distresses of marriage, loss of occupation, disapproval, temptations, sadnesses: none of these matter except to unite us more closely to Him. I know that you know this. It's our only rock of safety.

With much love and prayer, and encouragement to send books, dear Robert!—let me help you empty your stockroom,

Sister Wendy

---

12. *Mother Maria Skobtsova: Essential Writings*, ed. Helene Klepinin-Arjakovsky (Maryknoll, NY: Orbis Books, 2002).

Further enthusiastic responses followed as Sister Wendy delved into her new stack of books.

May 23, 2016

My dear Robert,

I've finished Etty Hillesum and Charles de Foucauld and am just about to start Bede Griffiths and Thomas Merton.[13] Both books are inspiring, but it struck me that each is a very clear example of the effect of temperament on holiness. Charles de Foucauld was passionately, extravagantly intent on imitating Jesus, the poor workman, while Etty, with her charm and innocent self-centeredness, was so convinced of the goodness of God and the beauty of His world that she could always move forward "singing." Each is a one-note saint, I think, but what a beautiful note.

With love and prayer,
Sister Wendy

————

May 23, 2016

Dear Sister Wendy,

When people ask me, "Who is your favorite saint?" I often think that it depends on what I need. Yes, so many of them sing one or two notes. The reason we need so many of them.

Last night I dreamed that I was supposed to give a talk about Anne Frank at Boston College. I realized that instead of bringing my talk with me I had packed all kinds of random items from my past: a trombone solo, drawings from my childhood. (I suppose we carry much of our past with us in every endeavor to talk about what is deeply important to us.) I had only

---

13. Anthologies by all these authors were included in the Modern Spiritual Masters Series. Etty Hillesum (1914–1943) was a young Jewish woman living in Amsterdam during the Nazi occupation. She was ultimately deported to Auschwitz, where she died in the gas chamber. She left behind a remarkable diary of her inner life, reflecting her eclectic spiritual vision and her effort to hold fast to God in the midst of her terrible circumstances. In a final note to friends, tossed from a boxcar on her way to Auschwitz, she wrote, "We left the camp singing." Charles de Foucauld (1858–1916) was a French aristocrat and soldier, who, following a dramatic conversion, became a desert hermit in Algeria, where he sought to imitate the "hidden life" of Jesus in Nazareth. He was beatified in 2005 and canonized in 2022. Bede Griffiths (1906–1994) was an English-born Benedictine monk who moved to India and tried to pioneer a model of monastic life integrating the spirituality of East and West.

about a half hour to prepare and I began imagining the talk I should give—
thinking that I might compare Anne Frank to Etty. It fascinates me that such
a person, with her temperament, background, and under such circumstances,
could have been drawn so deeply to God. She reminds me a lot of the many
"nones" (as they are referred to)—the young people who feel no attachment
to any particular institution or tradition, and yet feel an innate spirituality.
Not many follow that desire as deeply as Etty did. She reminds me also of
Dorothea Brooke in *Middlemarch*—whom George Eliot compared to St.
Teresa, equipped with a kind of spiritual grandeur, tempered by "the meanness of opportunity."

Yes, holiness is so shaped by temperament. We cannot aspire to be other
than the saint we are meant to be—with all the quirks and idiosyncrasies
that make us who we are. Don't you think so?

Sister Wendy's salutations took on a new note of intimacy.

May 25, 2016

Dearest Robert,

I think the glory of a rich sacramental life with the privilege of having
been drawn into the meaning of our Church's teachings—able to enter a little into the richness of St. Paul for example—is what raises a temperament
to a song of many notes. Of ourselves, there is only one holiness that He intends for us. We blessed ones though are not just of ourselves, we have been
drawn so deeply into the Spirit of Jesus, into the Trinity, that it is the Lord
who sings in us.

This was not possible for Etty. And not really for dear Charles, because
his psychic imbalance would not allow a deeper understanding. This was in
no way his fault.

Won't you write an autobiography some day? You've known so many
interesting and holy people, not always the same.

With love and gratitude,
Sister Wendy

Sister Wendy's interest in my life prompted me to share more about my per-sonal story, in particular the story of my father, Daniel Ellsberg,[14] *a famous whistleblower who risked his life for the cause of peace, and whose influ-ence loomed large over my own journey. At this time I was helping him complete a second volume of memoirs:* The Doomsday Machine.[15]

May 25, 2016

Dear Sister Wendy,

I have considered writing some kind of memoir—not so much because my own story is so meaningful, but because I am very interested in encour-aging people to look at their own lives as a spiritual text. I have indeed known many interesting and holy people—as you observe, correctly, not al-ways the same.

I am attaching here an article I wrote some years ago about my father, Daniel Ellsberg (possibly someone you have heard of). You can imagine that I had an unusual childhood. Now my father is 85 and I have been helping him finish his own memoir—a very rewarding experience for a son. Last week I helped him get through a patch that was blocking him by drafting a chapter about the Cuban Missile Crisis. Someday maybe I will write my own story.

But I wish you had found the time for this: what you most want to share, what you have learned, how it was rooted in your journey and adven-tures in grace.

———————

May 27, 2016

Dearest Robert,

My heart leapt to know that you were working with your father. I know nothing about him, except in the Nixon context. Is he a Catholic? Christian?

———

14. Daniel Ellsberg (b. 1931) was a government defense analyst who, in opposi-tion to the Vietnam War, photocopied a top-secret history of the war—the Pentagon Pa-pers—and provided it to the press in 1971. He was charged with multiple felonies and faced a possible sentence of 115 years in prison before his case was dismissed on the grounds of gross government misconduct. He went on to devote himself to the cause of peace, in particular, opposition to the threat of nuclear war. See Biographical Glossary.

15. Daniel Ellsberg, *The Doomsday Machine: Confessions of a Nuclear War Plan-ner* (New York: Bloomsbury, 2017).

God-fearer? Noble atheist? My heart would leap even higher, Olympic standard, to know that you were writing your own memoirs; not only is there such rich material in your relationships, but as you show in your "Lives..." you are so acutely aware of how God reveals Himself in the actualities of personal history.

Here is where I would always disappoint you, dear Robert, because I don't feel I have had a real "history" or "journey." No special insight has come to me through people or books, or even events, I'd say. I've just been held by the love of God and carried, a grateful passenger who wants only to praise and thank Him. But I haven't actually done anything: I've responded. And these responses have been on the periphery, as it were; the center has always been just still in Him.

I love admiring people, don't you? And I'm always sad when I can't be wholehearted about it.

With love and prayer,
Sister Wendy

———

May 27, 2016

Dearest Sister Wendy,

It occurs to me that you have responded and written about art the way I have written about holy lives. And you have suggested that if I just take

My father in 1971

away the other lives I will find sufficient material within my own story. Perhaps the same is true for you and art! Just what you have said—about being held by the love of God and carried—touches me deeply (and reminds me of St. Hildegard of Bingen's description of herself as "a feather on the breath of God").[16]

My father was raised in a strict Christian Science family of Jewish origin, though he has maintained no religious affiliation and is quite critical of institutional Christianity and its dogmas. One time he gave

———

16. St. Hildegard of Bingen was a twelfth-century German Benedictine abbess and mystic. Her holistic vision has earned wide interest in modern times, and in 2012 she was named a Doctor of the Church.

me a long lecture on why he rejects God. He asked me how I reacted to that. I said, "I don't believe in the God you don't believe in."

And yet there is no doubt he is a great soul. So deeply committed was he to ending the war in Vietnam—which he had witnessed firsthand—that he risked going to prison for the rest of his life to reveal a top-secret history of the war [the "Pentagon Papers"]. Since then his life has been dedicated to peace, to pursuing truth, exposing lies. He has been arrested close to a hundred times. Now, with all the strength left to him, he is trying to awaken the world to the threat of nuclear war—what he calls the "Doomsday Machine" —though he fears nobody will listen.

It is difficult to be the son of a Great Man—and for much of my youth he felt very distant. Now we are very close; we talk every day. The thought of losing him grips at my heart.

————

Sister Wendy entertained complex and competing opinions about the Trappist monk Thomas Merton. She was fascinated by him, constantly reading and rereading his writings and admiring his wisdom and brilliance. But always she detected something "obtuse and fragmented" in his relationship with God—or perhaps in his relationship with the monastic spirit. More than any other figure, his name would recur in our correspondence. I began to sense that in wrestling with Merton, Sister Wendy was struggling with something deeper.

May 28, 2016

Dearest Robert,

Thank you for the piece about your noble father. I enjoyed this very much and I feel this spurt of communications has been spiritually a true grace. As for your father's faith, isn't he rather like Etty, though of course so dissimilar a character? She knew so little about God and yet lived such a radiant life of closeness to him. Your father knows very much less about God, but what he is and what he does shows he is close to God, even if it's only an implicit and anonymous closeness. You are very blessed to have his spiritual clarity as part of your heritage.

I am almost finished with the volume on Thomas Merton. I must confess to you that I have never met a real contemplative who found Merton useful. That he should write about prayer and yet in his journals show such a fragmented and in fact obtuse relationship with God, is a never-ending puzzle and the source of my interest in him. It sounds so patronizing to say that he meant very well and was never consciously dishonest or untruthful, and I feel shame at even writing these words. The one really encouraging thing for me is that right at the end, in [his journals from] Alaska and California, he begins to speak about prayer quite differently, with the voice of experience. Only then does he say that prayer is not about ourselves, though finding your true self and becoming yourself has been such a constant theme in earlier years.

Sister Lesley's a bit weary today because she's had a dear friend visiting and a lot of talking is not a Carmelite thing, and I'm very weary, though thanks be to God, I have no visitors, but I have to struggle with being 86 and having poor lungs and trembling legs.

With very much love and gratitude to a most kind and supportive friend,

Sister Wendy

―――――――

May 31, 2016

Dear Sister Wendy,

It is interesting what you say about Merton—that you have never met a real contemplative who found him useful. But perhaps that is the thing: the vast numbers of people—not "real contemplatives," you might say—for whom he opened the world of contemplation. Some years ago I remember looking through a Catholic journal that listed all the retreats being offered over the summer around the country; almost half of them used the word "contemplative," and I wondered how much Merton had contributed to that. In the old days that would have been a word and an experience reserved only for those in religious life. Do you think that is true?

What you say about having poor lungs and trembling legs reminds me of something in Dorothy's diaries that always moved me. She writes, "No matter how old I get…no matter how feeble, short of breath, incapable of walking more than a few blocks, what with heart murmurs, heart failure, emphysema perhaps, arthritis in feet and knees, with all these symptoms of age and decrepitude, my heart can still leap for joy as I read and suddenly assent to some great truth enunciated by some great mind and heart."

Your keen engagement with the various things I have sent you makes me think that you can identify with these words.

Thank you for your prayers—which I am sure are most efficacious. Hoping that life continues to afford you many opportunities for delight.

―――――――

June 1, 2016

Dearest Robert,

   Your beautiful and stimulating letter opens vistas of delight in my mind. I can see those vistas, but don't know if I will be able to travel far into their world. I say this because on Corpus Christi, at night, and two days later, on the [Feast of the] Visitation, at night, I had a small heart attack. It is small. I am almost out of pain now and only feel very tired, which of course will, please God, pass. I'm not going to the doctor or the hospital, but our infirmarian is anxious that the doctor come, so charity leaves one no option there. I can't see what the doctor can do, but . . . perhaps a painkiller??

   No time or energy to discuss it, but although it is good that "contemplative" should be a word that the average person doesn't fear, it may not mean what it should mean. Personally, I think all prayer is contemplative, because we have to be still and look at God and I'm not sure that labels are of much use. We could have a good discussion if I were well.

   Very much love and gratitude,
   Sister Wendy

———————

June 1, 2016

Dearest Sister Wendy,

   Thank you so much for sharing the information about your health. Now it is my turn to pray for you—that you will suffer no more pain, and that your energy returns. You will need that to read all the books you have, and those I have recently sent.

   I will keep this brief, so you can rest, and don't feel obligated to write except when it pleases you. If there is any change in your health, whether good news or bad, I will be so grateful for a brief word.

   Wishing I could give your hand a gentle squeeze.

Sister Wendy acknowledged the arrival of new books, and noted, "I don't really feel I'm on the point of death, but if I were, I would have to live until I've read these books." I replied that if besieging her with books and other things to read kept her alive, then that was a good motivation for me to keep writing. I also mentioned another trip to the hospital to deal with kidney stones.

———————

June 9, 2016

Dearest Robert,

Every day since you told me about your kidney stones, I have been praying for you, knowing what a very painful experience you've been enduring. Be assured that I know you have been suffering and perhaps still are suffering, but that I know you understand what suffering is. To share in Our Lord's Cross for the redemption of this poor world is such a grace that it makes pain an unwanted, but very real, blessing. It doesn't damage us, it unites us to Our Blessed Lord.

Very much love,
Sister Wendy

———

June 12, 2016

Dear Sister Wendy,

Thank you so much for your dear expression of concern. I wrote a chapter on suffering in my book on happiness so I am familiar with the counsel of the saints. But while I am in severe pain I find it hard to think of the Lord's Cross or anything—just PLEASE LET THIS STOP!

———

June 15, 2016

Dearest Robert,

As it happens, I've also got some new pain in my life. I thought the two heart attacks a fortnight ago would just pass away, like the one I had a year or two before. But, no, pain comes every now and then, a peculiarly intimate pain that gives no hint as to whether it's going to balloon out into something more serious or whether it will fade away. I'm sure this is nothing like the pain of your operation, but it's made me very aware of the potential grace pain is. I don't think we have to feel happy about this gift, but as you know so well yourself, it is a great gift and, whether we feel it or not, to enter into the passion of Our Redemptive Lord is one of the most wonderful things that can happen to us.

One of the beautiful things God has done for you is bring you into contact with so many spiritual and intelligent people. I know it's not been passive, you've sought them, but dear Robert, you've found them. You have the most amazing roster of friends.

> With love and prayer and admiration,
> Sister Wendy

————————

June 16, 2016

Dear Sr. Wendy,

Dorothy Day had congestive heart failure—diagnosed only by a jail doctor one time. She suffered a lot of these episodes you describe. I would think it is very frightening—never knowing if it will get much worse or pass.

I am glad you are enjoying the St. Therese[17] book. You must have a special understanding of her, living as you do amidst her [Carmelite] sisters.

Yes, God has brought me in touch with many wonderful people. But apart from the ones I have met I feel that I have been blessed to become familiar with so many great souls—the ones I write about—who have become like friends. And I think you must also feel that way, having spent so much time communing with great artists, and so many beautiful works of art. But the wonderful thing about a true friend is not just to know, but to be known. I wish my great friends were not mostly so far away.

————————

I felt very concerned about Sister Wendy's frequent references to suffering. I wondered whether her sense of being "at the end of her life" was one of the reasons she chose now to share herself so personally. Her reply moved me deeply.

June 17, 2016

My dear Robert,

Your experience of people graced by God with minds and closeness to Him is special, I think. You compare my interest in art, but this is not even a shadow of what you have been given. In fact, although I revere everyone

———————————

17. *St. Therese of Lisieux: Essential Writings*, ed. Mary Frohlich (Maryknoll, NY: Orbis Books, 2003).

and believe that in some way that I don't understand, they are close to God, there are very few I have met with whom I feel I can talk. You are a rare exception and another is Sister Lesley, Our Lord's great gift to me at the end of my life. Not that we talk all that much, either you or she, but I know there is understanding without words.

With love and prayer,
Sister Wendy

June 17, 2016

Dear Sister Wendy,

My pains are all gone, though I have some new worries about my daughter, and about another friend who has just been diagnosed with cancer. The sorrows of those we love touch us so deeply, and there is so little we can do but listen and pray.

I am incredibly touched that you put me in the category of Sister Lesley as one you can talk to—or at least understand beyond words.

June 20, 2016

Dearest Robert,

I'm so sorry about your daughter and your friend. It's so much easier, I think, to bear one's own pain than to bear that of those one loves. We can give our pain to Our Blessed Lord and rest in Him, and of course we can give our beloved's pain to Him, but we can't make them give their pain to Him, and it's that act of individual surrender that changes pain from disaster into redemption. All I can do is pray for you, your daughter, and your friend.

I'm reading your beautiful edition of Flannery O'Connor.[18] Her whole way of life, so profound and so real, gives me a sense of a dimension in

---

18. Flannery O'Connor (1925–1964) was a southern author of novels and short stories whose life and writing were deeply shaped by her Catholic faith. She died of lupus at the age of thirty-nine. The posthumous publication of her letters, *The Habit of Being*, brought new appreciation of her art and of her stature as a spiritual teacher. I edited an anthology of her writings for the MSM series: *Flannery O'Connor: Spiritual Writings* (Maryknoll, NY: Orbis Books, 2003).

your life that may not show on the surface. I feel awe before Flannery. God's way with me has been so very different, I feel like a child before a woman, a real grown-up.

I deduce that you're a grown-up too, and it's that deep Christian maturity, painfully won, or rather painfully accepted, as God's gift and kept alive through, maybe, constant struggle. If this is your way to holiness, like Flannery's, I feel it's an even deeper privilege for me to be in contact with you. What He has given me, however, enables me silently and peacefully to give myself to prayer and that, dear Robert, I will certainly do.

So with love and compassion, and gratitude for what we share,
Sister Wendy

———————

June 20, 2016

Dear Sister Wendy,

Are we ever really grown-ups? Sometimes I mark some measure of wisdom—especially in no longer feeling I have to have the last word or prove that I am "right." In being able to forgive more easily. Or not being overly troubled by passing things. And at other times, I am struck low by the sense of how far there is to go—how much more growing up I need to do.

The other day I received a remarkable letter from my friend Yushi Nomura, a Japanese artist and lay theologian, whom I met through Henri Nouwen. I last saw him several years ago in Tokyo, where I was giving a retreat. He is in the late stages of terminal cancer, and I think he must have worked on this letter literally all day while he was receiving chemotherapy. He said that since he received his diagnosis—which was two months ago (they said that without treatment his prognosis was four months)—he has been reflecting on two themes. One is the image of an hourglass. He reflected that rather than think of the

Yushi Nomura

waning sand in the upper glass, he should concentrate on the growing sand in the lower glass; he is not losing life, it is being poured out, and it is not wasted or lost. It is being converted into another form. Much as when he gives a gift to his daughter—it is not measured in his financial loss, but in the transmission of love.

The second image was a sustained meditation on what he calls "Eschaton Reality"—the confrontation with what is ultimately real. He reflected on the whole story of Jesus in this light: how Jesus lived in that reality from the time of his baptism. How it is reflected in the lives of so many saints—including Merton's (!) epiphany at "4th and Walnut,"[19] in Augustine, in Thomas Aquinas, when he dismissed all his writings as no more than straw burning. He said that for a long time he was like a passenger in a car; but now he is strapped to the front of a bullet train headed directly to Eschaton, and in that light everything appears in a different dimension.

Flannery O'Connor understood this so well. It was a theme in many of her stories, in which her characters were stripped of their illusions and confronted with the truth. In one of her stories, a foolish old woman comes to a deep insight in the last moment of her life. The desperado who kills her says, "She would have been a good woman, if it had been someone to shoot her every minute of her life." O'Connor herself, living with a debilitating illness, knew what it was like to live in the presence of "Eschaton Reality."

I am immensely pleased to know how deeply you have responded to O'Connor. Her writings played a very deep role in my life. I was working as a night orderly in a home for terminal cancer patients, run by an order of Dominican nuns—the very community that O'Connor befriended (in Atlanta). This was a very conducive atmosphere for spiritual reflection, of which I was badly in need after several years of working at the Catholic Worker, numerous stints in jails for peace protests, etc. I came across *The Habit of Being*,[20] O'Connor's letters, and I was absolutely won, and this played a deep role in my decision to become a Catholic. It was truly my catechism. Of course for a while this made me into an insufferable Defender of the Faith. I had much growing up to do. But so much followed.

I have returned so often to the beautiful prayer to St. Raphael that appears at the end of the book:

> *O Raphael, lead us toward those we are waiting for, those who are waiting for us: Raphael, Angel of happy meeting, lead us by the hand toward those we are looking for. May all our movements be guided by your Light and transfigured with your joy.*

---

19. The reference is to the location of a famous event in Thomas Merton's life as a monk, an epiphany in downtown Louisville in which he realized his unity with all the people on the street. It was, he said, "like waking from a dream of separateness."

20. *The Habit of Being: The Letters of Flannery O'Connor*, ed. Sally Fitzgerald (New York: Farrar Straus & Giroux, 1979).

St. Raphael, the angel who guides us toward those we are meant to meet. Surely, that prayer has been answered in my contact with you.

Please remember Yushi in your prayers.

———————

June 22, 2016

Dearest Robert,

I am just about to begin a rereading of Flannery's letters. I do know her and marvel at the depth of her understanding of the truth. It struck me as strange at first that Dorothy had not brought you to the faith, but I can see how God uses natural attributes to speak to us through them, in this case Flannery's brilliance. She by nature and grace was the one to open you up to the full power of what Our Lord is. Dorothy prepared the ground, Flannery brought forth the flowers. I feel that among the extraordinary number of people you know or have known that are very close to God, I'm right at the back of the multitude. What your friend with cancer has written to you is of extraordinary depth and beauty. It's especially wonderful to see suffering purifying the spirit and opening new vistas of God's love.

I can't thank you enough for the insight you have given me into a world where He is truly loved.

With joy and gratitude,
Sister Wendy

———————

June 22, 2016

Dear Sister Wendy,

I had a letter from someone complaining of my referring to previously baptized Christians who have entered the Catholic Church as "converts." He cited a statute from the Episcopal Catechumenate that this is to be discouraged, on grounds of ecumenical sensitivity. It seemed strange to me that figures like Newman, Hopkins, Merton, Day, or Elizabeth Seton should not be described as converts, when that was so much a part of their identity; in some cases it involved a radical change in their social status, their relationship with their family, friends, etc. (Seamus Heaney has told the story of asking help from a caretaker at the cemetery in Dublin in finding the grave of Gerard Manley Hopkins: "Oh, you mean the convert?") But I don't really think of conversion as switching denominations—but really part of that turning toward

Christ that is the vocation of all Christians. My mother, an Episcopalian, was initially hurt when I became a Catholic—but I didn't see it as rejecting her or the church in which I was raised, so much as that I found my Christian identity anew within the Catholic Church.

The thing about my time with Dorothy and the Catholic Worker—it was possible for a while for me to think of the CW as my "church," the real church. I actually functioned as editor of *The Catholic Worker* for a couple of years with this sort of attitude. But at a certain point I couldn't keep that up. I collapsed under the pressure. That is when I took up this work in the cancer home and discovered Flannery O'Connor and realized for the first time that the church is very much wider than what I had known. Dorothy of course knew this. And so this really helped me to understand her in a much deeper dimension.

I dreamed of her last night, as I often do. I was supposed to give a talk at the Catholic Worker, and I was trying to figure out what to say. Suddenly I noticed that Dorothy was standing there, but in my dream I was realizing that this was a private vision I was enjoying, which no one else could share. She walked up to me, looking younger than when I knew her, and gave me a warm embrace. I said, "Dorothy, look how old I have become, whereas you haven't changed a bit." She stepped back, smiled, gave me a playful slap on the cheek, and said, "You should see a doctor about that!" Then she disappeared, and I woke up!

Along with my letter I attached a very delightful surprise: two pictures of me taken with Dorothy in 1977, which her granddaughter Kate Hennessy had recently discovered.

July 19, 2016

Dearest Robert,

Those are wonderful photographs. Two strong, focused faces, strangely alike, and in

With Dorothy Day in 1977

the seated photograph, in almost eerie alignment. Flannery may have converted you, and her rare, rich iconoclastic spirit has always been with you, but there's something about Dorothy's intense seriousness that I identify as very Robert.

I simply cannot tell you dear Robert what sustenance and what joy your series gives me.

Very much love and gratitude,
Sister Wendy

P.S. Sister Lesley says sternly that I have not mentioned my health. I am obviously still alive and rejoicing in the wonder of the world through which He comes to us. I'm fading a little, but I have no idea how long the weakness will last and then increase and overwhelm. We who live in the Will of God can only greet each day with joy.

———————

In a previous letter Sister Wendy had offered brief, succinct assessments of each of the volumes in the Modern Spiritual Masters Series she had read.

July 19, 2016

Dearest Sister Wendy,

When I was a child one of my favorite books was *Anatole the Mouse*. It was about a French mouse, with superb taste, who sneaks into a cheese factory and writes beautiful little reviews of all the cheeses he tastes: "Needs more salt"; "More cream." The proprietors don't know his identity; all they know is that his judgments are impeccable, and they leave him a note welcoming him to sample any cheese he wants. I feel that way when I read your precise evaluations of the MSM volumes.

"We who live in the Will of God can only greet each day with joy." I wonder if you have always felt this way. Is it a matter of temperament, or did you have to work hard to achieve this attitude?

For many years I was just drowning in a sea of stress. I think I learned to escape through my writing, and my immersion in the lives of the saints. I wish I could say that I am a great pray-er. But that would not be true. And yet I do try to greet each day with joy. I struggled a lot with the idea of the Will of God in my book *The Saints' Guide to Happiness*—so many of the saints truly lived in the will of God. For me it is a resolution to find the way to God that lies in every situation, a way to be more forgiving, more patient, more loving. That is one of the lessons I have taken from Dorothy, which means all the more because I know how much struggle it involved for her. By nature she was quick to judge and capable of sarcasm and anger. When someone once told her to "hold her temper," she said, "I hold more temper in one minute than you will in your entire life."

"*Rejoicing in the wonder of the world through which He comes to us*"— that is something I can identify with.

As Dorothy liked to quote from the Psalms: "Rejoice, and again I say Rejoice!"

————————

Sister Wendy admired those (unlike herself) who were capable of analyzing themselves, though she judged herself "quite good at sensing what other people are like, especially good at sensing their holiness."

July 20, 2016

Dearest Robert,

I wish so much I could help you. I think of Dorothy Day who lived her life much as you live yours, it seems to me. There were always burdens, always anxieties, no prolonged periods of rest, yet it was clinging to God with trust amidst all the pressure that surely made her holy. I would add though, that she went to daily Mass. I think you pray implicitly all the day, but Mass is that great objective prayer into which Jesus draws us.

Nothing can compensate for it. All we need to bring to Mass is desire and a Yes, and of course, time. But the time given to Mass is never wasted in the busiest of days.

I have always been aware that God was all that mattered and that He held me to Himself, which has spared me a lot of unnecessary turmoil. I don't think though that, temperamentally, I'm all that placid. (Sister Lesley nods approvingly.) But dear Robert, I have always been absolutely unable to make judgments about myself. I can only trust to God that I'm not in dire need of spiritual reform, living in a cloud cuckoo-land of illusion. But you know, even if I am, I don't really care because Jesus is our life and He will put all right and tell me if something needs to be done.

I'm always deep in admiration of those who can analyze themselves and I got into a lot of trouble with the novice mistress because I couldn't tell her my predominant vice. (I could only say hopelessly, "I think I've got all of them, Sister.") And as for predominant virtue, I couldn't find a single one. This was frowned upon and I was told that all spiritual authorities insist on self-knowledge as the foundation of virtue. I tried to suggest that perhaps God's knowledge would do, but this went down very badly. But I am quite good at sensing what other people are like, especially good at sensing their holiness, which I think is infinitely more common than realized.

Thank you for giving me the joy of a letter from you. Remember this is heaven, whether you feel it or not.

Lovingly and prayerfully,
Sister Wendy

————————

July 20, 2016

Dear Sister Wendy,

I am glad to know that you didn't quite fit in the categories of the novitiate. As Merton wrote, "One of the first signs of a saint may well be the fact that other people do not know what to make of him. In fact they are not sure whether he is crazy or only proud. . . . He cannot seem to make his life fit in with the books." Of course that was a self-serving statement on his part.

I believe self-knowledge is a very valuable aspiration—though difficult to achieve; we are so prone to self-delusion. Do we ever truly know ourselves?

Yes, heaven is right here. As Dorothy liked to quote St. Catherine of Siena, "All the way to Heaven is Heaven . . . because He said, 'I am the way.'"

————————

July 21, 2016

Dearest Robert,

Of course I'd love you to have an admiring, supportive, deeply Catholic family and I'd love that there were ample funds for your apostolate at Maryknoll and that the sun always shone for you and that you always felt the embrace of the One Who carries you along the way. But since it is His dear will that these things should not happen, then I can only join with you in thanking Him for what He does and trusting that it is for the best—not just your best, but the universal best. After all, if Jesus Himself took up the Cross, what a privilege that we share that with Him.

I was reading Evelyn Underhill's[21] advice about confession this morning —absolutely excellent. (I am myself a great lover of this sacrament, which I don't see as connected, necessarily, with sin, but with lack of love. We hold

———————————

21. Evelyn Underhill (1875–1941) was an Anglican spiritual writer who did much to popularize interest in the study of mysticism. See *Evelyn Underhill: Essential Writings*, ed. Emilie Griffin (Maryknoll, NY: Orbis Books, 2003).

up our lovelessness and sacramentally He pours in His love. I must add I have made several attempts to convert people to this view of the sacrament and have not succeeded.)

Much love, dear, brave, loving Robert,
Sister Wendy

July 21, 2016

Dear Sister Wendy,

Have you hung up your writing quill? I would love to see a book of daily reflections from you, beginning with your beautiful reflection on confession as something that concerns a lack of love.

There is a new center for Catholicism and Culture—the Sheen Center, in New York City. They have invited me to give a series of lectures on "my favorite saints." They asked me for five to start with. I proposed: St. Therese of Lisieux, Bd. Oscar Romero,[22] Bd. Franz Jägerstätter,[23] Dorothy Day, and Thomas Merton. (Forgive me; if only you could be present to play devil's advocate.)

Who would be on your list?

July 23, 2016

Dearest Robert,

I know your gentle heart would not be writing sarcastically, but I greeted your proposal that I should write such a book with a disbelieving laugh. I think I possibly "could" write a book if there was somebody asking me questions. I can nearly always answer questions and of course dear Sister Lesley writes down what I say. I don't think I could "create" a book anymore, yet I think that, with very few exceptions, I haven't created most of my books. I've looked at a picture and responded, which is another thing all together.

---

22. Oscar Romero (1917–1980) was the prophetic archbishop of San Salvador, assassinated while saying Mass because of his defense of the poor and his strong condemnation of injustice. He was recognized as a martyr and canonized in 2018.

23. Franz Jägerstätter (1907–1943) was an Austrian peasant and devout Catholic who was beheaded by the Nazis for his refusal to serve in Hitler's army. He was beatified as a martyr in 2007.

What an entrancing invitation: Your five favorite saints. I'd agree with you on the Little Flower [St. Therese] and Dorothy. I think I would choose St. Elizabeth of the Trinity,[24] perhaps Mother Teresa,[25] perhaps one of our recent popes, John XXIII, or John Paul II, or dear Benedict XVI. Although there were days when we shuddered at the mention of Ratzinger's name, grim watchdog of a very narrow faith, it would seem. His books are so profoundly alive with the joy of the faith. He hasn't the sweetness of Pope Francis, but one can only love him for what he's given us about Our Blessed Lord.

Although the most interesting figure of your five is, of course, Thomas Merton, I simply cannot accept him as a saint. I'm sure he did his best, but that's not the point. As soon as Sister Lesley has left my cell with her machine, I shall probably think of lots of saints I would choose, but on this very hot July afternoon I can only gasp out these few. I wish Elizabeth were better known. Our mutual friend Thomas Merton says she's not as well-known as St. Therese, because she's not as pretty!

Very much love and gratitude, you write wonderful letters,
Sister Wendy

———————

July 25, 2016

Dear Sister Wendy,

"*I think I possibly* could *write a book if there was somebody asking me questions.*" That almost sounds like an invitation! Would you like to try that? I have endless questions. I only wish I could ask them in person, though I am sure I would not be allowed inside the cloister.

———————

24. St. Elizabeth of the Trinity (1880–1906) was a French Carmelite mystic. Soon after taking her final vows she was diagnosed with an incurable disease and spent the next three years in increasing agony. A passage in one of her letters well reflects Sr. Wendy's own spiritual disposition: "We carry our heaven within ourselves, because he who satisfies the saints with the light of vision gives himself to us in faith and in mystery. It's the same thing. I feel I have found heaven on earth, because heaven is God and God is in my soul. The day I understood this a light went on inside me, and I want to whisper this secret to all those I love."

25. Mother Teresa of Calcutta (1910–1997), founder of the Missionaries of Charity and winner of the Nobel Peace Prize, was widely acclaimed as a living saint for her work among the destitute and dying. She was canonized in 2016. Both Pope John XXIII (d. 1963) and Pope John Paul II were canonized on the same day in 2014.

I do love the idea of composing a book with you through questions and answers. A very Socratic way of writing a book. I am sure there are many implicit masterpieces within you waiting to be born. Let me know if that idea appeals to you. If not, no worries.

As for my saints, you will be amused to hear that some years ago I visited Merton's home, the Abbey of Gethsemani. I was pleased to learn that they had spent a year reading aloud in the refectory from my book *All Saints*. I asked whether the monks had any trouble with some of my unconventional choices. I was told: "Well, there were some smirks about Thomas Merton."

July 26, 2016

Dearest Robert,

The type of book you are adumbrating would require work. I'm not going to say that I couldn't do it, if Sister Lesley could spare the time and we'd tackle a question a day. I think you have to think seriously though, with Orbis's finances fluttering in the wind, whether this would be a profitable book for you. Who wants to hear my opinions? Even I'm not interested.

Very much love, dear Robert, and please keep as well as the Lord allows,

Sister Wendy

P.S. from Sister Lesley:
Of course I will make time for a book between you and Sr. Wendy!!

July 28, 2016

Dear Sister Wendy,

I would love to pursue something with you in the form of questions and answers, and will try not to overwhelm you. Who wants to know your opinions? I DO!

For example: Could you describe what your day is like? What is the life of a contemplative? What is the nature of your relationship to the Carmelite community, and how did this come about? And how has it changed over the years? Do you feel a particular resonance with Carmelite spirituality? Was that always an attraction for you?

Maybe I should ask you: If you were to pose questions for Flannery O'Connor or Dorothy Day, what would you ask them? I am sure I could be instructed by your example!

Apropos of nothing—my youngest, the scientist, told me something very interesting. She asked me, "What is your conception of what happens to a caterpillar when it goes into a cocoon and comes out as a butterfly?" I said I supposed that it sort of grew wings. She said no—they have studied this only fairly recently, and discovered that it basically turns into goo, and then goes through a complete physical reconstitution into a completely different form. I thought this raised a completely new image of the resurrection: to sow a physical body, to raise a spiritual body, as St. Paul says. Somehow I found this information terribly moving and inspiring. And I am told that the struggle of a butterfly to break out of its cocoon is absolutely necessary to develop its strength and capacity to fly.

———————

July 30, 2016

Dearest Robert,

Let me start with your end observation—the wonderful image of the worm losing everything and when it is formless and almost a nothing, being reconstituted into something beautiful. I share the wonder and emotional involvement that you and your daughter feel. As to the need for the butterfly to struggle, I have never forgotten reading about a cocoon that was placed in a container that was too small. The butterfly did emerge, but it was crippled and deformed because there had been no room to exercise its powers. In a way that's also an image of becoming close to God, isn't it, in this life? "I live now, not I, but Christ lives in me," is another form of that disintegration and resurrection.

I can't refrain from giving you my final six, unfortunately (?) all women: Therese of Lisieux; Elizabeth of the Trinity; Bernadette Soubirous;[26] Julian of Norwich; Flannery O'Connor; Dorothy Day.

---

26. St. Bernadette Soubirous (1844–1879), a peasant girl from the small town of Lourdes on the northern Pyrenees slopes, was gathering firewood near a remote grotto when she saw a young woman. Her companions saw nothing. In subsequent encounters the woman identified herself as "the Immaculate Conception" and gave her instructions which uncovered a spring. This was the origin of the cult of Lourdes, the most popular pilgrimage site in Europe, famous for its healing miracles. Partly to escape unwanted attention, Bernadette entered an order of nursing sisters, where she died, after great suffering, at 35.

The only one not of our times, of course, is Julian, yet one cannot but feel a very strong link to her. I didn't mean it to be one-sexed and I struggled for favorite men. Charming Thomas Merton I exclude because he has given us every single detail of his actual life as a monk. I sometimes think he had no conscience, since he describes the most extraordinary breaches of the rule without the slightest contrition or even awareness that he promised to live otherwise. But let me not get on a hobby-horse.

The trouble about asking questions about Dorothy or Flannery is that there's nothing I would want to ask them. I'm afraid you'll have to accept that I'm a very uninteresting person, Robert—perfectly happy just to live in silence. Your own questions depressed me because they start with such factual and material matters. I feel very unattracted by them, alas. I can't think of any question about me that would attract me, though as you can see I enjoy discussing the saints we like and am finding your series a wonderful source of delight.

Very much love,
Sister Wendy

———

August 3, 2016

Dearest Sister Wendy,

Your reply to my questions made me smile! Yes, I did deliberately start on a boring note, thinking that would be an easier place to begin before working up to the Big Questions. But don't worry. I will give them more thought, and if you continue to find them unattractive, then I shall resign myself to unrequited curiosity!

———

August 5, 2016

Dearest Robert,

I think it's because I myself have always felt an oddity, though not, thank God, a stigmatic, that I feel a tenderness for Padre Pio.[27] In fact I feel a tenderness for all people whose vocation has been to be on the outskirts.

---

27. Padre Pio (1887–1968), an Italian Capuchin friar, was famous for bearing the wounds of Christ on his hands, feet, and side. Even as he lived he was credited with numerous healing miracles. He was canonized in 2002.

I think perhaps there's not much mileage in me, compared. But I don't want to break off our correspondence, which I find nourishing.

Very much love,
Sr. Wendy

————————

August 5, 2016

Dear Sister Wendy,

I have already apologized for imposing on you with my various jottings. But I wonder if you can indulge me if I attach the reflections I shared at my mother's memorial service. It was three years ago, but she has been much on my mind on my son's 30th birthday. She gave me so much, as you will see. From my father I acquired a passion for peace and justice, and for standing behind one's conscience. But my mother taught me so much about what it means to be a decent person. She implanted the seeds of faith, and I would not be writing about the saints today without her. Thank you for being someone I can share this with.

With my mother

————————

Though Sister Wendy doubted that anyone could find this interesting, she volunteered to answer my initial questions, describing some of the day-to-day aspects of her contemplative life, and opening a window onto her understanding of prayer. Increasingly, as I had hoped, this opened a window on deeper aspects of her inner life.

August 7, 2016

Dearest Robert,

I will be honored to read what you say about your mother. You have a wonderful heritage, and of course it will have passed on to your son. I envy you being able to articulate what you feel about your parents. I love mine and feel very grateful to have had such thoroughly good people who, though undemonstrative, I knew quite well would have died for their children. But I can't even formulate a sentence about my mother or father that I can feel is "true." Might this be because I entered [religious life] so young, at 16, when they were still mythic figures of power and love, and not mere human beings, as an adult child knows well?

Celibacy has enormous strengths and graces, but it can't break open the heart as can parenthood. You have a sort of built-in insight into the love of God the Father. Yours is a great privilege and you certainly have three most interesting children, for whom I pray.

I felt a little guilty about being so high-hat over your questions, so here is an attempt to answer your first one—not, dear Robert, that anybody would be interested:

When I came to live in solitude, it was solely to give myself to prayer. In those early days, at the beginning '70s, I took it for granted that part of that prayer would be a sharing in the Divine Office and I walked up from the caravan for every hour, except Compline.[28] But I began to realize that apart from the disruption of leaving the caravan so often during the day, the psalms were just too much for me. A line, perhaps only a few words, so fills me with light and joy that it is difficult to continue with the chant. I've realized that I'm not large enough a soul for this privilege. I rejoice to be in the ambit of that great praise of God, the sacred duty of the consecrated religious. As for me, and although it hasn't the same ecclesial significance, it is still ecclesial prayer. I just sit silently letting the Lord take possession.

I have a very minimal rule, discussed with a saintly Jesuit before I came. He was quite insistent that I not spend more than seven hours a day praying. But of course, the whole day is prayer of different levels. When I'm not sitting silently with my eyes shut, I'm reading, sometimes spiritual books and sometimes novels or art, and I consider all of this a type of prayer. So I have a very blessed and silent life.

I live in a room now at the far end of the monastery and leave it once a day when my dear carer wheels me to Mass. It's a lovely room with a tiny kitchen and a tinier bathroom on either side, and it has two big windows. They only look out on brick walls, the sisters' choir, and the back of the monastery, but I can see a little triangle of sky at the top. When I read Thomas Merton's heart-felt ecstasies about nature and its necessity for a full human life, I have

---

28. The Divine Office, or Liturgy of the Hours, is a central feature of monastic life—a schedule of prayer services throughout the day, beginning with Matins in the morning and concluding with Compline, or Evening Prayer. Recitation or chanting of the psalms forms the basic structure of these services.

to smile a little sadly. I would also like to have the natural world back again, but if God hasn't given it, it's because He gives me something else.

When the prioress decided that it was time for me to leave the caravan because I was too frail to continue living alone, she didn't know how to break it to me. She asked the chaplain to tell me. But as soon as I realized what he was saying, I had no problem. If God was waiting for me in the monastery, how could I want to stay in my hazelnut glen?

I've never regarded asceticism as anything but a means to an end, the end of being totally there for God. So getting up at about 11:30 p.m. every night and going to bed at about 6:00 in the evening is simply to give myself more time for undisturbed prayer—also I like praying in the night, which is a difficult time for many people. I don't eat very much and I don't eat after midday, simply because this fits into my normal pattern.

I never feel hungry. My room is luminous with icons and at the windowsill there's some most beautiful glass and I have huge bookcases with art books in them. Everything I look at speaks to me of Our Blessed Lord.

Dear Robert, this seems to me absolutely uninteresting. I have a small hope that having read it you'll decide that asking me questions is not a good idea.

Very much love, and looking forward eagerly to your books,
Sister Wendy

In light of her admiration for St. Bernadette, I had asked whether she had ever made a pilgrimage to Lourdes, noting that Flannery O'Connor, who was grudgingly dragged to Lourdes by her mother, had said, "There is some of us would rather die for our faith than take a bath for it."

August 8, 2016

Dearest Robert,

I realize I forgot to answer your question about Lourdes. No, I have not been, and I feel very much like Flannery did. I would only hope that I would have the grace to respond as she did when faced with the inevitable. I am convinced it is a holy place, but in the Mass every day I have my own holy place. I don't want to travel. My love for St. Bernadette has nothing to do with Lourdes. Although spiritually Lourdes was the greatest event of her life, in spiritual terms a transforming encounter, in worldly terms it was a disaster. If only Bernadette could have been alone with Our Lady! But the immense public attention marked her out as different and forced her out of her natural habitat, an uneducated peasant from the very lowest level of society, into the genteel surroundings of a middle-class convent. She was never at home, never accepted, always the subject of both scrutiny and suspicion. Although she wasn't clever, she was shrewd, shrewd enough to know that people looked down on her for her lack of refinement, her poor table manners, her ignorance of conventions, her lack of interest in book-learning. Although the humblest of women, she had an innate peasant dignity that was deeply aware of the scorn, especially since she was considered too crude a creature to mind. Oh dear Bernadette, what Our Lady gave her in that embrace of love was the start of a long Calvary of small humiliations.

Love,
Sister Wendy

August 8, 2016

Dearest Sister Wendy,

Having asked you such a banal question, I am terribly grateful for the thoughtful and really inspiring answer you were willing to share. I suppose if your spiritual director had not restricted you to only seven hours a day, you would not have had time to write me at all, so I am very glad. It does sound very much like the world of Julian of Norwich, though I'm not sure whether she had even as much as a little triangle of sky. (I think of Anne Frank and her beloved chestnut tree). But I know what while you no longer travel, and though your physical world is limited, for those who are so plugged into the spiritual realm, there are no horizons.

In my book of women saints[29] I wrote about a very dear friend, Daria Donnelly, my son's godmother, who died much too soon of a terrible illness. She wrote, "My getting sick increased my attention to the everyday heroism of refugees, the depressed, the arthritic, the mourning, the lonely, all those who know how good it is simply to get through a day." I remember how you wrote me about the grace of being able to connect one's sufferings to the passion of Christ (as Julian did). But Daria showed me how to connect one's sufferings to the sufferings of everyone—and thus to exercise compassion. I wrote about a nun who was dying of cancer. She said that she felt her sufferings connected her to "the wounds." The wounds of Christ? she was asked. "The wounds of everyone."

---

29. *Blessed Among All Women: Women Saints, Prophets, and Witnesses for Our Time* (New York: Crossroad, 2006).

And I am struck by the sense that if your goal is to be completely present to God, that can be done anywhere. I know that Merton is not an ideal example for you, but I think about his struggles to find the solitude he desired: "It does not much matter where you are, as long as you can be at peace about it and live your life. The place certainly will not live my life for me. I have to live it for myself." As for the solitude he sought: "Here or there makes no difference. Somewhere, nowhere, beyond all 'where.' Solitude outside geography, or in it. No matter."

Your present room also reminds me of Dorothy Day's final room in Maryhouse, where I used to visit her, and where she was pretty much confined at the end of her life. She was surrounded by books and icons, and picture postcards that she used to tape to the wall.

Anyway, what you have shared with me is INTENSELY interesting, and it has given me much to meditate on. If you had hoped this would deter me from asking questions, I am afraid you have failed. Don't worry whether your answers will interest me—but only answer if the questions interest you.

For instance: You say that everything you look at speaks to you of our Blessed Lord. Is this because you are a natural contemplative? Is it a gift? Or is this something that you needed to cultivate? Did it require a long experience as a solitary? Was there a time when you did not experience this? (Lots of questions but all aspects of the same question.)

August 9, 2016

Dearest Robert,

Questions: Dearest Robert, no questions interest me. There's really nothing I want to say. As to the one you have put to me in your message, I think as a child I was very aware of God in Himself, but far less aware of God in people, things, and events. Perhaps hardly aware of Him there at all. But from about 15 on, I did see that we were held always in His hands and with us, everything else. So although I would not say I'm a natural contemplative (I think I'm too superficial), I can't remember a time when I found any obstacle in my path. By the way, don't think I'm being humble, I just cannot express my triviality of mind in ways that would make it understandable to anybody but God. Once or twice I have had letters from people lamenting what they call a poor self-image, but I am quite happy with this poor image. I don't have to look at myself or feel any concern because there is God to look at, infinitely more wonderful.

However, let me remove a misunderstanding: I have never had, or wanted to have, and even shudder at the thought of having, a spiritual director. I think they are, on the whole, NOT A GOOD THING. This was merely a priest that the Notre Dame nuns asked me to consult before I came into solitude.

Merton: The last thing I would want is to in any way disturb your affection for this fascinating man. Just remember though, dearest Robert, that whenever you quote him somebody who knows his work will remember that in a page or two he will have gone back completely on what he says. Part of his essential makeup seems to be an inability to make a decision and stick to it. He is innocent in this. But whereas anything Dorothy says, or Flannery, or Therese, etc., one accepts as what they think and it becomes a guiding light. Knowing that Merton thinks he thinks this, but will soon be taking active steps to disprove it in practice, is disturbing, or maybe it just is in me. I don't want to pursue this.

Parents: You have been blessed to make an adult contact with your father and your mother. On the 5th of this month it was my brother's birthday and I spoke about our father's overwhelming joy in 1939 when Tim was born. In his reply Timothy said how sad he was that he never got close to our father and now it is too late. Dad was in the army medical corps from '40 to '45 so he began his life with only our mother and he never quite got over it. It made me ponder on the mysteries of these intimate relationships. Mostly I think they're part of the "wound" of which you speak so movingly.

With much love and prayer,
Sister Wendy

August 12, 2016

Dearest Sister Wendy,

I am sorry to have suggested that you had a spiritual director!—not knowing that this would evoke a shudder. And please don't worry that we don't hold exactly the same estimation of Thomas Merton—I actually see your point. I don't know whether you have ever delved into the Enneagram[30] but it is a useful measure of people's psychological and spiritual make-up.

---

30. The Enneagram is a model of the human psyche that posits nine interconnected personality types. It has been adopted as a device by many spiritual directors. I should have known that Sister Wendy, who on the whole believed that spiritual directors are "NOT A GOOD THING," would have no interest in such a concept. In fact, the topic made her "slightly ill."

Merton was in some ways more of an artist than a natural contemplative, with a sense of his own specialness, which made it very hard to submit to rules, vows of stability and obedience. And yet without those structures—though he constantly pushed against them—he would have achieved nothing (I think). Many of his admirers treat his abbot as the bad guy, but I think he must have been a very wise man. No matter—I won't keep needling you about him!

I am very struck by the great mystery that we can spend much of our lives in a situation that we think is where we are supposed to be, and then when we find the right place everything seems to click. I take it that for you, your early life in a teaching order was not really the proper milieu for your gifts and your yearnings. But everything has its purpose if we listen to where God is calling us.

———————

August 13, 2016

Dearest Robert,

Yes I do know about the Enneagram, which the sisters here have enjoyed at times. I feel I must make it quite clear to you dearest Robert, that I really don't know myself and that any statements I make may not be true. This doesn't bother me at all, because I can't see any point in trying to know myself. I feel that's God's business and He will make it quite clear to me if something that I do or think has to change.

Going back to my earlier confession that I don't feel I can say anything truthful about myself, do you think there's any point in asking me questions, dear Robert?

Much love and prayer,
Sister Wendy

P.S. Sister Lesley doesn't want you put off with your questions and I don't want to be selfish about this, but beloved Robert, what is the point?

———————

August 15, 2016

Dearest Sister Wendy,

As for the Enneagram—I was quite taken with this when I first heard Richard Rohr OFM talk about it. For many years I believed I was a Type 5, "the investigator"—the one who quietly observes and studies everything from the back row, and who has to struggle with active engagement—and this became a very fixed part of my identity. Then I recently took an actual diagnostic test and was astonished to discover that I am a Type 9, "the peacemaker." This was quite disorienting. It was as if I had grown up believing I was Irish, with all the store of pride and resentments that implies, only to discover that I am actually Italian. But it suddenly made lots of sense of things in my life—especially my constant effort to make peace, to resolve conflict, and to restore balance around me. At times this has served me well, while at other times it prevented me from changing things that needed changing.

But do we ever really know ourselves? That is a deep question. We know a certain story that we tell ourselves—but we get such a small glimpse of the whole picture, the impact we have on others, for good or ill, the effects of our small gestures, the things we do or leave undone. And there is so much capacity for illusion and self-deception.

I remember the words of St. Catherine of Siena,[31] which I recited in a homily for my daughter Catherine's baptism: "My cell," she said, "will not be one of stone or wood, but of self-knowledge." In what did this self-knowledge consist? She received the answer in a vision of Christ: "Know daughter that I am He who is, and thou art that which is not."

I am sure the answers you provided to my questions were "truthful"—even if you thought they were not interesting (at least not to you!). But I don't want to make you feel interrogated.

One of the mysterious aspects of the cult of saints is the question of miracles —still a prerequisite for canonization in the Catholic Church. As Sister Wendy noted: "A BIG SUBJECT."

August 16, 2016

Dearest Robert,

There is always such rich material in your letters, and I feel that if I had enough energy I could write quite a good deal in response. Lucky for you that we are meeting in the late twilight of my life.

I am reading a book on Marian apparitions, and the thing that struck me is that if one simplifies them, there's just a sense of the loving sense of Our

---

31. St. Catherine of Siena (1347–1380), a mystic and Dominican tertiary, is among the few women to be named a Doctor of the Church. After experiencing a "mystical betrothal" with Christ, she set out on a public mission to heal the world and reform the church.

Blessed Lady. Authenticity in its strictest sense doesn't come into it, though I must say that I don't think in any apparition stories there is deliberate falsehood. I think something happened, people became aware—oh, what a grace—of a loving, strengthening, motherly presence.

It's when they start to put words to this that I think we're into dubious waters. I've always been put off by these prophesies of doom; it just struck me now that these prophesies have actually come true. We're living in a very terrible world, one that gravely needs help and protection.

But I was also struck by how casually rationalistic I had been, convinced that it must all be a psychic projection, and never really considering that this psychic projection might be exactly the way that she shows herself.

Anyhow you will be amused to know that Sister Lesley is also a 9 in the Enneagram and she was chuckling happily to herself while she read your description. It makes me feel slightly ill to even think of the Enneagram, so you can see how any idea of self-disclosure has been sabotaged from the beginning.

Do you like writing letters (and obviously I think of emails as letters)? I find communication valuable and beautiful when one has something to say, otherwise it seems so trivial.

Very much love dearest Robert, and God bless you,
Sister Wendy

————

August 19, 2016

Dearest Sister Wendy,

The question about Marian apparitions is of course closely tied to the subject of miracles—which play such a big role (still) in the cult of saints. Certainly there is reason to regret the way that attention in the past seemed to focus on miracles or evidence of sacred power in the lives of the saints, quite overshadowing their actual lives. And yet the certification of miracles continues to be a prerequisite for canonization. And even though, in this scientific age, the range of recognized miracles has been reduced almost entirely to the realm of medical cures, still, it is the case that miracles continue to occur. I recognize that this is the case, yet I don't really know what I think about it.

One of the problems is not the question of whether God can suspend the laws of nature or physics—but why should God do this in very particular cases, curing one individual, while "ignoring" so many other deserving cases? Just to increase our faith? Yet it is striking what a great role healing plays in the gospels—not in some metaphorical sense, but actual physical healing.

I sometimes think the problem is that we tend to take too small a view of miracles, looking just at cures for which there is (as yet) no scientific rationale. But we don't see the larger role of grace and providence—not just in preventing terrible things (how is it possible that we have avoided nuclear war this long, what with all the accidents and near misses?), but allowing remarkably good things to come out of bad.

I confess that for all the time I have spent pondering the lives of the saints, I have never felt entirely comfortable praying to them for assistance. And yet sometimes I do feel a special sense of their presence in my life. They often appear in my dreams. One time, when I was suffering over one of my daughters, I dreamed that I was at a dinner party in which the guest of honor was Mother Teresa. She invited us to go around the room and present any special petitions we had. When it came to me, she put her hand on mine and said, "I know what your heart desires. Have no fear."

To your question—yes, I do very much enjoy writing letters; but it is not so much having something to say, as having someone to say it to that is important to me. I don't think what I have to say is terribly important, but genuine communication is a rare thing, and it means a lot to me, and there are not many people I know who share that capacity.

August 21, 2016

Dearest Robert,

Certainly I regard your letters as a great gift. With you, in your letters, comes a whole world of grace, of people of all kinds reaching out to God and rejoicing in Him. As for your dreams, I think they have a biblical quality. I'm sure that is one way that God communicates, but it's rare. I have beautiful dreams too, holy dreams that make me immensely happy, but I do think they are just dreams. Yours seem to have that extra edge on them that says that they are not just from you, but from above.

Thinking of the famous quotation from St. Catherine of Siena, it suddenly struck me that it is an absolute, whereas we live in a world of relatives. When I entered in 1946/7, we were taught to say on rising a prayer that said we only got up to praise Our Blessed Lord and that we united ourselves with the praise and adoration of His rising. The final line says that "I give and surrender myself to You without reserve," but how can I give myself if I don't exist? No, I do exist, I am, because that was God's good pleasure, to share His Being with his creatures, so that we can know what joy is. So I've moderated my enthusiasm for the great Sienese Doctor of the Church.

It sounds wonderful, but when you look at it, it doesn't really mean what it seems to mean. I remember the enormous happiness I felt as a novice when I realized that we are contingent, but that contingency is a real being, because God is real and all He makes is real.

I hope this is not a boring—Sister Lesley says no it isn't, so I won't go any further.

Much love, Dearest Robert, and much gratitude. Happy feast tomorrow for the Queenship of Our Lady,

Sister Wendy

P.S. I also have a difficulty with miracles. So much that in the past we thought was miraculous can now be explained in natural terms and I'm not sure whether, as it were, forcing God to act miraculously before we canonize His friends is the best way of going about things. We need no miracle to tell us Dorothy is a saint, but if there isn't a miracle she won't be canonized, and like you, I like the trust and devotion that people feel for a complete unknown, in worldly terms, whose holiness of life has convinced them that they can expect help there. This a BIG SUBJECT.

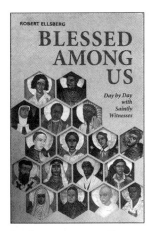

August 23, 2016

Dearest Robert,

Your most beautiful book, *Blessed Among Us*,[32] arrived today and I can't congratulate you warmly enough. I think if I knew somebody depressed I would give them your book, because it is so alive with the wonder of God's action. Each of those lives is a little miracle and each of those lives is completely different—stupid people, clever people, rich and poor, old and young, all centuries, all classes, in fact all religions. Some have been canonized, some are on the way, some will always be a source of local joy, some are what one might call secular saints. But in each one there is the Glory of

---

32. Beginning in 2012 I had been writing a short daily reflection on saints and holy lives for *Give Us This Day*, a monthly prayer resource published by the Benedictines at Liturgical Press. *Blessed Among Us* (Collegeville, MN: Liturgical Press, 2016) was a collection of many of these entries, two per every day.

God drawing the human being into His own largeness and gladness. I'm not myself given to depression, thank God, but if I were, a look through your book would fill me with happiness. And Robert, you don't just enumerate these holy people, you tell their story so beautifully. Incidentally, your very book answers your final question in your letter, as to why not everybody gets a miracle of healing, in fact, very few. Isn't it because every vocation is very different? If you need a miracle to open you up to God, you will get one, but perhaps you need something very different, and you will get that too.

Very much love,
Sister Wendy

August 23, 2016

Dear Sister Wendy,

This makes four books on saints that I have written. The Franciscan book for next year will be five. So I think I may justly claim the title of "hagiographer." Unfortunately, not the same as being a saint—but perhaps for some, this is their path. I do like to hope that what we contemplate, at length, may shape what we become. This is a good argument for prayer, whatever form it takes.

Sister Wendy had mentioned that in reading the authors featured in the Modern Spiritual Masters Series she noticed that many of them seemed to embody one or more "root ideas" or themes that characterized their spiritual message.

I wonder, if someone were to try to characterize your own spiritual "message" what three or four root ideas would they/you choose? Probably you would find the question disagreeable, uninteresting, or preposterous. But it would have to be something that connects your contemplative nature, your deep connection to the risen Lord, your ineffable prayer, and at the same time your special attraction to art—your ability to see so deeply into the spiritual and human realities transmitted through an artist's gifts. Maybe all these are aspects of the same thing, whatever "that" is.

Have you ever tried your own hand at drawing or painting?

Sister Wendy offered a beautiful summary of her attraction to art ("a delight in the beautiful"), her discovery that talking about art was a form of prayer, and that it also had an "apostolic element": that "for people who didn't know God, beauty was perhaps the surest way of finding Him."

August 24, 2016

Dearest Robert,

I can't but feel that a life spent immersed in the holiness of people's lives must have an effect on your own life. It is clear when you write that you feel the wonder of their open-hearted response to grace. And this wonder must also awaken in you the same desires.

I think my love of art is simply a delight in the beautiful. Remember, I've led, for most of my time, a life that is physically circumscribed—no plays, concerts, movies, travel, TV—so between the pages of a book I have been able to find such transcendent images of man's greatness of spirit, and of course, having tried to bring in some money for the community by writing on artists—contemporary artists, because I didn't feel my scholarship was sufficient to tackle a great master. I then became drawn into a world of art that I would never have considered possible. I also felt very strongly that for people who didn't know God, beauty was perhaps the surest way of finding Him. So this apostolic element, which I began to see actually worked, became a sort of secondary way of praying for me.

Also, in talking about art, though usually of necessity in a muted and hidden way, one can dwell upon the essence of the Godhead. His joy, the overflowing happiness that is in God, and which He specifically created us to share, is something that matters overwhelmingly to me. And it's all Him, His happiness, His creativity; all He asks of us is to receive, to accept His love, to enter into His joy. Awareness of all this means that nothing else really matters terribly much. The sufferings of other people are our sufferings, but we can take them into His peace and pray that there they can be assuaged. It's the other people's pain that hurts me. The Lord has spared me from having much of my own, as it were. It's the Passion of Jesus that is my pain, in which Passion are subsumed the sorrows of the whole world. Does that answer your question? I'm really not very good at this, dear Robert.

Very much love and prayer and gratitude,
Sister Wendy

Gradually I had been sharing more information about my fiancée, Monica, and the life we were sharing. Monica had initially been puzzled by my intense correspondence with an elderly hermit in England, but as I began sharing with her some of Sister Wendy's letters, her heart was won. And Sister Wendy, who had a preternatural ability to take the measure of people on the basis of slight information, quickly returned the affection.

August 24, 2016

Dearest Sister Wendy,

The new house (which my fiancée Monica and I are renting) is very old (by American standards): mid-nineteenth-century, part of an old Dutch settlement on the Hudson River called Sleepy Hollow, which goes back to the early eighteenth century, and which was made famous by the work of Washington Irving, author of *The Legend of Sleepy Hollow*. There is a large backyard which slopes upward, which makes it look like a wall of green, behind which is the Croton Aqueduct, a pathway that you can walk for many miles. The flowers outside the kitchen window attract butterflies and hummingbirds. It is quite a change from the one-room seventh-floor apartment overlooking a parking lot where I have lived for the past three and a half years.

In the last few years, in part thanks to Monica's influence, I have steadily lifted my eyes to take in natural beauty—after too many years with my head stuck in books. Now I take much delight in clouds, sunsets, trees, flowers, rocks—and am wondering how I missed all this.

Today is my daughter Catherine's 24th birthday. She says that in Paris, where she is studying for a master's degree, it is terribly hot now, with no air conditioning. But she has a year-pass to the Louvre and is spending a lot of time in museums. When she was young she could stare all day at a painting. It was very difficult to visit a museum with her because she would get captivated by the first gallery and never proceed. Perhaps you can understand.

August 25, 2016

Dearest Robert,

Now I can think of you with beautiful Monica in that beautiful house with beautiful pictures on every wall and God's own beautiful nature delighting you at every window. I also have come of late to a far greater appreciation of nature, because now I haven't got it. I only realized in retrospect what a joy I took from looking out of my two small windows. Because they were small windows, and I was in a little hollow inside a small copse, Fr. Steve, our chaplain who arranged the whole move for us, said to me, "Well you haven't lost all that much," and I cried out to him, "Fr. Steve, I had the world!" Well now I haven't got that world, but I have stocked up with flower paintings and books on trees. I feel a new insight has been given me, now that I no longer have the actuality of these lovely things.

Incidentally, I didn't answer your question about painting. No, Robert, I am completely uncreative. All my books are responses to the creations of other people. I don't think I've ever wanted to make anything, not even a cake or a rock garden or a flowered skirt. Interviewers tend not to believe anybody could be so helplessly lacking in this vital quality, but there it is. I can quite believe though that you could have been an artist, because I think you could have done many things. I'm grateful, though, for what you have done in your very unusual, but profoundly fulfilling, vocation.

I think of Catherine in Paris and hope her deep longing for beauty takes her beyond the material.

Very much love and gratitude,
Sister Wendy

August 26, 2016

Dearest Sister Wendy,

I wonder if you are able to call to mind all the beautiful images you have contemplated? From my office at Orbis, where I have now spent a

Mother Teresa

good deal of my life, I see a brick wall, but I have a beautiful patch of sky. When we moved to these offices I let others have the offices that look out across the Hudson Valley, all the way to the river and the Palisades beyond. During the winter, with an early sunset, there are tremendous views. I presume you are familiar with the great paintings of the Hudson River school.

Next week Mother Teresa will be canonized. I did meet her. She had come to the Catholic Worker to visit Dorothy. A homeless woman was sleeping on a bench at the front door and asked her, "You got a smoke?"

My main recollection was that she was very small. And she said to those of us there (in her familiar, lilting accent), "We are all doing the same work—something beautiful for God." Our paths crossed on a later occasion. After my five years at the Catholic Worker, I eventually returned to Harvard, and there, at my graduation, Mother Teresa of all people was the graduation speaker! She talked about the great spiritual poverty in the United States—so different from the material poverty in India, but just as real.

———

Sister Wendy elaborated on the contents of her room.

August 27, 2016

Dearest Robert,

There is very little wall space left in my room. Large bookcases are left, right, and center and I have icons on two tall layered stands elsewhere. The prioress does not want nails put in the walls, so there is a vacant space behind my bed, but I really wouldn't be able to see it from my chair anyhow. I have a succession of postcards on a little table on my right, the Metropolitan daily calendar on the little chest of drawers next to that, and I have several great reproductions balanced on top of one another on the lowest shelf of books. I have a great medieval annunciation triptych (Master of Moulins); balanced to the right of that I have two of Fra Angelico's angels; behind that the wonderful Poussin Annunciation, the greatest of all versions of this holy scene; and above that Duccio's Madonna and Child. I can always fit in postcards, but there's no space for anything larger.

I'm very touched by your generosity in allowing other people to have the beautiful views. Oh, I hope I would have been able to be so selfless, but I doubt it. I think I would have made ineffectual attempts to take the viewless room and allowed other people to persuade me into the visual delights of what you describe. I'm glad God has not put me to the test too often. What a disappointment I would have been to Him. Fortunately He is quite content with our disappointingness because all He asks is that we should accept our need of Him, and let Him be that wisdom and holiness that St. Paul speaks about in 1 Corinthians. If only people knew that looking at God and forgetting themselves open out a world of joy.

Very much love dear Robert,
Sister Wendy

———

August 29, 2016

Dearest Sister Wendy,

Thank you for permitting me this imaginative tour of your hidden cell. It is a special privilege to allow my mind to visit you there.

I came across this line from Henri Nouwen today: "It is remarkable how much consolation and hope we can receive from authors who, while offering no answers to life's questions, have the courage to articulate the situation of their lives in all honesty and directness. Kierkegaard, Sartre, Camus, Hammarskjold, and Merton—none of them have ever offered solutions. Yet many of us who have read their works have found new strength to pursue our own search. Their courage to enter so deeply into human suffering and to become present to their own pain gave them the power to speak healing words."

This was cited by my friend Gabrielle Earnshaw, who has just edited a collection of letters by Nouwen entitled *Love, Henri*.[33] It will be a beautiful book, and I was honored that she asked me to provide some editorial consultation.

Gabrielle was a professional archivist who was asked to take on the Henri Nouwen archives when these moved to Toronto after his death. She knew nothing previously about Nouwen. Then she experienced a terrible loss, the death of her young son. It was extraordinary how the gift of Nouwen's presence in her life came at just the time when she needed it. She has emerged out of this a very deep person—shaped by her loss and suffering, and her desperate efforts to find her way back to meaning, wholeness, and insight.

It reminds me of Leon Bloy's statement: "There are places in the heart that do not yet exist, and into them comes suffering, so that they can exist." We would not ask for such places in our hearts (well, unless we are Julian of Norwich or St. Therese)—but it is extraordinary what God can do with this suffering, if we let Him.

————

August 30, 2016

Dearest Robert,

If we're to speak of hearts, yours must be continually on fire with the flames caught from the people among whom you move. Love is catching.

I love the sound of your friend Gabrielle, so noble and so real, and I think she's just the right person for Nouwen. What makes everything he

---

33. Henri J. M. Nouwen, *Love, Henri: Letters on the Spiritual Life*, ed. Gabrielle Earnshaw (New York: Convergent Books, 2016).

says so striking is the earnestness of it. He may be talking more of what he desires than what he can do, but he really does desire it. I wouldn't have liked to meet him with his human neediness, but the thought of him is very consoling. I must say he makes a great contrast to "him who is not to be named" [*Thomas Merton!*], who seems to be lacking in precisely that quality. But I shall not go into this.

Your heaven is so full of stars, dear Robert, so many that you can't number them anymore, but they all sing for joy and take you beyond your one small life into the wonders of theirs.

You know you need never feel that you need to write to me because there's always such a fullness in your letters that it rejoices me for quite a long time.

Much love and gratitude,
Sister Wendy

————

John Leary

Sister Wendy often commented on her daily reading from my book All Saints, *such as this response to the entry on John Leary, a young Catholic whom I had befriended in Boston, where he divided his time between peace work and the local Catholic Worker house where he lived. His evident goodness and holiness were recognized by many, who mourned his sudden death at the age of twenty-four.*

August 31, 2016

Dearest Robert,

This morning Sister Lesley and I were quite bowled over by your essay on John Leary, who was new to both of us. I know canonization doesn't really matter—Mother Teresa and Dorothy are luminous without any sacred titles—but it does mean that people pay attention to someone whom the Church has visibly honored. I would love to know that this young man's cause is moving forward, or as Sr. Lesley points out, even started.

With love and gratitude, with joy and prayer,
Sister Wendy

————

August 31, 2016

Dear Sister Wendy,

I am glad you were touched by the story of John Leary—one of my personal "saints." He was my best friend when I went back to college after the Catholic Worker. It was only after his death that I really had a sense of what a wide community he had touched in his short life. It would have been interesting to see whether he could have sustained such purity, goodness, and generosity if he had lived. But then that was not his mission. He was an eternal youth.

It would be nice for other people to know about him—especially young people, to show how it is possible to live a full and complete life no matter what time is given us.

"Alas, there is no Saint Wendy." On the origins of her unusual name.

September 8, 2016

Dearest Robert,

How wonderful for you to know that this loving and surrendered young man chose you as his friend.

I too had a special friend, not saintly like John, but a woman of the utmost integrity. We met when we were both 14 at boarding school, and I always felt astonished that Val should have chosen me as her friend. It made me feel I must be more than I thought myself to be.

Alas, there is no Saint Wendy. I have always very much disliked this name and have constantly sought to find some saint who would illumine it. The best I ever found was Saint Wendolin, patron saint of cows. I cannot feel drawn to this virtuous woman. But do you know the derivation of the name? J. M. Barrie had as neighbor the poet William Ernest Henley who wrote the poem "Invictus" ("I am the master of my fate, I am the captain of my soul"). There was a little daughter in the family, I think a four- or five-year-old of whom Barrie grew very fond. She was an exceptionally loving little creature, advancing with open arms to everyone she met and calling them her "friendy." Since she could not pronounce her "r's," something that I'm also a little weak on, this came out as "fwendy" and when Berry needed a name for his very loving mother-of-all-the-world, little heroine for Peter Pan, he called her Wendy. So I can sort of ring out a spiritual meaning from my wretched name.

I was greatly rejoiced when I entered the convent to be able to leave Wendy completely behind me and receive a new religious name. I wanted one of dignity that did not reveal too much about my inner life and I was very happy to be Sister Michael. When Vatican II suggested that there was a sort of unreality in this practice, and that nuns might consider taking back their baptismal names, I knew with sinking heart that the Church was pointing straight at me. The only consolation in descending from the angelic Sister Michael to the poor wretched Sister Wendy was that I knew it would give pleasure to my mother. After all, she chose the name. She was a beautiful, petite little woman and I think she thought she'd have a beautiful, petite little baby. Instead she got me.

I hope you are settling down into your lovely new house with its butterflies and paintings. Thank you for all your goodness to me.

Lovingly,
Sister Wendy

––––––––––

A surprising proposition!

September 8, 2016

Dearest Robert,

I would like to raise a very serious question. How would you feel about giving a retreat here? This is not my own idea but comes from discussion between the prioress and Sister Lesley, both of whom are very keen. This would be for next year, and of course, if this wonderful thing is possible, I would bow out of the picture (I don't go to the retreats anyhow) and you would be fine-tuning arrangements with Sister Stephanie, the prioress. When Sister Lesley reads your books in the morning, first *All Saints* and then *Blessed Among Us*, it sometimes seems to me that we have you actually there in my cell speaking directly. This morning was quite overwhelming, listening to Blessed Frédéric Ozanam saying, "The Church would be better to support herself upon the people, who are the true ally of the church, poor as she, devout as she, blessed as she, by all the benedictions of the savior." Afterwards I said to Lesley, was that a quotation or was that Robert? These lives of service to the poor move you so much that it could have been you.

With renewed gratitude and very much love,
Sister Wendy

I responded, of course, that I would be very glad to lead a retreat for the Sisters, knowing that this would not involve Sister Wendy, but expressing the hope that if I found myself in her neighborhood there might be an opportunity to meet. This would indeed come to pass in the following year.

———————

September 10, 2016

Dearest Sister Wendy,

I have a friend who is going through a period of deep agitation about a community that she left; she is now wondering whether she made a mistake and whether she should consider returning. She is searching for some sign of what she is being called to do. I told her that I was sure that God would make it clear. That is the way everything else in her life has occurred so far.

I wonder whether you went through a time of terrible agitation when you were facing the question of leaving your congregation after so many years. It is remarkable how in your case God also led you to a kind of life and work you could never have imagined, and the possibility through art of speaking to such a wide secular audience about the love of God for his creation.

When I look back on my life it is remarkable the way so many things unfolded—always in response to prayer, though I did not even know to call it prayer at the time. I could tell a story of my life in which each new step seemed to appear at hand, as conveniently as Tarzan's vines in the jungle—from the chance that led me to the Catholic Worker, the chance introduction that opened up a scholarship to study Spanish in Bolivia with the Maryknoll Fathers, a connection that later led me to Orbis Books; the unsolicited invitation to edit Dorothy's diaries and letters, or to write the daily entry on saints for *Give Us This Day*, or within weeks of my uttering a prayer in a time of desolation, that I might know what it means to love and be loved, receiving a note from Monica, whom I had first met when I was 17, telling me that she had just read one of my books. . . . I don't know whether such a red thread is evident in every life—or only for those who have eyes to see.

Of course it makes it all sound terribly easy. Almost each of these steps was preceded by uncertainty, doubt, and anguish. And I could tell a different story: about my parent's divorce, the years when I saw so little of my father, then watching from a distance as he was put on trial, facing 115 years in prison; my mother's depression; my flight from home when I was sixteen; my struggles about whether to register for the draft; my sense of failure as a "Catholic Worker," and then jumping forward, the hard years as my marriage unraveled, the sufferings of a child with anorexia. . . .

And yet even these shadows are part of a story of grace, so that I can truly look back on it, as St. Augustine did, and see that all the while God was hovering in the background, guiding and protecting me, even when the thought of God was far away.

I am not, in fact, a very "good Catholic." The wounds inflicted on the Body of Christ by the sex abuse scandal have affected me deeply, as they struck close to home in my former parish. Perhaps this is what motivates me to turn to the saints. When I became a Catholic, a former nun gave me a little Penguin book of saints and said, "Welcome to the Catholic Church—the saints are the best thing about us!" And when I went back to Harvard, after becoming a Catholic, I surprised my mother by saying: "I have just bought my Christmas present from you, and I hope you will pay for it." It was the four-volume set of *Butler's Lives of the Saints*, which sits in front of me on my desk at this moment.

I'm sorry—I fear I will have overwhelmed you, taking up all your allowable "recreation" for the week.

Thank you for your friendship, one of God's most recent and precious gifts in my life.

September 13, 2016

My dearest Robert,

Your beautiful autobiographical letter is not "recreation," no, it is spiritual reading. It is prayer in a very moving sense. I think you should seriously consider writing an autobiography, because your awareness of the thread that leads always on, that comes from God and leads to God, is so exceptionally clear. One comment I would make, and that's about your sense of the Church. I am overwhelmed every day with my awareness of the Church as the Mystical Body, that sacred holy community in which we truly find Jesus.

Without the sacraments that the Church gives us, how immeasurably poorer and harder life would be. But together with this holy and Mystical Body that is Jesus Himself, the Church is simultaneously a collection of people who range from saints to miserable sinners. No revelation of child abuse and episcopal lying has any effect upon the reality of the Body of Christ. These poor people are wounds in the Body, never the Body itself. In fact, I think our love and dependence on the Church grows deeper when we contemplate these terrible suppurating wounds. To lose faith in the Church because of this ugliness and betrayal would be like turning from Christ and His Passion—the wounded Jesus in whom there was no beauty. Dearest Robert, the Church needs strong and prayerful hearts like yours all the more now that we've seen such painful things.

In the course of this correspondence information about our respective journeys emerged somewhat haphazardly, so that it took me some while to understand the chronology of Sister Wendy's religious vocation. Born in South Africa in 1930, she and her family moved in 1939 to Scotland, where her father was training as a doctor. At sixteen Sister Wendy joined the Sisters of Notre Dame de Namur, a teaching order. Following her novitiate in England she studied at Oxford (living in a local convent and enjoying no interaction with her fellow students), where she received a congratula-

Young Sister Wendy (then known as Sister Michael)

tory first class honors degree in English literature. (The great J. R. R. Tolkien, her examiner, urged her to continue on for a doctorate, but she declined.)

In 1954, after earning an additional teaching diploma, she returned to South Africa to teach at one of her order's schools for girls in Cape Town. She later moved to Johannesburg, where she was appointed superior of the local convent. All of this was a great frustration of her deep calling to contemplative life.

In 1970 she suffered a physical breakdown, whereupon she received papal permission to withdraw from her congregation and become a consecrated virgin and hermit. She moved to England and was welcomed to live in a caravan on the grounds of the Carmelite monastery at Quidenham in Norfolk. In was from there, in the 1990s, that she embarked on her accidental apostolate as a commentator on art through television productions and a succession of books. But eventually, that public phase of life receded, and she returned, happily, to an anonymous life of solitude and prayer. When her declining health made it impossible for her to live alone, she moved to a room in the monastery enclosure, receiving only a single visit from Sister Lesley, who brought her daily meal and wheeled her to a loft overlooking the Sisters' chapel to attend daily Mass.

Increasingly, as I shared my own story with Sister Wendy she reciprocated in kind.

I would never have left Notre Dame of my own will, because although I was convinced that I needed much more time for prayer, I had given myself to God. If the Order said no, I happily, if with pain, would have died trying to do what obedience asked of me. After all, it doesn't really matter what we do and whether we like it or not, or feel we have absolute needs that are not being met: all that matters is to do the Will of God and whatever it is, in that Will is our happiness.

People have said to me that I must have been very unhappy in those difficult years as a teacher, but I never thought of myself as unhappy. I was clinging to God and moving through the waters in which He had led me. I was convinced that if He wanted to "rescue" me, it would happen, and so it did. I got more and more unwell and had two or three very public epileptic fits, one at a major superior's meeting, about which the order was not at all happy. One doctor, who I think must have been a romantic, said that he thought I was dying of a broken heart.

Whereupon the order itself said they would release me in order to try a contemplative vocation. I really think they thought I would come back to them, but of course it was pure joy from then on. But as you can see, I didn't have to make any decision. My decision was to trust and obey, and look how wonderfully it all turned out. The most I have ever hoped for was to be a Carmelite, yet my life as a solitary has been infinitely more prayerful, more silent, and secluded than I could have imagined would be my good fortune.

I couldn't have lived this life without those years in Notre Dame, which stripped off at least the outer layers of selfishness. I'm afraid there's still a great deal left for God to do. I also think that the active work, the television and the books, which I only undertook in the beginning to earn some money for the convent, were a great blessing in disguise. I never wanted to leave my caravan, but having to do so made me aware of the needs of the world and the hunger and longing of people has become a central factor in my prayer life.

I think the dark side of your life has been as fruitful as the lighted side, but in a way our life isn't up to us. It's Our Lord who holds us by the hand and draws us into His mysteries.

Very much love, dear Robert,
Sister Wendy

September 13, 2016

Dearest Sister Wendy,

I will look forward to hearing from Sister Stephanie in good time. Whether I have anything deep to share with the Sisters is a question, but I will not cast doubt on your and Sister Lesley's endorsement, as you have a pretty good idea, by this time, of where my strengths and limitations lie.

On the latter point, I accept your maternal correction, if I have not shown sufficient appreciation for the church. Of course I consider myself a part of the church—I could not think otherwise. There were many years where I wore this identity uncomfortably, as one after another of my Orbis authors was treated with so much harshness. (And now so many of these same theologians have been embraced by Pope Francis.) Dorothy was keenly aware of the failings of the church, but she recognized her own sins and weaknesses, and included herself under judgment. We all fall short of what Jesus calls us to be. But as you say, we must not confuse the Body of Christ with its wounds.

I am very interested to hear about the mysterious route that led you from the convent to your blessed solitude. Many saints—Julie Billiart, Hildegard of Bingen—seemed to have experienced mysterious illnesses that blocked one path in order to open another. (If you had lived in a different age, do you think you would have liked to be an anchoress, like Julian? When I write to you I feel almost as if I had a magic postbox that connects me with her anchorhold in Norwich.)

The will of God is a very mysterious thing. I wrote at length about this in *The Saints' Guide to Happiness*. There is a distasteful side to this phrase when it is used to imply, for instance, that poor people should be resigned to their poverty and the early death of their children, because it is the "will of God," when it is much more likely to be the result of unjust social structures. At the same time, it seems to me that this phrase has been invoked all too often in religious life by religious superiors who believed that their will was effectively the will of God. To me, to submit to the will of God implies a confidence that in every situation, no matter how difficult, there is a way to God—a way to love, to fullness of life. How to find that way? It may be by way of obedience—by saying Yes. There are, on the other hand, situations when it is by saying No—and discernment enters in to help us distinguish one from the other.

———

Sister Wendy shared deeply personal reflections about her family, and on the early signs of her longing for solitude.

September 15, 2016

Dearest Robert,

I can't resist telling you that my earliest longing was to be an anchoress. It seemed to me the perfect way of life. Now that I know more, I realize I would greatly have disliked the window open to the world.[34] The thought of the dear people coming every afternoon is more than I have the generosity to live with. No, what I have is the perfect way and it came purely from God's gift.

You had asked me if I have siblings. I have a younger sister and brother. But there are five years between each of us and, since I entered when I was 16, I have never got to know my brother. He was about six or seven when I left and when I came back to South Africa seven years later, he was a very obnoxious and spoiled teenager. This is a harsh judgement and maybe unwarranted, but I could find no point of contact at all. There never did come a time when I could meet him as a person. All I could do was pray for him and always send birthday and Christmas cards (never reciprocated). But he's had a very good life and now in Australia seems to be becoming a rather saintly man, working full-time for the Church. He does communicate now, often in a most beautifully pious style that I cannot quite emulate.

My sister, whom I also did not know, accompanied my mother on her visits to me after I became a solitary. I then realized that she and I would have been very great friends. We have the same sense of humor and enjoy the same books. I grew to love her very deeply and her death of lung cancer two or three years ago has left a gap that nothing will fill. But she was a great grief to me. With all her gifts and charm and leadership qualities, she was not a happy woman—in fact an angry woman, though this she would not admit.

All my attempts to speak to her about the meaning of suffering and God's love only made her cross. I think this was partly her humility; she felt this talk was beyond her—quite untruly, of course.

However, underlying all this is the fact that the greatest sin of my life is my unkindness to my sister. I once said that on a television program and the reviewer got very upset and said that all siblings fight. But it wasn't that I fought with her, I simply blotted her out. As far as I was concerned there was only one child in the family and that was me. The cruelty of this attitude is something that I have to live with, though I have many times asked for forgiveness and of course I know that in Our Lord's eyes forgiveness is given as soon as we look at Him.

A psychologist who heard that interview wrote to me saying that she thought I might have mild Asperger's, and if that were so I would not have been able to relate more to my family. My friends used to say to me that I never seemed to need people, though, of course, I liked and took great de-

---

34. In many cases, the enclosed cell of anchoresses like Julian of Norwich featured a window on the outside world, where people could come to them for spiritual guidance. Sister Wendy preferred her more secluded arrangement.

light in their company. But Sister Rachel[35] told me once that she'd seen a change since I came here. She felt there'd been a real movement of love that involved me with people in a way that would never have been natural to me. If this is true, then it was a miracle of grace, a miracle unfortunately coming too late for my poor siblings.

The will of God is such a mighty mystery that I would not like to approach it without more mental energy.

Very much love and thank you,
Sister Wendy

P.S. Perhaps I could just say this: it's never God's will, ever, that bad things should happen to us. He made us to share His joy. But when bad things do happen, it is His will that we turn to Him for help and let Him draw us through and out of them without damage. It's a convoluted question because I think devout people find their only consolation in great sorrow in saying "It was God's will," just as other people get irritated by it. It's hard to explain how God is in the suffering, in the loss, and as Julian would say, all is working towards the great goodness, but it doesn't feel like that. I'm sorry, that was even more muddled than my letter.

––––––––––

September 15, 2016

Dearest Sister Wendy,

I was very touched that you shared with me the information about your siblings, especially your regrets about "unkindness" toward your sister. Whether you blotted her out in earlier years, it sounds as if you grew to know and love her in later years, and that surely meant a lot to her—as well as the fact that she had the benefit of remaining close to your mother, while she lived.

I am probably closer to my sister than to anyone (she is three years younger), and yet I still wake up crying for forgiveness for how I treated her when we were young. We never fought. But I too feel as if I blotted her out— as if it was an embarrassment to have a younger sister who looked up to me

35. It was Sister Rachel, as prioress at Quidenham at the time, who originally welcomed Sister Wendy to live on the grounds of the monastery. Because Sister Wendy was not formally a member of the community, she and Sister Rachel were able to enjoy a deep friendship, each encouraging the other along their respective spiritual paths. And, under the pen name Ruth Burrows, Sister Rachel would become famous in her own right as a spiritual writer.

and always wanted to follow me and do whatever I did. She is in many ways a more admirable person. But it took me a long time to appreciate that.

I was puzzled by the doctor who raised the matter of Asperger's syndrome. Many people might assume that is what attracts certain people to a contemplative life. But from what I have seen of you on television that seems highly unlikely—your powers of intuition, empathy, and human insight are so keen. Though maybe Sister Rachel is correct in observing that you have changed since you took up the contemplative life.

I would have also said of myself that I seemed not to need people, "though I liked and took great delight in their company." But at some point that also changed for me. So maybe one can grow and change.

And on "the will of God"—of course God does not will that we suffer. But what it means to me is that there is no suffering, or situation so terrible that there is no access to God—so to seek that path, to continuously ask for it, is God's will.

I am very happy that in the last two days I have had very sweet dreams. In one I was talking with Pope Francis, telling him about my life, and when it was time for him to leave he said, "We should continue this conversation. Please give me your telephone number." And last night, a dream of meeting Dorothy Day, as we were both in line to enter a museum. I was so glad to see her and catch her up with what is going on in my life.

––––––––––

Sometimes Sister Wendy and I exchanged reflections on more theological topics. In one letter, Sister Wendy reflected at length on the topic of "original sin," stimulated by a "not-very-interesting book" she had happened to read. Sister Wendy's insights, in contrast, were very interesting. In one letter she wrote, "The big difficulty, I feel, is the wrong name, because there really isn't any sin involved. I remember a priest saying that this is the one dogma for which one doesn't need faith. Yet I think this term really refers to that sense of incompleteness that we all have, and our feeling that this is not how things should be. That Jesus saved us from this by His incarnation is very true, but I think without His death we would never have seen the extent of God's love, nor would we have known the malice of which our race is capable. I've not put this well and we may come back to it sometime if you would like."

Sister Wendy's attitude toward sin—that it is such a small thing in contrast to the immensity of God's love—was, as I often came to observe, one of the many points she shared with her beloved Julian of Norwich.

September 16, 2016

Dearest Robert,

Original sin: The wonderful thing is that the closer we come to God, the more acutely we become aware not of sin so much as of sinfulness, and the more acutely we become aware that God doesn't care. He forgives, He provides all that we haven't got, His joy envelops us. The sinfulness which is not act, but disposition, our innate inability to be what we would like to be, enables Him to give Himself more fully than if we were strong and controlled.

I rejoice in your beautiful dreams. You have saints in your mind and in your life and now in your dreams, too, blessed Robert.

Thank you for your sensitive understanding of my weakness.

Very much love,
Sister Wendy

———————

In reply to her reflections on sin, I mentioned to Sister Wendy how one of my authors, the Jesuit theologian Jon Sobrino of El Salvador, has said, "Sin is what puts Jesus to death."

Julian of Norwich

September 18, 2016

Dearest Robert,

What you said about the crucifixion showing us the meaning of sin is a beautifully expressed belief of something very important to me. That's why I think, as opposed to the Eastern Church, Our Lord had to die on the cross so that we would understand exactly what sin was capable of. But this of course should just make us cling more joyfully to Our Lord as redeemer. I do feel the one person who really got all this right was Julian, and I love that she accepts paradox, that on the one hand things are not right and on the other hand they are right. Of course she puts it far more poetically and convincingly than that. But it's living in the paradox that I think we find peace. Isn't it the same for the will of God? It's never His will that we should suffer, and yet in suffering we find His will, because there He is waiting to lead us to resurrection.

I'll pray for you to have peace and that you pray for me to have light upon my desires.

Very much love, dear Robert,
Sister Wendy

————

Sister Wendy had mentioned that among her icons was "a very clumsy early eighteenth-century icon of Sts. Laurus and Florus, you know, the ones with the horses. And since I love horses, I love to see them galloping with their patrons."

September 19, 2016

Dearest Sister Wendy,

I was interested and surprised to discover your love of horses! My daughter Christina, who came to dinner last night, displayed her latest tattoo—the face of her beloved horse Leroy, who died some years ago. He was a rescued police horse, which meant that he was fantastically well-trained. After the retirement of his police owner, he went into a depression and wouldn't eat. Christina adopted him and nursed him back to health. He was an extraordinary creature—deeply empathetic and expressive. He took to me—I think because he was more accustomed to men. And he would walk across the paddock to wrap his neck around my head and just hold me close. It was a very sad day for all of us when he developed laminitis and had to be put down. This inspired my daughter, while still in high school, to participate in a scientific trial that actually developed a technique for early diagnosis of laminitis.

I agree with you about Julian, and her profound reflection on the passion of Christ as a window on the immensity of God's love. And of course I love her conception of creation as no more than a hazelnut in the hand of God—so tiny, yet so precious, as reflected in the price God was prepared to pay for it.

I will definitely pray for light upon all your desires.

————

September 20, 2016

Dearest Robert,

I've never had the privilege of knowing a horse, as Christina has, but I've seen horses and I watched them on television when I was out filming. It's their beauty and their courage that so enthralls me—their heart. I was always hoping our filming would be over in time to watch the races, and if I had had any money to bet, I might now be a wealthy woman. It somehow turned out that I had a strange "gift," not so much of knowing which horse would win, but of knowing which horse most wanted to win. And since racing, like most things, depends on what you want, I was nearly always right. A friend of mine, Annie, who took me to Mass in London, was so impressed by this gift that she said that when it came to the Derby, she would go to the betting place and put on a bet for me for the first five. It turned out that I got right first, second, third and fifth.

But next morning at Mass she told me that she'd never been in a betting place before, and she couldn't work out how to do it! Annie told me she would gladly give me the money if I was in need, but of course it hadn't the same triumphal ring to it.

I'm reading again books on [modern saints who received the marks of Christ's passion]. I'm very moved by their story and yet there is a certain reserve that I can't but feel. Is this just because of the strangeness of the phenomenon, which we today tend to shrink from? Our Lord still speaks to those who listen to Him, but I would imagine, perhaps wrongly, that He speaks in silence. I would feel that an actual voice, exterior to me, was a diminution of our closeness. But of course every person is so different and their relationship with Him is different. How fatal to make comparisons.

Today Sister Lesley wheeled me out to the front porch to have my photograph taken with Sister Rachel (Ruth Burrows). We've been friends since 1970 and since we now have a novice who takes very good photographs, the sisters are using the opportunity to take one of Rachel. I was very reluctant to be in on this and could not bear to look at the finished product. Rachel is an extremely beautiful woman, lovely bones, austere mortified face, where I have a round

Sister Rachel and Sister Wendy

face with no character at all except protruding teeth. I was asked to do it, so I've done it.

Thank you dearest Robert and God bless,
Sister Wendy

———————

September 20, 2016

Dearest Sister Wendy,

That is fascinating about your natural skills as a bookmaker. Christina (the horse girl) is not fond of horse racing, since it is so dangerous and hard on the horses. You might well have made a much greater impression on the public if you had gone in for wagering on horses instead of merely commenting on art; it might even have earned you an OBE. But it does not surprise me that you have great powers of communicating with animals.

I am delighted by the stories of saints who had animal companions. Long before St. Francis, there was St. Gerasimus and his lion. And all those Celtic saints who befriended and made disciples of wild animals—bears, badgers, otters, and the like. I wrote about a saint who restored a favorite trout to life (after a hapless younger monk had caught and served it to him). St. Hugh of Lincoln had a pet swan that protected him. I read of an anchoress who shared her cell with two snakes who drank from her bowl. It is a picture of the Peaceable Kingdom!

I had a friend who served a very long term (25 years) in a nearby women's prison. They had a program in the prison called "puppies behind bars," which allowed the women to train service dogs. I thought the companionship of a dog would transform any cell into a loving home. Do you think there is any truth to the notion that Julian had a cat in her anchorhold—to keep down the mice?

I admit that I have a hard time warming up to victim souls, like St. Gemma Galgani and other modern stigmatists. Perhaps they bring to my mind the suffering my daughter went through with anorexia. The worst of it lasted about a year, with three long hospitalizations. She looked like a concentration camp inmate—which was possibly her aspiration. She felt a deep identification with the sufferings of Anne Frank and other victims of the Holocaust. It was the most terrible ordeal—like a form of demonic possession. In the midst of this I went to Mass one day and heard the gospel text where Jesus raises the little daughter of Jairus who seemed to be dead. But he says she is not dead but merely sleeping: "Little girl, arise!" The text notes that Jesus commanded them to "give her something to eat." I was overcome with emotion.

And now she is well! She, whom I feared would never finish high school, has graduated with honors from college and is enrolled in a master's program in Paris.

So I know that God hears our prayers. As for hearing the voice of God, I like what Hildegard said of her visions: "These visions which I saw I beheld neither in sleep nor dreaming nor in madness nor with my bodily eyes or ears, nor in hidden places; but I saw them in full view and according to God's will, when I was wakeful and alert, with eyes of the spirit and the inward ears."

We do not do enough to cultivate the eyes of the spirit and the inward ears—well, perhaps you do.

————————

September 21, 2016

Dearest Robert,

Unless Sister Stephanie says no, I would like to give you my icon of Sts. Florus and Laurus for you and your daughter. It's two or three hundred years old and not technically very good, but it's a joy to behold. There is one great masterpiece icon of Florus and Laurus, and this one makes an attempt to copy it. As you know that is the traditional way of writing icons: copying. I would love to see a picture of your icon of St. Dymphna.[36] Today a young artist who sometimes writes to me sent me a delightful little holy card of St. Dymphna with a medal. Sister Lesley groaned at the medal because I like keeping medals in my pockets, those very large nun pockets, like horses' nose-bags, that sometimes make my habit very heavy. I also have a large medal sewn into my veil at the back, but that's to try and keep it down because I have a curved spine and a funny neck and my veil is always sliding over my shoulders.

All who know you must have ached for you during those painful years your poor little girl was struggling in her own way to distance from the world by immersion in the Holocaust. How wonderful that Our Lord in the end did take her hand and lift her up. Isn't it better in retrospect to have had early suffering and grown through it, than to have had a carefree youth and a very troubled adulthood? I think your life has been marked by these little touches of notice from the saints.

————————

36. An icon of St. Dymphna, patron saint of the mentally ill, was a precious gift from my friend, the artist Fr. William Hart McNichols. See Biographical Glossary.

Very much love and gratitude, with prayers for all the many things that you know need praying for,

Sister Wendy

September 21, 2016

Dearest Sister Wendy,

I reply in haste to say that I am overwhelmed and moved by your offer to send your icon of Sts. Florus and Laurus for me and my daughter Christina. This is a most extravagantly generous offer, and I will entirely understand if Sister Stephanie objects.

I shouldn't have spoken lightly of victim souls. That is a kind of holiness that one can only approach on one's knees. "Victim soul" was perhaps not the right expression. That is a concept that fascinated Dorothy Day, as she believed she had known people who had deliberately prayed for the grace to take on the sufferings of others.

The reference to the artist who sent you a medal of St. Dymphna reminds me that you must receive piles of mail from so many people, and yet you are so good to take the time to write to me so faithfully and with such beautiful attentiveness.

September 22, 2016

Dearest Robert,

I used to have a lot of letters and I can truthfully say that although I answered them all, it was purely as a duty of love. I don't like writing letters. This is where you are the great exception, in that what you write to me is so interesting and inspiring that I feel desirous of responding.

I had sent Sister Wendy a book I edited of wood engravings by the great Quaker artist Fritz Eichenberg, who contributed many famous illustrations to The Catholic Worker.[37]

I've a sneaking feeling that I should be looking at more art of this kind and that I am a coward. Your very name reminds me of those great suffering

---

37. *Fritz Eichenberg: Works of Mercy*, ed. Robert Ellsberg (Maryknoll, NY: Orbis Books, 1992).

masses, the people who are oppressed, misused, threatened, and deprived. I don't think I pray for them explicitly enough. What I tend to do is just embrace them in the Love of God and hold them silently to my heart, while I look past the suffering, as it were, to the joy that is Jesus. Your father has never been able to do this—you understand what I mean—and you who know Jesus have never been able to do it either.

Moreover, when Our Lord spoke of the sheep and the goats, He didn't let the goats off because they suffered interiorly and prayed for the hungry, the homeless, the sick. It may be that I am too limited a person to do more, or it may not be. I just have to look at Our Lord and trust Him that He would let me know if He wants more.

Thank you for all your beautiful letters.

Lovingly,
Sister Wendy

September 23, 2016

Dearest Sister Wendy,

You may have noticed yesterday in *Give Us This Day* my inclusion of Daria Donnelly, my son's godmother, whom I have previously mentioned. Here is where I truly regret the limitations of these short little entries. A much longer version appears in *Blessed Among All Women*. After the birth of her second child she was found to have multiple myeloma—a very terrible cancer that caused her bones to be very brittle. She experienced excruciating pain. She certainly didn't ask for any of this, or imagine that God liked her to suffer more. But the way she coped with her suffering—with grace, courage, and generosity—was a true martyrdom, in the original sense of witness. I'm not sure she identified with the suffering of Christ, but she certainly felt great solidarity with the sufferings of others. She prayed to be healed, if that was God's will. But as a mother of young children, she was torn, as she said, between "thy will be done / hell no, children need their mothers."

She is the one who pointed out how limited my stories of saints were by the omission of "saint-mothers/fathers." The church has so often validated the sufferings and sacrifices of religious, without acknowledging the daily/hourly sacrifices that parents make: the noise, the confusion, the constant demands on one's patience, charity, and self-sacrifice. Of course not all rise to the challenge. And of course there are wonderful compensations. But Daria for me really modeled a kind of holiness in the world. At her funeral there was a curious sign: a little rainbow that hovered over her house in a

James Cone

clear blue sky. (I witnessed another strange prodigy at Romero's beatification: a rainbow-colored nimbus that surrounded the sun on an otherwise clear day.)

Yesterday I had lunch with one of my best-selling authors, James Cone, the father of "Black Liberation Theology."[38] I asked him whether he has taken part in any of the "Black Lives Matter" demonstrations, provoked over the past couple of years by the rash of police shootings. He said, "I demonstrate with my pen." I liked the sound of that—because I feel I do so little for peace, for the poor, for justice. I am not in any sense an "activist." But I like to think that with my pen (or computer!) I do my part to protest the darkness in the world, largely by focusing attention on the light. As you do with your silence and your prayer.

———————

I had previously asked Sister Wendy whether she thought Julian of Norwich had a cat, as I had heard speculated. Though Sister Wendy had a fondness for cats, she felt they were out of place in a life of solitude.

September 24, 2016

Dearest Robert,

One of the most striking things about you is your work for peace and justice, work as you rightly say that you do in literary form. So the light you shed reaches far more people than can be done by activism. It's an essential element of you, that great desire to bring His Kingdom into reality on earth and it's very heart-warming.

You asked me about Julian and a possible cat. There is no evidence whatever that Julian had a cat. The very suggestion comes from the *Anchren Reule*, which says that anchorites might like to have a cat, and in fact that

---

38. James Cone (d. 2018), a professor of theology at Union Theological Seminary in New York City, was renowned as the father of "Black Liberation Theology," an integration of the perspectives of Malcolm X and Martin Luther King Jr. Orbis reprinted his early works, including his first book, *Black Theology and Black Power* (1969), and later added original titles, including his classic, *The Cross and the Lynching Tree*. We worked together for more than thirty years, and at this time I was working with him on his final work, a memoir: *Said I Wasn't Gonna Tell Nobody*.

the author knew of anchorites who did so. Judging from myself, I would be very surprised if Julian had one. Sister Lesley and I are wildly enthusiastic about cats, which we think God's most beautiful animal (just that little inch more beautiful than the horse). There's a small group in community that are fanatic ailurophiles and if any one of this small group gets a cat picture, it goes the rounds. When I first came to Quidenham our doctor had the most beautiful cat and it was a very great joy to caress her when I went to the surgery. Anyhow this exquisite creature had kittens and the doctor was very keen for me to have one, but I explained that I couldn't live with another person. If your vocation is to solitude, as Julian's was, and in its humble way mine, then solitude it must be. God fills your whole being and you really haven't got room for a close friend of any species.

Those are wonderful photographs [the rainbow for Daria, the solar nimbus for Romero], and how fitting that the sign in the heavens appears for a great martyred archbishop and equally for an unknown wife and mother. I feel very strongly, just as you do, that countless saints are overlooked because they haven't got the heft of a religious order to promote their cause. But they are luminous in their own sphere. Sister Lesley and I were very struck by Daria Donnelly and it is lovely to know of the personal link you had with her. I'm sure everybody could produce saints that they've known and been affected by.

As I write this the sun is shining on all my icons—my small chapel of prayer. I have some beautiful colored glass on the window ledge and the afternoon sun shines through them and fills my cell with sparkles, little rainbows really, just like Daria's, though not as impressive as Oscar Romero's.

Very much love and prayer,
Sister Wendy

September 26, 2016

Dearest Sister Wendy,

I imagine you enjoyed today's story of St. Therese Couderc, who received a vision in which the word "Goodness" was stamped in gold letters on every creature.

As a dog lover, I am less inclined to appreciate the goodness of cats, who always strike me as cunning and devious. I will grant them, they are soft and lovely to pet, but they also make me sneeze. I take it the allowance of a cat in an anchorhold was to keep down the rodent population. And so if

Julian did not have the company of a cat, she might well have had other, unwanted company.

It is funny that you feel there is nothing worth writing about your life, yet you have encouraged me to write my own story, which is certainly lacking in external drama. Meanwhile I am helping my father finish his memoir, which is due to the publisher in three weeks. Last night, characteristically, he said, "I could just work for twenty hours a day, straight, even if it breaks my health, just to get it in." I said that sounded very romantic, as if his heart would burst just as he turned in the finished book; but the more likely outcome is that he would break his health and thereby not finish the book, which would profit him nothing.

———————

September 27, 2016

Dearest Robert,

I hope your father's book is as inspiring and interesting as it deserves to be. But I think your biography would be so too. Just count up the number of exceptional people you know and whom you could talk about. Of course, it would be too private to talk about your previous sorrows. I absolutely agree with you that married life, to become the sacrament of God's love that He intends, demands a selflessness that is very rare. The only consolation is that since God asks it, He will give it. I think priests and nuns should tremble at the relative ease of their lives and remember constantly that this peace is not given for their own enjoyment, but so that they can pray and be there for the people who struggle. I'm sometimes baffled as to how excessively demanding it must be to live with another person, to fulfill them and accept their fulfillment of one's self, and yet this beautiful and terrible interchange of love is written into the human body. It's the normal way of holiness. Anything that highlights this is a great blessing.

I think you have misread the nature of the cat. Cats do not have that easy trustfulness and need of humanity that makes the dog so lovable. Dogs are lovable, I quite agree. But the dignity of the little cat, its comic curiosity, its easy and unstudied beauty, are God's gifts to us. I have sometimes thought that in some homes, poor deprived homes, even if wealthy, the only beautiful thing is the cat. You may add, the dog is beautiful, too, to which I graciously assent.

Very much love,
Sister Wendy

P.S. Thinking about your autobiography, I remember how you said one event led onto another and so you were always guided, even though you had no idea in which direction you were moving. You have seen that very clearly in your life, but I think it's in everybody's life if they're helped to realize it. There are very few movements in my life, but I too can see how giving oneself to God, even in what seemed a dead-end situation led inexorably to another opportunity to love Him. We just have to keep our eyes open.

––––––––––

Sister Wendy really only wanted to talk about God, yet the things she wanted to say "have no words."

Elizabeth of the Trinity

October 7, 2016

Dearest Robert,

    This is a short letter. One thing, though, I don't want to forget to say, when I wrote to you that only in Julian and Therese did I find a teaching of the truth of Our Lord that never in the slightest opposes what one has learnt from experience of Him in prayer. I should have added a third name, Elizabeth of the Trinity. I'm not used to using the word "resonate" but if I were to use it, I would use it of my response to her heart. I feel I know what she is talking about, even when there aren't any words for what she wants to talk about. I so wish she were better known and loved. The trouble is there are so few anecdotes about Elizabeth. We know so very much about Therese, so very little about this contemporary of hers. It would be wonderful if you could commission a really spiritual person to write about her in terms that will disclose to the people of today the deep silent beauty of her simple surrender to the Blessed Trinity. There's almost something miraculous I think about the depth of her theological insight, considering her lack of education and the paucity of the spiritual reading at her disposal. The only thing she was ever really taught was music, where she excelled as a pianist, but from within she knew the Catholic truth.

A very old friend came to see me a few days ago and I managed an hour in the parlor since I really felt that was a duty of love. She said how well I seemed, which of course in one way is splendid to hear, but in another makes me wonder whether I'm not doing enough. I thought to myself, could I write another book? It would be one on my usual method, picture and commentary, but then, dear Robert, I thought, I really only want to talk about God. And the things I want to say have no words. In fact I don't want to say them, but I want them to be said, if you follow me. My relieved conclusion was that God does not ask this impossible task of me.

Lovingly,
Sister Wendy

––––––––––

October 10, 2016

Dear Sister Wendy,

My daughter Christina called me the other day. This was itself banner news. While she will usually return my calls, I don't think she has ever called on her own initiative, just to chat. She said she had been terribly moved by my talk on my favorite saints (the one I gave you) and it had prompted her to delve into the New Testament. "I just love Jesus!" she said. She said she wept to read about Peter weeping after his betrayal. She wants to read more! She has always had a deep instinctive spiritual sense, but it has been unformed (which reflects badly on me). Anyway, this made me very happy.

I am very glad to hear that you are looking—and I trust, feeling—better. And that this has inspired thoughts, no matter how fleeting, of writing another book. How I would love to have a book from you about God. Not anything systematic. Just short reflections, as they occur to you. The things that remind you of God. Perhaps you would find inspiration by contemplating various words, like the Desert monastics of old. Anything that comes to you in prayer—even just a few sentences or a paragraph. Or thoughts suggested by your reflection on scripture. If this thought plants any seeds, or prompts any feelings of consolation (as Ignatius would put it), then see where that goes. How I would love to publish such a book! I am sure it is not an impossible task—especially if you don't think in terms of a book, but simply one little thought at a time! If they are not said by you, then by whom?

––––––––––

October 11, 2016

Dearest Robert,

I can hardly contain my joy at what you tell me about your daughters. I shall pray very specifically that this opening bud comes to beautiful flower. And Catherine, too, another girl with a deep spiritual sensitivity, perhaps God will come to her through beauty. How she will love the blue of the Chartres windows.

You know Robert, I don't really have thoughts. Nothing I have written to you in our correspondence would I have said or thought if you had not said something or put a question that made me want to respond. When Sister Lesley reads to me in the morning, from your two books, and from *Magnificat*—from which she reads me the collect, the Epistle, the Gospel, and the homily—I nearly always have comments, and usually on all four, but I can't see that they would be worth immortalizing in print. I suppose what we should do is have a tape recorder and just send the whole thing off to you every now and then.

Unfortunately Lesley's face brightened when I said this and she said, "That's an idea!" But truly, dear Robert, I think it's a very bad idea and I really only said it to show the unlikeliness of my producing anything. I think a kind of scrapbook of a book would not attract readership. Scattered little comments are not really what you could call ideas. Naturally, though, writing to a publisher, one does think of a book, especially since, I'm ashamed to say, I produce books very easily. I don't think I've ever rewritten anything to get it better, though probably everybody thinks I should have done. You remember how Shakespeare never blotted a line and how Ben Jonson said he would have written much better had he done so? I don't think I've anything more to give and the absence of any words that come near to describing what I see and feel suggests that I'm not asked to.

Lovingly,
Sister Wendy

———

October 11, 2016

Dearest Sister Wendy,

I am amused by your saying that you do not have thoughts—though I know what you mean. I really don't know what I think except in response to questions. That is one of the reasons I enjoy interviews and answering questions after talks, especially if they are questions you haven't heard before. So I empathize with your feelings about that. Clearly you do best when you have something in front of you to inspire you. I wish I could suggest something. But that is for my own selfish desires and not because you need to do anything that is uncongenial.

—————

October 12, 2016

Dearest Robert,

Some days I feel that I'm not as sick as I think I am and I certainly am beginning to feel pretty sure that the terminal diagnosis of Pulmonary Fibrosis is incorrect. So if there were a way to work for the Lord, I would accept it. But I can't think of anything that I myself would want to write.

I think I may have told you that of my numerous books, there were only three I wanted to write, the others were all commissioned, except for the first, *Contemporary Women Artists*, which was not commissioned and which I only wrote to earn money for the community. It was the two little icon books that I really wanted to write to share with people the holy wonder of those pre-iconoclastic images, sixth and seventh century.[39] But I know that if asked to comment on a passage or asked an interesting question, I would be able to speak freely and fluently and in grammatical sentences. So I feel I should say to you, dear Robert, that if you throw off a ball of this nature every now and again, I will try to return it. But they have to be real balls, things you think are really interesting or passages on which you would really like to hear what I think. I can't see you having another triumph, but I'd have a go out of a desire to express my gratitude to God for His enormous goodness to me and to share the deeply held convictions that perhaps unconsciously dominate my life.

From your exhausted but loving,
Sister Wendy

—————

———————————

39. The North American editions of these two books were actually published by Orbis: *Real Presence: Sister Wendy on the Earliest Icons* (Maryknoll, NY: Orbis Books, 2010); *Encounters with God: In Quest of Ancient Icons of Mary* (Maryknoll, NY: Orbis Books, 2009).

Icon of Sts. Laurus and Florus

October 12, 2016

Dearest Sister Wendy,

After returning to the office from my trek to the city I found your package waiting for me! How beautiful. I immediately kissed the precious icon and begged Sts. Laurus and Florus that I might be worthy of their blessing.

Thank you so much for such a beautiful and meaningful gift. I can't wait to share it with Christina.

———

On the way to the Frankfurt Book Fair, I stopped in Paris to visit my daughter Catherine.

October 16, 2016

Dearest Sister Wendy,

I am now in Paris—a city I assume you know well. Today we went to Sacré Coeur—a church much more striking from the outside than in. And then to Saint-Agustin, a church with much spiritual power: the place where Charles de Foucauld returned to the Church.

I presume you know the museums very well. Is there any place else you are very fond of?

I remember so well when I brought Catherine here when she was 12. She said then, "Someday I will live here"—and so it has come to pass. It is fun to rely on her fluent French and *savoir faire*.

———

October 17, 2016

Dearest Robert,

You make me smile with your confidence in my knowledge about Paris. I have been there several times, but always with the BBC to film, so that I know the hotel where we stayed, the church where we went to Mass, and the part of the museum in which we filmed. This is true for everywhere I've been: church, hotel, museum. In other words, I don't know anything. The thing about the museums of Paris is that they are, as you know, extraordinarily rich.

Just to really look at one gallery in the Louvre or in any of the other museums would take a day. If I knew somebody had a short time in Paris, even though I'm speaking from relative ignorance, I would say, don't miss the Cezannes and don't miss the Poussins. Of course there are hundreds of other great paintings, but those are my two favorite artists, both very profound, morally significant artists, as well as overwhelmingly beautiful. This would mean one leaves with one's soul fed with a heavenly nourishment.

Very much love and joy,
Sister Wendy

––––––––

November 8, 2016

Dearest Sister Wendy,

I have been thinking about Pope Francis quite a lot, of course—planning another letter to him. We are publishing a wonderful book of his addresses to priests, *With the Smell of the Sheep*.[40] Perhaps this inspired a dream I had the other night: I dreamed I was at the Vatican, waiting to meet with Pope Francis. He had just walked into the sacristy to disrobe after Mass and I was standing just outside, when Pope John Paul II walked up. He was young—like when he was first pope. I felt a deep sense of awe. He nodded in the direction of Pope Francis, with an affectionate chuckle, and said something like, "Dear Pope Francis—such a master of the liturgy that he can depart from the liturgy." Then he looked at me and said, "Look at this," and he held out a couple of odd-shaped cards with his picture on them. They had evidently come in the mail; I could see a postmark on them. "I just received a notice from the Academy that I have been selected to receive a special academic honor." He shrugged and said, "I don't know if this is proper, but would you like one of them?" I said yes, and he handed me one of the cards.

––––––––

40. Pope Francis, *With the Smell of the Sheep: The Pope Speaks to Priests, Bishops, and Other Shepherds* (Maryknoll, NY: Orbis Books, 2017).

I said, "Holy Father, I am Robert Ellsberg. I am the publisher of Orbis Books, with the Maryknoll Fathers. We publish books on mission, theology, and spirituality." He shook my hand warmly and said something like, "Well, we're all doing good work." I took off my glasses (a strange thing to do, I realize) and bowed my head and said, "I pray that you will bless our work." He made the sign of the cross. I could see that Pope Francis was almost ready and Pope John Paul II smiled and said, "I think we're in pretty good hands with Pope Francis, don't you?" I said "Yes!" Then he seemed to disappear and Pope Francis appeared and said, "Ok, shall we go?"

————

November 9, 2016

Dearest Robert,

I'll answer properly, but this is just to share your wonder over that extraordinary dream. Now you move forward with the blessing of St. John Paul II. And such visible tokens of his interest in your work. Perhaps he's especially strengthening you because he knew what horrors the day would bring. Every day these next four years we must pray for poor Mr. Trump. God created him and loves him and it's up to us to help him to understand what his responsibilities are. Not by words of course, but by prayer.

Much love,
Sister Wendy

————

I had been sharing my premonitions about the pending presidential election of 2016. As it turned out, my worst fears were realized. Sister Wendy's counsel, in the spirit of Julian of Norwich, was that "all shall be well."

November 9, 2016

Dearest Sister Wendy,

There are so many others who will need our prayers in this time of Trump. The world has endured worse demagogues, but the stakes were never so high for the future of the world. I tremble. A day when words simply fail me and all one can do is pray.

————

November 10, 2016

Dearest Robert,

It could even be that this bizarre event opens up America to a renewal of its true spirit. Anyhow, God made Mr. Trump and loves him, and in our prayers we will love him too.

I think everybody is rather speechless at the moment. I can't help thinking of poor Mrs. Clinton who must be devastated. But for her, too, this is a moment of grace and I pray that He enables her to rise to it.

Very much love and gratitude for all you give us,
Sister Wendy

I replied: "Yes, I know that God loves Trump—as he did Herod, and Caligula, and so many others. And that he can draw good even from terrible things—which is one of his signatures in history."

November 11, 2016

Dearest Robert,

What with grieving for Mrs. Clinton and President Obama and the whole civilized world, there's not much to do but to put the whole mess on the altar where Our Blessed Lord can deal with it. As St. Teresa says, all passes except for God, and you rightly remarked it's the divine specialty to bring good out of evil.

I hope America is getting over the cataclysmic election results. To my incredulous horror, a devout Catholic woman who often writes to me says that she voted for Mr. Trump because "he's pro-life." She says she didn't expect him to get in, but she felt it was her duty to make a protest against abortion. It's a terrifying example of how dangerous it is to see all moral questions through a single lens. I wonder how many people voted as a kind of mute protest against something or other, feeling quite safe because he was unelectable, surely???

With love and hoping that you get a good rest,
Sister Wendy

November 14, 2016

Dearest Sister Wendy,

I agree with you entirely about the way the "pro-life" banner is suscep-tible to manipulation. If it is detached from a more comprehensive commit-ment to the dignity of life in all its form, it becomes a kind of fetish. Last night I heard Trump on television say that his two big constitutional com-mitments are to the "pro-life" cause and the "second amendment" (the right to bear arms). But he is also the candidate who said we have to bring back waterboarding "and a lot worse.... Frankly we have to be willing to con-sider things that are considered unthinkable." He is the person who has spo-ken of targeting the families of terrorists; of banning Muslims; of the desir-ability of our allies acquiring nuclear weapons; of allowing guns in churches and schools; whose response to police shootings of African Americans is the need for more "law and order"; who has demeaned women, Mexican Ameri-cans, people with disabilities; who says that climate change is a "hoax" per-petrated by the Chinese; who wants to build a wall along the entire southern border.... I could go on and on.

Already this is beginning to invade my dreams. I hope I have not done the same for you! Only prayer can drive out the demons that are loose in the world.

Meanwhile, the most constructive things I can do are right at hand: I am working hard with my father to finish his book on the "Doomsday Machine"—the mad apparatus of nuclear war planning. Last night I edited a chapter that dealt with the serious concern, at the time of the original testing of the atom bomb, and later the H-bomb, that this could start a chain reac-tion that could ignite all the hydrogen atoms in the atmosphere and ocean, reducing the earth in minutes to a spinning cinder. The scientists determined that the odds were quite low, though not zero, so they proceeded anyway.

And I am helping Sister Helen Prejean finish her memoir, which tells the story of her formation as a nun, and the changes that led her to take on the issue of the death penalty, which she has battled so valiantly.[41]

And I am finishing my book on Franciscan saints.

At present I am writing a letter to Pope Francis. Instead of my previous, more business-like letters, I thought I would write to him as I would if we could actually meet and talk—what I would tell him about Dorothy Day,

---

41. Sister Helen Prejean, a Sister of St. Joseph, is the author of a bestselling mem-oir, *Dead Man Walking*, about her immersion in the world of death row prisoners. She became an internationally known activist, with considerable influence in both the Church and American culture for raising opposition to the death penalty. For seven years I helped her work on a second memoir, *River of Fire: My Spiritual Journey*, pub-lished in 2019 by Random House.

what I would say about my work on saints, and the mission of Orbis. I see him increasingly as a great gift that God has offered in our time—and a crucial counter-voice in this time of fear and hatred.

November 15, 2016

Dearest Robert,

There are so many counterbalances in your life. You live amidst beauty and you're working actively to share your vision of God's holiness, open to all of us. You show especially how this holiness shines forth in the lives of his saints. I think it is in these beautiful holy things that you should make your home and blot out all these reports of what poor Mr. Trump has said. Agonizing about these things will not remove them, they will only disturb your peace, and as you know, where there is no peace, there is no prayer.

Your voice sounds weary and sad. You don't have to feel sanguine to trust that God will look after your country: it's not a matter of feeling, but of trust. Out of so many disasters, doesn't He bring healing? You and I can both think of times in our lives when it seemed we had met with heartbreak and yet out of that very suffering came something far more beautiful.

With love and hope and joy, knowing that you understand the duty of delight, even in Mr. Trump,

    Sister Wendy

I shared with Sister Wendy a personal letter of thanks and appreciation I had sent to Pope Francis. Unsurprisingly, I did not receive a reply, yet I continued to write him regularly over the following years.

November 16, 2016

Dearest Robert,

That's a most beautiful letter for the Pope. I hope it reaches him because I think his sad fatherly heart would rejoice at everything you say.

This is a great time of grace for America. I can see Flannery O'Connor understanding the ignorances and deficiencies of your poor president-elect as a true way of entering into the mystery of redemption. When it's all too smooth we don't go deep enough. Mr. Trump forces us to grasp at our roots. If they are rooted in self, they'll come up easily in our hands, but if, as we hope, we're rooted in Jesus, they will be deep, life-giving sources of strength for us. So perhaps America is in for a conversion experience where it least expected one.

Very much love and prayer,
Sister Wendy

––––––––

November 16, 2016

Dearest Sister Wendy,

Your dear words send my roots rain (as Hopkins would say). Yesterday I gave an hour-long interview with a radio program called "Radio Maria." The interviewer ended by asking me what I think of Pope Francis, and I rather gushed on. Apparently for him and his listeners this was by far the most controversial part of my interview. Afterward he wrote to tell me how he and so many others are baffled by Pope Francis and what he wants to do. He sent me a link to a story about Cardinal Raymond Burke and three other cardinals who had put a series of questions or "dubia" to Pope Francis about the meaning of his exhortation on the synod, *Amoris Laetitia*, which appears to offer the possibility of "sinners and adulterers" receiving communion.

I often think of how eager so many Christians are to adopt the attitude of the scribes in place of the good news of God's mercy and forgiveness. So eager to reinstitute the enforcement of the law, so eager to cast the first stone. (America, with the Puritans, was conceived in this godly righteousness.)

I reflect on those words in light of your reflections about Holy Saturday. A time of seeming dejection and darkness. And that brings me also Pope Francis's beautiful words on the Resurrection from *Evangelii Gaudium*:

> Christ's resurrection is not an event of the past; it contains a vital power which has permeated this world. Where all seems to be dead, signs of the resurrection suddenly spring up. It is an irresistible force. . . . Each day in our world beauty is born anew, it rises transformed through the storms of history. Values always tend to reappear under new guises, and human beings have arisen time after time from situations that seemed doomed. Such is the power of the resurrection, and all who evangelize are instruments of that power.

How can one not be stirred by such words?

––––––––

In a significant turning point, Sister Wendy nodded for the first time toward the possibility that our correspondence might hold value for other readers. Perhaps all along we had been writing a book unawares.

November 17, 2016

Dearest Robert,

That is a great feast of praise of God that you have shared with us today. Thank you. I am quite confident that the holy power of the Risen Lord, in whose transforming grace we all live, will overcome all the darkness and lack of love. It's very sad, though, to find that unloving darkness actually within the Holy Church itself and to find cardinals unable to see that any law which keeps people back from God is not from Jesus. But the more we pray and rest on Him, the more scope he has for teaching these good men, teaching them not to be Pharisees but Christians.

Again and again you've told me that you would like to publish something personal from me. Robert, I say this very hesitatingly, but could you cobble something together from our letters? Sister Lesley has often been very moved by the interchange between us. I know there would be much more work to be done, and you may feel that whereas exposure is fine for me, it would not be for you. I just mention it.

Your letter to the Pope stays in my heart as something so luminous and true, so warm and simple, so childlike and yet so adult. I hope very much it gets to the Pope.

With love and prayer and gratitude for all that is happening,
Sister Wendy

P.S. I read Flannery yesterday and she was telling a friend that she'd never been anywhere which she didn't feel was the right place to be. That kind of instinctive awareness of God as He comes in happenstance, in good things and in bad, is what makes me convinced she was a very holy woman. Nice to have a tart saint, isn't it?

———

November 17, 2016

Dearest Sister Wendy,

I am very touched by your suggestion to think that there might be a way of drawing something out of our correspondence. It has seemed that you have shared very deeply with me, and I have no doubt that we could make something of this—though there is no immediate urgency (trusting that you are feeling somewhat more robust). I hope that there will be many more letters to come!

Flannery O'Connor said she had never been any place that didn't feel like the right place to be—but she also said that she had never been anyplace but sick. ("In a sense sickness is a place, more instructive than a long trip to Europe, and it's always a place where there's no company, where nobody can follow. Sickness before death is a very appropriate thing and I think those who don't have it miss one of God's mercies.")

I appreciate your saying that my letter to the Pope was both "childlike and adult." Indeed, I felt as if I were talking to a father—from my heart, not as the publisher of Orbis. When I read his words, in turn, I experience such a feeling of love. It pains me to think that there are Catholic leaders who don't feel the same.

––––––––––

I was interested to learn more about the mechanics of this correspondence on Sister Wendy's end. Of greater interest was learning that it was through her reading of my daily writing on the saints, which reflected "a non-judgmental love and interest," that she had found it possible to write with "a candor that is completely unprecedented."

November 18, 2016

Dearest Robert,

How the email correspondence works is that, as you realize, Sister Lesley comes into my cell in the afternoon with her machine [laptop] from which she reads me emails. Thank God there are usually not very many, though I have a very dear old hillbilly Georgian who tends to write, send me a poem or a drawing or a photograph every day. Dear Lesley who has a tender heart always wants me to reply to these messages, but I feel the occasional word is more appropriate for a hermit, not a daily interchange. Then for the emails that need answering I dictate and answer off the cuff. I think it's this off-the-cuffness that Lesley especially likes. It is in fact the way I write my books—no re-reading, no improvements, which means that none of my books is very good, but I feel perhaps "good enough." Time is precious, I am the very opposite of a perfectionist.

Every morning Sister Lesley reads to me from your two books. You have the special gift for showing the beauty of each life, its struggles and its fulfillment in Our Blessed Lord, and obviously this orientation comes from something deep within yourself. This non-judgmental love and interest must be why I have written to you with the candor that is completely unprecedented. I have tended since my youth never to speak about personal experience because I was so traumatized by finding that others did not share it. Oh how certain I was that once I entered the convent we would all speak the same language and I would understand everybody and they would understand me. One cannot but smile at such adolescent foolishness. Anyhow in its oblique way I think this was a grace, because why do we need to speak about things? Or even think about what God is doing in us? That is His business.

Very much love,
Sister Wendy

It was, in turn, Sister Wendy's non-judgmental love and interest that encouraged me to share with her my dreams.

November 24, 2016

Dearest Sister Wendy,

Last night I had a very extraordinary dream. Once again I was introduced to Pope Francis. He had just said Mass and was preparing to go home. Somehow he caught my eye and came over to greet me. He suggested that we walk together. It was on a long pathway next to a river, and there were huge crowds of people, but they seemed to part effortlessly to let us pass. He spoke to me in Italian and I said I couldn't speak Italian. But then I realized I could make myself understood in Spanish. So the rest of the dream I spoke to him in Spanish. I told him about Orbis, what kinds of books we publish, including his titles. I thanked him for *Evangelii Gaudium*—telling him that I "read it every week" (which I admit is an exaggeration). I started to tell him about Dorothy.

By then we had arrived at his home, which seemed to be up on a rocky cliff, as if he were some kind of Irish hermit. We had to climb up these rocks, and I thought, *he is too old to have to do this*. We reached sort of a perch and stopped for a while. He said, "Thank you for telling me about your work and a bit about your life. But your life is more than your work. For instance, you should remember to pay more attention to Nicholas" (my son).

I was astonished that he knew his name, since I hadn't mentioned this. I said Nicholas is 30, and he is married. And I have two daughters (*dos hijas*).

"What do they do?" he asked. I said one is studying cinema in France, and the other—she has a "great passion to change the world." This made him smile. He said, it is late, you should spend the night here. We had to crawl through a precarious opening that led into a drab set of rooms that looked very institutional. I wanted to tell him: "Holy Father, I am divorced." But then I woke up.

I wish that I could say he told me something very significant. But you know, Sister Wendy, what came to my mind—a certain feeling, which, I realize, called to mind the pope's own motto: *miserando atque eligendo*. As you have probably read, he took this from a sermon by St. Bede about the calling of St. Matthew, the tax collector: "Looking on him with mercy he chose him." I take it the syntax is rather difficult to render in English— like *mercying and choosing*. Anyway, that is the sensation I had: that I had been looked on with mercy.

Forgive me for sharing my dreams. I know that there is nothing more boring than hearing about other people's dreams. Maybe that is what you meant when you wrote: "I have tended since my youth never to speak about personal experience because I was so traumatized by finding that others did not share it."

I wonder what you mean when you say you were "traumatized that others did not share it"—your desire to speak about personal experience? or the kinds of experiences you had? Did you mean experiences of God? I wonder what those experiences were, and if you would share some of those memories. Perhaps it is my delayed "adolescent foolishness," as you put it, but I am intensely interested in such things.

As is Monica. When she was a little girl she desperately wanted God to give her some sign that he existed. So she made up a little test. She asked her brother to name a number that she had in her mind, and when he guessed the right number she knew immediately that God was real, and she has never doubted it since!

November 27, 2016

Dearest Robert,

Your dreams are precious. And it would seem that this is one of the ways in which God is communicating Himself to you. The dream gave you one piece of practical advice, to think more about your son. Perhaps subconsciously you feel that he has moved away from you into a self-sufficient zone, but that can't ever be true, can it? You have things to give him that only you can give. And the other beautiful thing about your dream was the Pope's affection for you. He knew you were his true child (perhaps there's a sort of parallel here between you and Nicholas?). He wanted to be with you and to talk with you—just thinking about such a dream makes me feel happy.

No, I don't think dreams have anything to do with what I said in my last letter, and obviously "traumatized" was an exaggeration. What I meant was that God had always been so real to me, and it had been a shock to discover that He wasn't so real to the other girls at school. I was convinced that in the convent everybody would live in His presence, and I discovered that this was not so. The novices were nobly and courageously struggling to learn how to pray and how to center their lives on God, and I was baffled at the necessity of such struggle. I may have said to you before that one day the provincial stopped me and said that the novice mistress told her that I loved praying, and I replied in surprise that, "No, God loves it." It was always so clear to me that God gave the prayer, He prayed. I don't suppose I really wanted to talk about this even if I had been certain that everybody thought this way. After all, what can one say? But time and again remarks I made that were deductions from His presence were received with kindly disagreement.

I'm not putting that well and I know that technically and factually I was wrong very often. I could never imagine how anybody could hurt Our Blessed Lord and in fact got into trouble for "not believing in sin." I do believe in sin, and did, but I think it's something far more uncommon that people tend to think. Human weakness is one thing, but that's not sin, and it never bothers Our Blessed Lord, as long as we turn to Him in contrition. Mother Julian puts it so well when she describes God as not wanting us to get all upset about our "sins." I believe thoroughly in sinfulness, but I think it's actually rather difficult to actually sin. It never occurred to me that anyone in the convent would disagree. I think in many ways I'm still as foolish as I was at 16, though perhaps I disguise it better.

This is a rather dull letter, dear Robert, though it is you with the right to feel exhausted. However, my dear old friend Dr. Stutterford says that the two great symptoms of a failing heart are breathlessness and a crushing fatigue that can't be mistaken with just tiredness. These are excuses but I'm bold enough to make them.

Very much love and gratitude for your beautiful letters,
Sister Wendy

"If you knew what was going to happen in your life, would you want to know?"

November 27, 2017

Dearest Sister Wendy,

Monica and I were just talking about the always disturbing statement of our Lord—that only those who hate mother and father and even children are worthy of the kingdom. Of course one must allow for a certain hyperbole. I think obviously when it comes to our vocation, we can't be deterred by those who cling to us in a possessive way. But it goes both ways, and we must learn to let our children go.

I remember the conversation I had with my mother many years ago when I was 19. I had dropped out of college and I was setting off on an unknown quest that would lead me to the Catholic Worker. She was very upset with me. She thought I was "throwing my life away." She left for work that morning without saying goodbye. Then she called me later to apologize. She said she had been thinking more about this. She said, "We want our children to be mindlessly happy. But that is not what we want for ourselves. We want to explore, and find out who we are, and make mistakes and learn from them. So you go do that, with my blessings. You find everything you are looking for and let me know when you do."

I thought that was one of the most precious gifts I have ever received.

Christina came to visit the other day and surprised me by saying she is thinking of applying for a master's program at Union Theological Seminary! I cannot but feel that I am witnessing the fruit of seeds planted long ago in the course of my own searching, and in my mother's blessing.

Last night I went to see a very interesting movie called "Arrival." Since there is zero likelihood of your seeing this, I don't worry about giving anything away. It is about the arrival of strange alien space craft around the world. A woman linguist is compelled by the military to try to communicate with them. All the while she keeps having memories and flashbacks about her daughter, who eventually died of a rare disease. She is able to make a breakthrough with the aliens, who communicate through strange complex pictographs, which she begins to interpret. The aliens have come to bring humanity "a gift." The gift is actually their language. Once you master their language, you enter into their way of thinking, in which past and future are one. They have come to unite humanity with this gift, because, they say, "we will need you in 3,000 years." Meanwhile, through this experience, the linguist and her scientist colleague fall in love and you realize that the story of the daughter is actually in the future, not in the past. The linguist knows what will happen—her ability to see into the future actually gives her essential information to avert a terrible war in the present. She says to the scientist, who will become her husband and the father of her child, "If you knew what was going to happen in your life, would you want to know?"

There are certainly times when it would have spared me much grief if I could have known what would happen. I remember when my daughter's therapist said to me, "There will come a time when all this will be in the past, when she will be fine." I needed to believe that, but I didn't "know it."

I suppose that in a way, living in the presence of God, as you experienced at a young age, is a certain way of knowing the future: not of course everything that would happen, but knowing in some way that there is nothing really bad that can happen; that even if suffering or loss occurs, this can't separate you from the presence and love of God.

The love of prayer is obviously a gift you received at a young age, something the other girls had to struggle over. And I take it this made you rather an odd duck, even in a community devoted to prayer. It is funny when we realize that we have an ability or a gift that seems so natural to us that we don't even realize other people don't have it. Like having perfect pitch, or the ability to "see" auras.

I trust that among the Carmelites you are not so out of place.

Well, in my dreams about the pope, of course I am glad to receive a word from him, but mostly I think my heart is just reaching out to him to offer him love and support, to encourage him to feel faith and courage in continuing on his path.

It is funny when I write to you, I sometimes think I am jumping randomly from point to point, yet it always seems to be connected and make sense. At least I hope you find this true!

November 29, 2016

Dearest Robert,

Yes, your letters are all of a piece and one theme develops out of another. I feel mine, though, are rather choppy, but it's not worth bothering about epistolary style. You have no idea how unique it is for me, these letters we exchange.

I meant to say about your beautiful Pope Francis dream that I thought it was significant that he led you upwards. You know that in committing yourself to his guidance, you have put your hand into the hand of a very wise father, in God. I also kept remembering how Our Blessed Lord said to the pair of apostles who asked where He lived, "Come and see." In going to see where Pope Francis lived you were expressing your desire to live as he does, don't you think?

That's wonderful news about Christina. When I was a novice, my great desire was that my sister should become a nun and my brother a priest. It took me some time to realize that vocations were specific to individuals and that all the scope she needed to become complete would be offered Pamela in her marriage and that Tim would now in his old age be the most ardent of Catholics. I think in fact he would like to become a priest now, but it is only now that he has reached that point. So I mustn't be narrow-minded again and get all excited by seeing the word "theology," but I must just pray that all your children understand the wonder of God and the joy of His reality, in whatever way He wants to show them.

Your relationship with your son and with your mother makes me think about families. After my last letter it struck me to wonder why I had taken it for granted that everybody was aware of God and had this certainty of safety that you mention in your present letter. I say this because my parents were not explicitly pious, though of course they were solid Catholics. It never occurred to me to doubt that they were close to God, but I had in fact no evidence, as it were, except the evidence of never seeing them speak or act in a way that would not have pleased Our Lord: no gossip, no small-mindedness, no quarrels, no malice. Yet, I have never had a conversation with either parent of the type you had with your mother. They were reticent people, I suppose, but I was so conscious of their goodness that I didn't need any proof. I believed everybody was good and in fact still do, because only God knows.

I never felt the need of any deep conversation with my parents or indeed with anybody else. I remember feeling very uncomfortable when the novice mistress started to talk about God because I couldn't quite recognize her God as the God that I lived with. And anyhow, how can one use words for something that is of its nature ineffable? I feel a deep distrust of words, I'm afraid. I think this is why I find it very difficult to believe that anything I've written can truly be heard, whatever my intention. I suspect, too, its behind, though unconsciously, my terrible handwriting. I try to write clearly, but if I know no one can hear, I think the words just shrink in on themselves without my trying.

I also realized, thinking of my family, that although I tend to say I never knew my brother because he was only little when I left home at 16, he was in fact, nearly 8, and yet, do you know Robert, I can bring to mind only one memory of my brother, and that is of him as a baby, once. Of course I was at boarding school, but I was always home for the holidays, so for over eight years I lived with that child and so blotted him out apparently, that I have literally only that one memory. I think this shows a very selfish and maybe pathologically damaged psyche. What overwhelming mercy that Our Blessed Lord took me into His arms so that I always did have a deep loving relationship, even if it wasn't one that words could express.

Your dreams made me think about my dreams, which are remarkably passive in comparison. There you are skipping along hand in hand with the blessed Francis, him giving you good advice, you dutifully nodding. Whereas I am more often looking at pictures of Our Blessed Lord or Our Lady or explaining the faith. A few nights ago I spent the night trying to make my body like the crucifix, which was very difficult, but I knew worth struggling for. And last night I was explaining the omnipresence of the cross. It is always with us even in the slightest shadow, always something precious, always a source of grace. I explained (to whom?) that I thought the cross came in four different ways, from the very slightest shadow to the deepest agony, and I was telling (whom?) my mysterious dream companions that it is holding to our hearts the cross that brings us closest to the crucified Lord. So you see these are not very exciting dreams, though they linger happily in my mind afterwards.

I was also interested in what you said about Monica's challenge to God as a child. Books suggest that many children put God to the test and feel that He failed: mother didn't get better; I didn't pass my exam; no cake for tea. Monica was very fortunate in her brother's answer, but I think she must have had a predisposition to believe, or she would have queried it and tried again. So that's a blessed thing for you to have as your love—a woman who is attuned by nature to God. I think your children are too, and I hope you never give up on sharing with them what God has given you.

Very much Advent love, dear Robert,
Sister Wendy

In reply, I told Sister Wendy that Monica confirmed the correctness of what she had said about her challenge: "If God had failed that first test I would have given him many more chances!"

Sister Wendy would definitely not want to know the future. But she offered a beautiful definition of prayer: "Prayer is each one of us facing God in Jesus, with the Holy Spirit speaking His praise within us."

December 2, 2016

Dearest Robert,

In a previous letter, you described to me what must be a fascinating film with its interweaving of past, present and future, and you asked me if I would like to know the future. No, I would definitely not like to know. I love the constant little surprises of every day, even the painful ones, which are all experienced in the context of complete security in God. I don't even think it could be possible because we haven't an existence of our own, we're contingent; God's creating us every moment. We flow from God's being—or if we like He sings us, and only He knows what His song will be. I think of myself as a sort of breath that He breathes, only there because of Him and having no objective reality outside of that holy creative and sustaining Breath. It's a nice fantasy to play with, but I think the reality is so infinitely more beautiful and even exciting, because we have the adventure every day into what He will make of us, with nothing settled and nothing limited. It's all an eternal coming forth from Love.

Obviously I'm not just talking about myself, but about all of us, about what it means to be human.

I find it almost impossible to talk about prayer and I think books on prayer are very dangerous. Prayer is each one of us facing God in Jesus, with the Holy Spirit speaking His praise within us. Since each of us is different, how this comes about must be different. So I think the danger of prayer books and prayer talk is suggesting there's a right way to do this. I find that most people seem to think there is a right way, and everybody knows it except them.

We've had novices here bitterly lamenting "that they haven't been taught how to pray." These novices usually don't make it, because the nakedness and vulnerability of prayer, understanding that we are completely on our own, is of the essence. By on our own of course I mean we are there facing the Blessed Trinity and there can be no intermediaries.

Having said that, I think there are three levels of prayer. There's the completely silent and wordless deep prayer, which not everybody is offered (prayer being God's business far more than ours, the kind of prayer we experience is really up to Him—what we give is the time and the desire). And then there's the next layer of prayer in which we're thinking about God or talking about Him or reading about Him. And then there's the third layer which you describe in your words about Dorothy, everything is prayer at this level, whether we peel potatoes or read a detective story or do our taxes or drive a car, etc. If these are the elements of our day then that is where God is waiting for us. And receiving Him in these countless forms, cleaving to Him through them and beyond them is the texture of a genuine commitment to His will in prayer.

Very much love,
Sister Wendy

————

December 5, 2016

Dearest Sister Wendy,

I am feeling very happy to have finished my book on the Franciscans, just needing to write the introduction, for which I have a whole month.

When you read many of these stories, they tend to fall into a dozen or so typical forms. For instance: the princesses who refused to marry, and finally won permission to join a convent; or the ones who were forced to marry, but then were widowed and so got to fulfill their dream. There are the stories of the simple brothers who were thought to have very few gifts, but then somehow reveal their amazing spiritual powers: whether answering the door, begging for alms, preaching, or flying through the air.

Then there are stories that are absolutely *hors classe*: such as Louis Massignon, who was converted by his encounter with Sufi mysticism and became a Third Order Franciscan with the name Ibrahim, devoted to Christian-Muslim reconciliation.

The other night I showed Monica a wonderful movie she has never seen. Probably you don't know it, though it comes from England: *Billy Elliot*. It is about a poor miner's son in the north of England who discovers an uncanny attraction to ballet and ultimately wins a scholarship to the Royal School of Ballet. And it made me think that there are probably so many people who aren't gifted with words, and for "meanness of opportunity" (as George Eliot would say) have no chance of discovering they can express themselves with genius in some other form—as artists, poets, artisans, athletes. . . .

As Eliot notes, "Here and there a cygnet is reared uneasily among the ducklings in the brown pond, and never finds the living stream in fellowship with its own oary-footed kind. Here and there is born a Saint Theresa, foundress of nothing, whose loving heart-beats and sobs after an unattained goodness tremble off and are dispersed among hindrances, instead of centring in some long-recognizable deed."

How wonderful when someone finds their true vocation. But so many are truly born in the wrong time and place, never finding fellowship with their oary-footed kind.

––––––

December 8, 2016

Dearest Robert,

Today is the feast of the Immaculate Conception and the white-hot radiance of Our Lady's purity is spreading out all round the world, burning away at our nastiness and sinfulness. I know we don't see it or feel it, but that's what she's there for, to be a sanctifying presence through the death and resurrection of her son. In the context of this beautiful warm purity, all these sorrows and sadnesses seem less crushing, don't you think? How delicate and perceptive of your mother to give birth to you on St. Lucy's day [December 13]. You with your great capacity to shed light on the lives of God's friends. I think of you as a light-bringer, in the nicest sense, and an illuminator of what would be dull manuscripts. You haven't got a second name Lucius have you? Robert Lucius Ellsberg sounds good to me.

I'll be thinking of you on your birthday and asking for floods of light.

Very much love,
Sister Wendy

––––––

Sister Wendy's Christmas card carried the line from St. Paul: "I live now not I but Christ lives in me." I had been surprised in one of her letters to learn that at one time she had been a "reverend mother"—an office, I supposed, that was not entirely congenial.

December 9, 2016

Dearest Robert,

You are quite right in regarding the image of me as a reverend mother with a certain dubiety. I was imposed upon the community, who had not elected me and did not want me. I don't think for one moment I was a success, but it was a time that I'm sure God had things to teach me.

I was thinking a great deal this morning about what I have very inadequately put on my Christmas card, that "I live now not I but Christ lives in me." To know that when the Father looks at us, He sees His well-beloved

Son looking back at Him. Isn't that the source of the deepest joy and freedom that one can imagine? You remember how St. Elizabeth of the Trinity
offered herself as an extra humanity for the divine Person who dwelt in her
heart, so that Jesus could use her utterly, just as He used His own human nature. All these words are so utterly empty compared to the truth we're trying
to talk about. There are no words and no thoughts and no feelings, just the
truth of Jesus who is more ourselves than we are.

    With love and prayer as always,
    Sister Wendy

December 9, 2016

Dearest Sister Wendy,

    My mind is filled with words, sentences, and paragraphs, regardless of
whether I am writing a book. Even in my dreams I am often delivering
speeches, which is why I often awake exhausted.

    Monica has observed that my writing about saints functions for me very
much in the same way that her meditation practice does for her. I am very
fortunate that *Give Us This Day* has given me this great gift. I am now in my
seventh year. By the time I finish the current contract, that will represent
eight years of writing these stories. And it all goes back to my original pur-
chase of a four-volume set of Butler's *Lives of the Saints* when I found myself utterly engrossed—as much with the strange and fabulous stories as the
great ones. That was thirty-six years ago, and it is still my dear companion.
Have you read *The Way of a Pilgrim*, about the Russian pilgrim who walks
all over carrying his beloved copy of the *Philokalia*? And this reminds me of
a dream I had years ago:

    I dreamed I received a package of five books wrapped in brown paper
tied together with string. It was marked "Philokalia," (which of course
means "love of the Good, the Beautiful") and I thought someone was sending me these volumes. They were mailed from India. It was too heavy to
carry so I dragged it along on the ground. They began to unwind and un-
ravel. When one opened I saw that there was a little, brown-skinned baby
girl inside. I was scared and quickly opened the others. They each had little
shriveled up things like newborn puppies but they all turned out to be little
Indian girls. They all were fine once they were out of the boxes and I gave
them something to drink. The oldest one could speak. She said she was eight
months old. I named her Cecilia.

In another project, I have returned to editing the memoir of Sister Helen Prejean. It is about the story of her life up to the life-changing encounter with a prisoner on death row, which is where her other famous book, *Dead Man Walking*, began. She entered the convent when she was 16, back in the late 1950s, and the book is really about the journey from the black-and-white certainties of religious life when she entered into the experience of Vatican II, and her awakening to the social dimension of the gospel.

Sister Helen Prejean

I wonder if you have felt any similar evolution in your understanding of religious life since the time you entered. Of course, you always had such a deep vocation for prayer—unlike Sister Helen, who always assumed that she would be teaching and working with kids. But I wonder whether Vatican II, or the new openness to Scripture, or liturgical renewal had any similar impact on your own journey. Would you always have felt so open to recognizing the sacred in the world and in art? Or was that the fruit of an awakening?

December 10, 2016

Dearest Robert,

The work you're doing for Sr. Helen sounds both interesting and important. My experience, though, has been very different from hers. However, we both entered at 16, and we both expected to spend a life teaching. It dawned upon me in the novitiate that I had wanted to be a praying nun and found the idea of teaching very distasteful. I also thought that I might not be able to control a class and the thought of such a humiliation was terrible. It therefore seemed obvious (oh foolish youth) that this was the Cross and that there was no way to enter into closeness with Our Blessed Lord without embracing these distasteful and possibly humiliating things. It turned out that I never had any difficulty with controlling a class, but I never ever wanted to teach. This was especially so when prayer threatened to engulf me in the classroom.

You can imagine me as an English teacher trying to draw the children into the meaning of Gerard Manley Hopkins and the intensity of prayer

becoming almost unendurable. My degree, remember, is in English and although I was also asked to teach subjects about which I knew very little, like
botany and even math, I mostly taught English. That is a minefield of spiritual intensity and I think my struggles were partly the reason why my health
degenerated, and the Order very generously allowed me to seek a contemplative form of life. I had been asking for some years, having realized that in
fact I actually needed more prayer, but my superiors said no, I was essential
to the school system. At one stage I thought that I might die or have a breakdown, but I felt quite happy about this, because if that was what God was
asking, that was where He was. To live in God's will is our only happiness,
even if it comes in a form we would not have chosen.

But apart from those two likenesses with Sr. Helen, I think our paths
were different because we're different kinds of people. She's a heroic
woman going out and battling for suffering humanity. I've just continued on
the path I was placed upon all those years ago and the changes have not
made any obvious impact on me. I suppose I've had access to more scrip-
tural studies, which I have always greatly appreciated, but that also has just
been a slow development. When there were these recent changes in the
liturgy of the Mass, with vehement arguments for and against—mostly
against—a great friend of mine, who directed most of my films and in fact
became a Catholic after what he saw, wrote to me that he supposed I'd
hardly noticed the changes. That's true. The Mass is the Mass, and the bones
of the great surrender will always be there, indestructible.

That dream about the little Indian girls must have made a deep impression if you've remembered it all this time. Clearly it was a succoring dream
because you unwrapped them and brought them into life, the wee shrunken
brown creatures. In a strange sort of parallel that's what you do with many of
the lives of the forgotten saints. You drag them out of obscurity, you unwrap
them and you let them speak to you. Then you share them with the world.

Very much love,
Sister Wendy

————

December 11, 2016

Dearest Robert,

This is a sort of P.S. to yesterday's letter, when I hadn't got the energy
to tackle Butler's *Lives of the Saints*. I was probably about 13 (1943) and at
boarding school when my mother wrote to tell me that she'd bought the

complete set. I was longing to get home and read it. Butler's *Lives* weren't put in our usual bookcase, which was one of those wonderful many-sided cases that swiveled round—such a useful piece of furniture, I wish I had it now. No, Butler's *Lives* went into a glass-fronted cabinet in the front parlor. I sat down, all expectation, and can still remember the physical shock of reading about St. Agatha and discovering that she had her breasts cut off. Breasts were new to me and rather puzzling. I couldn't quite see the point of them. In fact, I never really have, because gender to me has always been something quite unimportant. If we love somebody for their goodness, their kindness, their charm, their sense of humor, does it matter if this friend is man or woman?

I have a complete blank spot here as you can see, which is one of the reasons I would never have been a good novice mistress—too odd. I felt physically violated by what happened to Agatha and felt my nose was violently pushed into the reality of what holiness might mean. God had to have it all. Your physical control of yourself was one of the many things you might have to surrender to Him. It would have to be surrendered gladly and trustfully, because however destructive experience might seem, this was only a seeming, because in everything that happened God was there holding us to His Heart. But I was so shocked that I couldn't read further. And those green volumes stayed in that glass-fronted bookcase as a perpetual reproach to me. I couldn't even read about a martyrdom.

This shame, which was very real, was a great grace, disguised as graces often are. It made me cling all the more trustfully to Our Blessed Lord: "When I am weak then I am strong." Since I really couldn't feel myself equal to a life in which breasts were cut off, or teeth shattered (St. Apolonia), or eyes pulled out (like your own St. Lucia), I had to realize from the start that it was God who would have to do all things for me. I was a failure before we even began, and that didn't matter because it was God's holiness and God's strength that I knew would be given me.

So you see, Butler has many profound associations for me. Quite apart from the question of what holiness might demand, it posed a question about sexuality. I entered without ever having met a boy, and my class at school never discussed these things. When my mother, gritting her teeth, bless her, offered to explain the "facts of life," I told her I didn't need to know because I was going to be a nun. During my novitiate, when it dawned upon me that I had somehow signed on to be a teaching nun, I realized I had a duty to know and I asked the novice mistress. She gave me a little book, a book so repulsive that I knew at once it had nothing to do with God. It explained how bodies worked, but surrounded it with dense mists of fear of sin. Even to think about the act of sex might mean damnation, according to this book.

I knew God well enough and had read enough secular literature to know how important sexuality was for people to be absolutely certain that He couldn't have made us with a deep-rooted need, which was also a supreme pleasure, that was in any way sinful. I saw that this whole question was not one that would concern me, except to be grateful to God for the beautiful things He gave His children, and to pray that people would use these gifts in the way He intended.

One of these days I must start Bishop Butler's work again, without all these associations. I smiled to think what a great guide and companion the dear father has been to you.

Lovingly,
Sister Wendy

December 11, 2016

Dearest Sister Wendy,

I do think it is not wise to raise children on stories of sadistic cruelty. Interestingly, even in my accounts in *Give Us This Day* people will write in to say how disturbed they were by some of the (mild) details I include.

Flannery O'Connor has a story where a little girl pictures herself as a martyr—standing in the arena, which is sort of like a circus. When she is attacked by ferocious lions she imagines that she would tame them and make them into her pets. She later learns that the Cross is quite different from what she imagined, and that it has more to do with charity.

Of course all these excruciating tales of martyrdom make us think that the age of martyrs was long ago, whereas our own recent history was marked by many more martyrs than the era of the Roman Empire. Furthermore, as Dorothy liked to point out, martyrdom is not just standing before a firing squad; the opportunity to bear witness, at some cost to our ego, reputation, or comfort occurs in our everyday life.

Nevertheless, I am touched by the innocence and natural purity you bring to these subjects, which makes me think that your parents were quite wise in naming you after Barrie's Wendy.

I have been thinking lately about the ways that our life takes turns that turn out to be absolutely providential, yet we could not have chosen them.

I think of Dorothy's own story, how everything that she did and that she became came about because of the frustration of her desire: her wish to marry Forster.[42] She wrote him desperately for five years, trying to get him to change his mind. In that time she didn't advance any further in her vocation. And then, when she finally realized it was hopeless, that same month she met Peter Maurin and within six months she was the editor of *The Catholic Worker* and the leader of a lay apostolic movement.

I wonder if that principle applies to your own life? What seems so interesting is that you obviously had a very deep vocation to a life of prayerful solitude, and you pursued this in a manner absolutely guaranteed to thwart your deepest longings. And yet somehow it all turned out straight.

You felt that your superior's word, telling you that you were meant to teach, was the word of God about where He wanted you to be. "To live in God's will is our only happiness"—but how are we to know God's will? And can it be God's will to place us in a situation that makes us think we will have to die or have a breakdown?

You knew instinctively in reading that awful book about sex and sin that it could not reflect God's will. But many people—particularly in the convent at that time—would surely not have known this, and they would have been responsible for creating much misery and guilt in the lives of their pupils.

How great God is to offer us clues and hints about what we are meant to do. Don't you agree?

December 13, 2016

Dearest Robert,

I completely agree with you that things that seemed disastrous in our lives turn out to be just what we really needed. You know from your own life that this has happened again and again, and so it is with me. You ask how I could be certain I was doing God's will. My certainty came from my

---

42. In *The Long Loneliness*, Dorothy Day's memoir of conversion, she describes her experience of "natural happiness" while living with a man, Forster Batterham, whom she deeply loved. When she discovered that she was pregnant, she found herself wishing to have her child baptized—though Forster, a committed anarchist and agnostic, would have no part in this. Nevertheless, she went ahead with this plan and then followed by becoming a Catholic herself, though this would mean separation from Forster, who did not believe in marriage. It was literally a choice, she wrote, between "God and man." And yet, in editing her letters, *All the Way to Heaven*, I discovered that she had continued for five years to write Forster, trying to persuade him to give up his "pigheadedness" and agree to marry. It was only in 1932, when she finally abandoned this quest, that she was free to discover her true vocation.

vow of obedience. What your superiors tell you may seem to you foolish and mistaken, but if they insist that that is what they want, then you know that you are obeying God. For people who do not have this security I think circumstances usually make it fairly clear because God is in what happens, isn't He? Whatever it is, He will be with us in it to make it beautiful.

A thought very much in my mind is what St. Elizabeth says about offering Our Lord an extra humanity. Her prayer is that when the Father bends over her, it's the face of His Son that He sees looking back at Him. And that just as Jesus, the second person of the Trinity, took on a human nature in which to live and die, so each of us can offer Him our nature for the same redemptive purposes.

We have an old sister in the house at the moment who is faced with terrible grief and I was so wishing that I could take it on myself and suffer it instead of her. This made me think it must have been such a joy to Our Blessed Lord to be able to do precisely this for us.

Lovingly,
Sister Wendy

———

Scrutinizing memories of childhood selfishness, Sister Wendy regretted the "lowly state of existence" she brought to the Lord, "shabby and shifty."

December 14, 2016

Dearest Robert,

I feel unhappy at letting your word "purity" go without a protest. I was ignorant. And I don't think you can use the word "pure," that radiant word that we associate so particularly with Our Blessed Lady, for somebody so profoundly selfish as I was. Also, looking back, I can remember two occasions, and perhaps there were many more that I've forgotten, when I told a lie to escape from a situation that profoundly embarrassed me. I remember the circumstances of both so well. The first when I was 8 years old and the second when I was 13. Foolish, childish lies, at that.

The very fact that I couldn't accept having made a complete fool of myself shows how far I was from understanding the cross. In fact, now I look back on a life that I have never looked back on before, it seems to me that I woke up completely, spiritually, when I was four—that under-the-table experience you know about. But then, you know, I think I went to sleep again, and woke up in my last year at school, 15, 16, ready to enter the convent, in

1947. I was almost sleepwalking those years, lost in a world I didn't understand and couldn't find my footing in. So you see it was a very lowly state of existence that I brought to the Lord, shabby and shifty.

Very much love,
Sister Wendy

December 15, 2016

Dearest Sister Wendy,

I was very touched by what you shared about St. Elizabeth, offering God a share of her humanity. I think we all do this, when we aspire to be followers of Christ—whether consciously or not. Our hands, our hearts, our eyes and ears. When we stand in solidarity with the vulnerable, or practice the works of mercy, what are we doing aside from offering God a share in our humanity?

I was also touched by what you shared about your recollection of the foolish lies from your childhood. I am sure most of us have much more to confess. But I realize that whether small or large, all lies or sins are made of the same thing.

I remember the last and perhaps only time my father ever spanked me (not, I can assure you, my last transgression). I must have been about 4 or 5. I had told a terrible lie, and my mother told me that I would have to wait for my (unfortunate) father to come home to punish me. He told me that this would require a spanking, and he instructed me to lower my pants. I tried to intervene, using what I thought was clever "reverse psychology": "Wait, wait, Daddy...! It hurts more with my pants on!!...I don't think you understand. I said it hurts more *with my pants on!!*"

The fact that you were far from understanding the cross at the age of 13 is hardly surprising—even if you, precociously, "woke up completely, spiritually" when you were four.

My Jesuit friend Jim Martin[43] says that he once said to his spiritual director, "This is not the cross I would have chosen." The wise director replied, "If it was the cross you had chosen it wouldn't be the cross."

---

43. James Martin, SJ, a Jesuit priest and popular writer, is the author of numerous books on the spiritual life, including *My Life with the Saints* and *The Jesuit Guide to (Almost) Everything*. Since publishing his first book—*This Our Exile: A Spiritual Journey with the Refugees of East Africa* (Maryknoll, NY: Orbis Books, 1999)—we had become close friends.

Yet how often do we try to outfox God: "It hurts more with my pants on!!"

Well, I hope you don't think I am making excuses for you—but I doubt that the Lord regarded the gift of yourself when you were 16 as something shabby and shifty.

There is a popular phrase today, of being "woke"—as in waking up to structures of injustice and prejudice. The first chapter of my *Saints' Guide* is called "Learning to Be Alive" and it includes many connections with the idea of "waking up." Thoreau concludes his *Walden* with the line: "That day dawns to which we are awake. The sun is but a morning star."

How much of our lives is spent sleepwalking and how much truly awake?

———————

Sister Wendy reflects on the meaning of the sacraments, especially the Mass: "a great objective act of love and surrender into which Jesus draws us."

December 18, 2016

Dearest Robert,

I'm puzzled as to why I told you in my last letter that I sleep-walked for eleven years as a young girl. I suppose these exaggerated and rather silly statements are the effect of my not ever thinking back to this time. Now that in writing to you I am thinking back, I think I'd put it like this: up until 15 I was always aware of Jesus as the Life, but I hadn't got much grasp of Him as the Way and the Truth. I lived in a rather muddled, non-focused way in the intimacy of that Life, and there were several times when there was an intense focus, times that when now I recall them fill me with joy and gratitude. But that Jesus was the Way, that there was movement and purpose and plan, no, I was sort of befogged. Only when I was 15 did I begin to focus more intently and that focus grew and sharpened until I was fully ready, at 16 years and 11 months, to enter into the absoluteness of religious life.

That gradually growing awareness of Jesus the Way, and other people, vague, anonymous, shadowy people on the way with me—that was a special time for me. It wasn't an awakening, but it was almost such. And then I became aware of Jesus as the Truth, but this happened slowly over the years. You know how St. Paul speaks of the double-edged sword—that x-ray brightness of His presence that leaves nothing hidden or overlooked and exposes us to Him in the full responsibility of His beloved One. That was personal truth as it were, which is of course as much agonizing as it is unitive.

There was also the truth of His revelation, which has grown and grown until it fills my whole horizon and I know I can never encompass it. I think quite early on I realized that the Mass was an encounter with the Risen Lord so profound that I don't think any mystical experience could be greater. My guess would be that if we could only go to Mass once a year, people would be fainting with joy during it. But whether we experience ecstasy or nothing at all doesn't make any difference. The Mass is a great objective act of love and surrender into which Jesus draws us.

I was slower to enter into the immensities of the other sacraments. What baptism means has become more and more important to me. St. Paul is the one who understands it best so far as this mystery can ever be understood, which isn't very far. Baptism means we are "in" Jesus, taken onto a completely new level of being. As St. Paul says, we die with Him and we rise with Him. Everything is out of our control now except that He enables us to say yes to this, to Him being our life and not ourselves.

I don't think anybody would query any of that, though that doesn't mean, very sadly, that people are living the implications of Jesus being our life. But I pray that people want to and that in the end He will bring it about. But I don't think there is a general understanding of the sacrament of reconciliation. I've tried several times to explain this to people I love and I always fail. I try to point out to them that it's not really about sin. I think it's very difficult to actually commit a sin, to look at God and say, no, I refuse. If such a tragedy has happened, of course the sacrament will explode the obstacle we have madly set up and catapult us into God's love again. But surely that's the exception. The average person has just small infidelities and unawarenesses, ways that they've missed God who was trying to draw them into joy. He only minds about this because of what they have lost. He couldn't give Himself to them during the washing up or the office meeting or the TV program because they weren't looking at Him.

So we only have to present ourselves in the sacrament, the sacrament that enables us to look at Him and ask to be made more loving. It's a sacrament that draws us out of our narrowness, out of those terrible confines of selfishness and self-absorption, and sets us free to receive the purifying and redemptive love of Jesus. I'm baffled why people don't go often, because we don't receive this purifying love for ourselves only, but to make it available to the whole world. It's like a heavenly air-purifier, to be rather vulgar. Sweetness and freedom and light course through us in this sacrament, out to the whole sad world of lonely, muddled people. It's a Catholic duty to go to confession for their sake.

I don't know if I've convinced you, dearest Robert, but if so you'll be the first one who has heard what I'm trying to say. It matters so much to me, but my words are not powerful enough. One would long to be a saint just so that His love could energize more the feebleness that we offer Him.

Very much love, dear Robert, as you enter your next candle-lit year, Sister Wendy

––––––––

December 18, 2016

Dearest Sister Wendy,

Last night I had two significant dreams. In the first I was part of a large group awaiting a visit from Pope Francis. When he arrived he greeted each person in turn. When he got to me he put his hands on my shoulders and looked deeply into my eyes, which immediately filled with tears. "What's the matter?" he asked. I said, "I can't find the words." He then took my head and pressed my forehead against his for a long time. He said, "They will come."

When I got up I immediately set to work writing my introduction to the book on Franciscan saints. It flowed out in one sitting. It took off from the inspiration that Pope Francis received, at the moment of his election as pope, to choose the name Francis—a name that no previous pope had dared to claim. The second dream was also very moving to me. I was walking with my mother in her old neighborhood (my mother never went for a walk in her life!) and I asked her, "Have you ever heard of Sister Wendy?" I proceeded to tell her all about you, everything about your life that I have come to learn. It was a very sweet dream.

––––––––

December 19, 2016

Dearest Robert,

That was a wonderful Pope Francis dream, not only beautiful in itself, but so functional. After that blessing the wellsprings were opened and out flowed the words that you needed. That is so exceptional to have a practical outcome from a dream that I think perhaps it was more than a dream. It seems to me to be verging on the visionary. One of the effects of a vision, remember, is that we are changed, something happens, and wasn't that the case with this dream?

I'm touched that you should have spoken to your beloved mother about me. This was however a real dream, though it has changed me a little, in that

I feel so pleased and moved. I think you are the champion of dreams. I can't help thinking of St. Joseph and how God communicated to him in what would have seemed just a dream, but it was an encounter with the Holy.

Very much love to you and Monica,
Sister Wendy

————

Sister Wendy had said at times that religious life, or at least the novitiate, was not exactly what she had expected. I wrote: "My impression of religious life, 'in the old days,' is that there was much emphasis on uniformity and trying to get everyone to conform to a particular model of the perfect religious." I had learned more about this while writing a history of the Maryknoll Sisters.

December 20, 2016

Dearest Robert,

I gave a wry smile when I read about the restrictions and prohibitions that the Maryknoll Sisters were faced with when they entered. It was just the same with Notre Dame de Namur. Somebody once hazarded that there was an early etiquette book in one order which made the rounds, because all you said was very familiar. But I must confess I hardly noticed. The two and a half years of novitiate were a sort of space in which I was being drawn into the God whom I had so longed to be one with. But I can remember that in those two and a half years, I once found myself alone for ten minutes and the feeling of bewilderment and discomfort was very strong, because from the time you got up until the time you went to bed, you were in community doing one task after another. Never a vacancy.

I didn't realize until I had left the novitiate and arrived at Oxford that it had also been two and a half years without literature, without poetry or drama or even good novels. We had our half-hour's reading every day, but it was solid hagiography or, more interesting, theology. If only we'd had Ellsberg to read. As a deeply selfish young girl I saw the benefit to me of never doing what I wanted or would choose, but always being under discipline. I wouldn't have changed a thing.

I had mentioned to Sister Wendy how much I missed memories of my children at this time of year—devoutly writing letters to Santa, opening their Advent calendars, and so forth.

Your delightful account of your children gave me pause for a moment. Santa Claus played no part whatever in my family life. I knew that poor little children who weren't Catholics believed in some ridiculous figure called Santa Claus, but we blessed little Catholic children, we knew that all our presents came from the baby Jesus. I can see that in theory this might have made them even harder to query, but I can't remember ever getting anything I really wanted anyhow. The very worst, the absolutely very worst Christmas present was a sort of toy kitchen, with a stove and a food cupboard. We had a cook and maids and I'd hardly ever been into our own kitchen. So this gift rather baffled me. But what made it so terrible, Robert, and I can't even think about this without pain, is that I absent-mindedly opened some of the packets and ate the contents. Only after a mouthful did I realize that I had broken the communion fast. I tried and tried to find a way out of this, but it was no good, and I had the great sorrow of going to Christmas Mass and not being able to receive Our Blessed Lord.

I suppose the benefit was that it deepened my desire, but it was cruel. What a joy that now there're no longer little children worrying about whether they've had a drink of water or swallowed their toothpaste. Thank God that our dear Pope Francis understands Our Blessed Lord's happy freedom from niggling little laws. I hope he can carry the Church with him because there is still this strange fear of "falling into error" when you lighten up some of the unmerciful restrictions that have found their way into canon law. I feel great hope, though, because not only do we have a great pope but he is in the hands, and knows he is in the hands of a great, great, great God. In the end all shall be well.

Very much love,
Sister Wendy

————

December 20, 2016

Dearest Sister Wendy,

It is funny for you to think back on the bafflement you felt in the novitiate at having ten minutes alone—now that you have all the time in the world to be alone.

If you were starting out in life today—if you can possibly imagine such a thing—do you think you would enter a contemplative order? Did your time with Notre Dame prepare you somehow for your later life as a solitary contemplative?

Another question that has occurred to me—about growing up in South Africa. Did the social realities of your country make an impact on you? I don't ask that in a provocative way. I wonder whether in church circles that you were aware of, was there any sense that apartheid was a topic of religious concern? I, of course, had a rather a peculiar childhood, in which there was no way to avoid the impact of war and political issues. Fortunately, I also had my mother to remind me that there were other things to life.

So now we are living in the era of both Pope Francis and Trump. One embodies all that I am for; the other all that I oppose. It is the contrast between Baby Jesus and Herod.

Just last night I asked Monica about her favorite Christmas presents, and she also remembered her worst: a toy kitchen—probably for different reasons. I remember how my mother used to give me things that she *hoped* I would be interested in (fulfilling her own frustrated longings as a child): chemistry sets, erector sets, and the sort. They held no interest for me.

———————

Though she spent much of her early life in South Africa, Sister Wendy "blushed" to admit how insulated she was from the political realities in her homeland.

December 21, 2016

Dearest Robert,

I never felt I belonged to South Africa. My childhood was in Scotland, and I was amazed when I was nine to be taken to this strange foreign country. Remember I left then when I was 16 to spend eight years in England, five at Sussex and three at Oxford, so I had very little idea of the political realities in South Africa. I blush to tell you I never had any ideas, even when I finally returned to England when I was 40. Enclosed in a small country boarding school for white children only, it was amazing how insulated one could be. I've always thought with sympathy of the Germans who said they'd no idea what Hitler was up to. One can't believe they didn't know, and yet I didn't know in South Africa. I didn't read the newspapers, we had no radio, no one came to give us talks. I now feel ashamed and am trying to make up for my obtuseness.

It was obvious to me early on in the novitiate that I had wanted to be a contemplative, not an active nun. But as I told you I thought I would be shrinking from pain and humiliation, and felt that God would make it quite clear to me if I was to have what I desired. When I asked permission to change to a contemplative order my superior told me no. I was quite content because this was obviously God's will and if I didn't like it, all the more chance to love Him in it. It was only when the doctors told my superiors that the pressure of trying to live a life for which I was not suited was destroying my health that they told me I could go. I felt far better to die doing what obedience asked than to live in the solitude I longed for. And I've never regretted that. For one so intensely selfish, the life of an active nun was supremely purifying and I don't think I could have lived in solitude without that "novitiate of suffering."

Now off you go to the happiness of your family Christmas, where St. Joseph will inspire you to be as loving as he was.

Very much love,
Sister Wendy

PART TWO

THE ART OF LOVING

With the beginning of a new year, Sister Wendy acknowledged my Christmas present: a subscription to Give Us This Day, *the monthly journal for daily prayer, to which I contributed a short daily reflection on saints and other "blessed among us." She also referred to a gift from my friend, Fr. William Hart McNichols[1]—Fr. Bill as she always called him—a priest and icon painter living in New Mexico.*

January 7, 2017

Dearest Robert,

    I received the January *Give Us This Day* some time ago, but I hesitated to write to you, and even now I'm not quite sure whether it's appropriate. You had all the human joy and stress of Christmas upon you and it could be that the last thing you want is to have to start writing letters again. On the other hand, you may be thinking that I'm still wrapped in spiritual bliss and am reluctant to return to the work-a-day world. In a way this is perfectly true, but Our Blessed Lord is in the work-a-day world as truly as in the depth of silent prayer and we will never find Him completely if we only want to engage with Him on the level we have chosen. He chooses the world and so must we.

Fr. Bill McNichols

---

1. Father William Hart McNichols (b. 1949). See Biographical Glossary.

I got an astonishing Christmas present from Fr. Bill who sent me his profoundly beautiful icon of Jesus Emmanuel with His wounds and seraphic wings. It's a very large icon so it draws the eye to it the moment you come into my room. It's perhaps the most contemplative icon I have, and I am very conscious of his kindness in thinking of me. When I have my 70th Jubilee next month I think I will ask Sister Lesley to put it in the community room for the day, or perhaps in the ante-choir, so it can remind everybody of the very great joy of serving Him—the privilege of contemplating His wounds and uniting our sufferings to His, and the wonder of His wings, wings of prayer, which He wraps around us and lifts us up. That's the point of a seraph isn't it? Two wings for flying and two for holding you in an embrace.

Lovingly,
Sister Wendy

January 7, 2017

Dearest Sister Wendy,

The first paragraph of your letter is such a rich source for reflection. I have been so blessed with work that makes it easy to be reminded of God.

As you have surmised, the last few weeks have been quite hectic, but Christmas and the New Year passed very beautifully. Monica's three children came for a week and it was a wonderful time to get to know them better. My three (Catherine back from Paris for the week) came over on the afternoon of Christmas Eve—the first time they had all met one another, and this was the greatest possible Christmas gift. I was able to unveil for Christina the beautiful icon of Sts. Laurus and Florus, and she was deeply moved.

I don't know if I mentioned to you that Fr. Bill almost died some years ago. He was hiking in the mountains when he had a massive heart attack. Somehow they flew him to a hospital and he was completely unconscious for weeks. I received frequent updates and they were reporting that he might die any hour, and perhaps if he lived he would never be able to paint or work again. I left a phone message for him, just to hear his voice. I told him that if he ever heard this message it would mean that my prayers had been answered and that he had risen like Lazarus.

He is a very deep person, a true man of prayer. He was of course able to resume his painting and ministry. But such an experience makes you think about the reason for your life, why it is given to you, what you are meant to do with it.

I described for Sister Wendy my intense work with my father, helping him complete his memoir, The Doomsday Machine: Confessions of a Nuclear War Planner.

My days of activism are behind me—those years long ago when I was constantly going to jail and sitting through long meetings and marching on picket lines. But I feel there is nothing more important I could do for the cause of peace than to help my father with this book. And what makes it all the better is that there is nothing more I could do to show my love for him than help him finish this great task. I was saying goodbye to him on the phone the other night, and I startled us both by saying, inadvertently, "Goodbye, Darling."

This year will bring the joyous occasion of your Jubilee! I am glad you are already contemplating how that can be an occasion of joy for the community, as it will be for your friends.

———

January 10, 2017

Dearest Robert,

It was so good to know that your life has been blessed and fruitful these last weeks. I was so pleased to hear from you, but I'm afraid this is not going to be much of an answer because I had a fall this morning and although there's nothing broken, there are some painful places in my body and I feel shaken. So this is not the time to write at length. Indeed, though, I don't think I would have had much to say about your letter which has as its strong quality the pleasure it gives me to read. I'm delighted about your book and your father's book, slightly awed about the amount of work you are doing for his book, but I share your gratitude on having this extraordinary opportunity not only to fulfill your vocation as an apostle, but also your vocation as a son.

In your letter you speak of my friends, which really amounts to about five people outside the monastery, and though we have never spoken, everybody in the monastery. I suppose though I must add you and the two other Americans who write to me, though you are in a special category, dear Robert.

Although my fall was minor, and since I pulled a whole rack of icons down on top of me, I was also very fortunate not to damage any of them. I still feel very grateful to Our Blessed Lord for letting me hold the hand of the Crucified Jesus, even if the pain is not great, it's still precious isn't it?

Very much love always,
Sister Wendy

———————

January 10, 2017

Dearest Sister Wendy,

I am so sorry to hear about your fall. How poetic and spiritually suggestive that you should be pummeled by an avalanche of icons! I am worried that today, afterwards, you will be feeling more pain than you did right away. I hope you will take it easy and not invite heavier crosses than you can bear.

I love the fact that you refer to your circle of friends as including "everybody in the monastery...though we have never spoken." I do feel that I would have to include among my friends many people with whom I have never spoken, including all my saints, and my unrequited pen-pal Pope Francis. Then there are the friends one has never met in the flesh, and I am glad to be included in that apparently select communion.

I had the most gratifying possible response from my father to the work I had done. He was overwhelmed. It was such a shot in the arm, since only earlier in the week he was ready to give up. Now, he says, "We will have a book!" So now he is motivated to get back to work and confident that we are going to cross the finish line together. It is a very wonderful thing to be able to give such a gift to another person—especially one's parent. My mother, of course, had no such notion that the meaning of her life was tied up with saving the world. She just wanted her children to be happy. And I was able to fulfill that desire before she died.

I hope your friends make up in quality what they lack in quantity. But I am sure if you include not only those with whom you have never spoken, but also those you have never met, and even those completely unknown to you (though they hold you in their hearts and prayers), they would be as numerous as the stars.

———————

January 11, 2017

Dearest Robert,

All the icons that cascaded prayerfully on me are safely back on their board and have suffered no ill-effects. As you surmised my teeny-weeny ill-effects are slightly greater today, but both wonderful Fr. Delp and Mother Teresa[2] (I'm reading your books at the moment) and St. Elizabeth, whom I read constantly, give such an example of gratitude for the gift of the cross that I feel a renewed eagerness to be with Our Lord in His suffering—even if what I suffer is so miniscule.

With love and gratitude,
Sister Wendy

———————

January 11, 2017

Dearest Sister Wendy,

I had a very deep call last night from a friend of mine going through a crisis of faith, following a prolonged and serious illness.

I told him that I think of faith as not about believing certain doctrines, but about a confidence that God is in our lives, and that we meet him along the way, as Pope Francis says, and that doubt, stumbling, and uncertainty are all part of that journey. I was touched that he would confide in me so deeply. I don't know what you would have advised.

His heart is operating at very low efficiency, leaving him so exhausted that he says he finds himself unable to pray.

———————

January 11, 2017

Dearest Robert,

What you said to your friend was, of course, absolutely right and true, but I am profoundly grieved that it needed to be said.

I don't know if it will help your poor suffering friend, but I wish you could convince him that we can always pray. When we are sick we pray in a

———————

2. Alfred Delp, a Jesuit priest, was executed by the Nazis in 1945 on account of his opposition to Hitler. See Alfred Delp, SJ, *Prison Writings* (Maryknoll, NY: Orbis Books, 2004). For Mother Teresa, see *Mother Teresa: Essential Writings*, ed. Jean Maalouf (Maryknoll, NY: Orbis Books, 2001).

sick way, in a feeble, hopeless, useless way, which draws the utmost love and compassion from Our Blessed Lord. Essentially, He is our prayer, praying within us, glorifying His Father. And in fact when we think we can pray, we may well be getting in His way. Blessed are those who have nothing. Oh how often Jesus spoke about this state of interior poverty, of littleness, of powerlessness, and how beautiful it all sounds when we read it or write it or speak about it. How terrible it is when we live it. But here's where we glorify Him—in that blind cold clinging. I must confess that it is never so with me, but I know that is how it is with those very dear to Him, and I think your suffering friend must be among them.

I will pray for him.

The small strains and aches are wearing themselves out, but I notice that a fall is destructive of physical confidence.

Much love and joy,
Sister Wendy

January 12, 2017

Dearest Sister Wendy,

I am not surprised that one consequence of a fall is a lack of "physical confidence." Any kind of traumatic experience leaves one shaken, physically and emotionally. My worst accident came some years ago when I slipped and tumbled down a whole flight of stairs. I ended up in the emergency room where they stuck a tube in my chest and drained a liter and a half of blood, and then admitted me to the intensive care ward. No icons were involved in this incident. But for a long time after I came home I felt tremendously fragile, and if anyone said a kind word to me I burst into tears.

Today someone posted the first online review of my book *Blessed Among Us*, awarding me 1 out of 5 stars, under the caption, "Not So Hidden Agenda," and accusing me of pushing "a liberal agenda." I have a whole file of letters along this line, accusing me of promoting the insidious "social justice agenda," or favoring heretics, or advancing the feminist cause. Fortunately, such readers tend not to renew their subscriptions to *Give Us This Day*, so they are gradually weeded out.

January 15, 2017

Dearest Robert,

I'm sorry for the poor threatened people who cannot see the beauty of your interest in the lives of those who seek to help the marginalized. It amazes me that they can't understand that that's where Jesus is, not in the courts of kings, as He said, but with the poor and the little ones. I'm very sorry that they're canceling their subscriptions because isn't that drawing down the blinds on their sad dark little rooms?

Would you believe it, Robert, it is snowing! I can't see the snowy world, but I can see the snowy stone of the balcony and I have the satisfaction of knowing that that snow will not be trampled on. It's a full moon at present and, as you know, I get up at about 10:30 or 11:00 to pray on until Mass time, so I imagine tomorrow there'll be a special brightness to the golden light that floods my room at about 1:00 and 2:00 in the morning. Just to have God is joy enough, but there are all these minor peripheral joys that gladden our lives.

With love and gratitude,
Sister Wendy

January 15, 2017

Dearest Sister Wendy,

The same full moon that shines on you has also been overhead here—always especially beautiful this time of year, when the light reflects on the snow. Not much of the latter yet, but we had a nice dusting the other night.

Regarding my friend—when he told me that he had trouble praying, I told him that the desire to pray is itself a kind of prayer. Maybe he should just hold on to that for now. He told me that this was actually very helpful. I have always been moved by the line from St. Paul about the Holy Spirit who prays through us, "in sighs too deep for words."

Another friend of mine, a Capuchin, has just been diagnosed with very serious cancer. He also wrote about how hard it was to pray in the middle of the night, when he was sleepless—and how words from the psalms, repeated over a lifetime, came to him in a most consoling way.

January 17, 2017

Dearest Robert,

Sister Lesley has been explaining to me that my full moon is your full moon—a concept I can't quite get into my head. But anyhow, it's nice to think that we're both living at night in that gentle brightness. If she's right about the full moon, I think we must both have had the same snow, because it really was just a dusting, though we hoped for more.

Your advice to your friend about the desire to pray being prayer is something that I absolutely agree with. People somehow seem to think there should be some kind of interior product for it to count as "prayer." But prayer is just a being there, a wanting for God to have all He desires. Sickness and fear and strong negative emotions: if that's how we're feeling, that's where God finds us and that's where we find Him. I will pray for your friend.

Very much love and gratitude,
Sister Wendy

Sister Wendy and I followed the impending transition from President Obama to his successor with sadness and foreboding.

January 17, 2017

Dearest Sister Wendy,

Now it is raining—what about there?

I heard a radio program about the arts, which mentioned that President Obama's favorite artist is Edward Hopper and Obama's staff arranged for two Hopper paintings to come on loan to the Oval Office. I saw them on TV last night—as Obama was being interviewed. It made me wonder what it would be like to have your favorite paintings on loan to gaze at. What would you pick? (Whenever Monica and I go to a museum we always play a game where we pick the painting in each room that we would choose to take home if we could.)

And what will Trump choose to decorate the Oval Office? And what will that reveal? In three days we shall know.

The rain has stopped, and I will close, with love,

Robert

January 18, 2017

Dearest Robert,

I'm not surprised at Mr. Obama's liking for Hopper, both of them such lonely self-contained men. I wonder what two he chose? I would choose a Cezanne and one could really say ANY Cezanne, because the mature Cezanne has no failures. And I would choose a Poussin, probably a landscape, but perhaps one of his two series on the sacraments—those marvelous solemn sacred works. But the wonder of living today, even if I don't understand all these new inventions, is that we can almost have works on our walls that are indistinguishable at a slight distance from the great originals. No, I understand it's not the same, but it's still a very great joy. I don't particularly mind living in my little box because in God one has infinite space and freedom. I've got books to look at too, to remind me what a tree looks like and how the sun shines.

I read today that St. Gemma Galgani[3] once said that there is no love and faith without suffering. I suppose it's the true test and yet how wrong it seems to us that good should be rejected and vilified. It makes all our little sufferings—or perhaps I should say mine, because I know mine are little and I don't know about anyone else's—seem precious. If this is the way that Jesus went, and the way that all His saints go, then how sad, really, not to have suffering.

Today it is two weeks to my Jubilee. And I can truthfully say that it has been seventy years of immense happiness. There was suffering, but really, hardly noticeable. I hope St. Gemma wouldn't consider me off the books with such a paltry amount of sharing in the passion.

Lovingly,
Sister Wendy

———————

January 19, 2017

Dear Sister Wendy,

I watched Obama's last press conference last night—and it was a melancholy occasion. His reasonableness, intelligence, and basic integrity were so evident. He talked about the need for resilience and to avoid cynicism, and how he and his wife have tried to model these values for their

———————

3. St. Gemma Galgani, who died in 1903 at the age of 25, was an Italian mystic who identified intensely with the Passion of Christ—even receiving the marks of Christ's wounds on her hands and feet.

daughters. I can think of no precedent for the transition that we are about to witness.

I do think it is difficult to live in a space without some glimpse of the sky. I think of Anne Frank and her family in their annex hideaway, and what it meant for her to be able to glimpse a single chestnut tree. (The recent death of that tree was a news item.)

My heart throbbed to hear you say, "I've got books to look at too, to remind me what a tree looks like and how the sun shines." I read a story this week about a man who was just released from prison after spending forty years in solitary confinement—the longest such sentence in American history. He talked about how he had to kill a part of his soul in order to maintain his sanity.

Back when I was young I was held in solitary confinement for sixteen days in a jail in Colorado, where I was arrested for trespassing on railroad tracks leading into a plant that constructed all the plutonium triggers for thermonuclear bombs. I fasted the whole time—hence my removal to solitary. It was a cell I would say about 8 x 8 feet, with no illumination except from the hall outside. There was a wall of bars, and beyond that a door to the hallway, which was open most of the time. When they closed it I was in complete, tomblike darkness, which was very claustrophobic. Within minutes I would begin to fear that they would forget me in there, and then I began calculating how long it would take me to suffocate, etc. Fortunately, that never lasted very long. (Truth be told—I much preferred to be in this solitary cell than in a cell packed with sixteen men, all sharing an open toilet, smoking cigarettes all day and night.)

I had a thin mat on the floor—no chair or other furniture—and a sink within reach of the bars where I could fill a cup with water. That was it. But I did have a Bible, and I spent many hours praying the psalms and meditating on the Gospels. It is interesting how such a perspective—being a prisoner, or being sick, or dying, I suppose—gives you a completely new perspective on scripture. The psalms, which I had recited in a rote fashion, suddenly became filled with urgent meaning.

Some of the guards were harsh. When I was chained with some other prisoners waiting to walk a few hundred yards to the courthouse, I squatted down to conserve my energy. I felt so weak. One of the guards shouted at me angrily. But another one put his hand on my shoulder and said, "Just a little bit more, Robert—you've done a good job. God bless you."

I am very glad the approach of your Jubilee causes you to look back on seventy years of "immense happiness." Surely you must have experienced a good deal of suffering if your superiors felt you might die if you weren't released from your congregation. But then that freed you for such a life-giving realization of your vocation. I have experienced something similar. At the time it seemed like unbearable suffering, but these were merely birth pangs that opened such a path of deliverance.

We see things in such a different perspective when we look backwards. I think that is why Moses was only vouchsafed a vision of God's "backside" passing by. It is looking back that we see so clearly the presence of God in our lives.

———————

January 22, 2017

Dearest Robert,

I am sitting here overwhelmed by your account of what you suffered for the principles of righteousness. Any comment I could make would be vulgar. What I think I should say, though, is that if I put my head back I can see a small semicircle of sky above the roof and the chimney that is opposite me. So I feel rather ashamed now that I might have sounded in want of sympathy, whereas I love everything in my life just as it is.

I think about Pope Francis, and all the nastiness and criticism he receives from those who will always be frightened and reject the teaching of love. Although we accept that the way of love is the way of the cross, it's so much easier to accept it for ourselves than for others—especially another whom we so hold to our hearts as our present Holy Father. I don't think the Church has ever had a greater gift than this man of sweet and humorous simplicity, whose love of God and belief in our capacity to love Him equally is so touching in all he says.

One of the graces you and I know so intimately is the glory of the Resurrection arising from the pain of what seemed like death.

I'm conserving my energies so I'll send you a kiss and love,

Sister Wendy

———————

Sister Wendy celebrated the 70th Jubilee of her entry into religious life. For the occasion, I dedicated one of my dreams in her honor.

January 31, 2017

Dearest Sister Wendy,

Silver and gold have I none to present to you on this glorious day of your Jubilee. Let me instead share a vision from a dream last night.

I was driving down a curvy wintry hill on a residential street in Ossining (where I used to live), when I looked ahead of me and saw the most glorious mountain—pointed like the tip of a diamond, with a sheer wall facing me, all covered in snow, caught with the sunlight on it so that it glistened like gold, with the most brilliant blue sky. It was enormous, filling the whole horizon, like Everest or the Matterhorn.

I had to catch my breath at the sheer beauty of it and quickly found a place by the side of the road to park my car. I walked back up the hill so I could just stand and take in this most glorious sight. I tried to photograph it with my phone, and regretted that I didn't have a better camera with me. And yet I felt that this most glorious vision—so HUGE, so distant—as if across a deep ravine that separated us—and at the same time magnificently close—would stay with me forever. When I awoke this image stayed with me. And all the day I was filled with such a deep sense of awe and love.

There—I present this lovely dream at the door of your cell, where you may contemplate it and make of it what you will.

I hope that you experience those emotions yourself on this day, and, if you will allow yourself, consider how many lives you have touched and enriched by your apostolate of prayer and beauty. How much you have enabled so many to experience the goodness and beauty of the Lord as reflected in the beauty of this world, and in its most wonderful and attentive witnesses.

Meanwhile, please know that I will be praying this day for your intentions, which I hope in one respect will coincide with my own (if that is not too selfish an application of prayer): that this year I will have an opportunity to visit Quidenham.

May my vision of the holy mountain delight you, and fill you with longing for the Kingdom.

How would Sister Wendy summarize her life? "A deeper and deeper living into Jesus."

February 2, 2017

Dearest Robert,

Well, you've given me many things, but your vision was a special gift. I cherish it in my heart, and I rejoice that you are so close to Him that He reveals His beauty to you under this unforgettable symbol.

My Jubilee card is from the Met. It's a most beautiful medieval Annunciation (oh, may we all receive our vocation with the completeness that Our

Lady did) and inside it has just one word: Rejoice. Rejoice is the only possible response to God's goodness to me. Nearly eighty-seven years ago (it's just twenty-three days to my birthday), I was baptized into Christ Jesus. Seventy years ago I had the joy of beginning to realize the wonder of that. I think I'd sum up my life as a deeper and deeper living "in Jesus."

My private joy is a public joy in that everything God has given me He has given for others, for the suffering world, which of course is true for everybody and their special gifts.

Very much love and gratitude, and may God bless your great work for the Church, which is Himself,

Sister Wendy

Sister Wendy's Jubilee card

With Sister Wendy I had discussed a new biography of Dorothy Day by her granddaughter, Kate Hennessy, which focuses on the relationship between Dorothy and her daughter Tamar (Kate's mother).[4] I had commented that it reveals how holiness is rooted in a person's full humanity, with all its flaws and ambiguities.

February 8, 2017

Dearest Robert,

I would like to have the book by Dorothy's granddaughter in my little Dorothy Day library. I always puzzled over the relationship with her daughter Tamar because one can sometimes see that Dorothy's getting it wrong. It's a most beautiful illustration of what holiness isn't and doesn't do. One tends to think that perfection comes with total love, natural perfection, with open mind and deep insight into practically everything, but of course it isn't so.

---

4. Kate Hennessy, *Dorothy Day: The World Will Be Saved by Beauty* (New York: Scribner, 2017).

The point is that I think this book will do a great deal to inculcate realistic thinking about the saints. I have sometimes felt despair when reading some very ill-chosen passages in *Magnificat*. How could a saint think that God was harsh? How could a saint think that Our Lady could change His mind, as it were, and coax Him out of His bad temper? I know that this is blasphemy, and I don't like even saying it, but this is more or less (sometimes more) what some accredited holy men have preached. So Dorothy's little misunderstandings with her daughter will gently disabuse those who don't know that what God takes to Himself and sanctifies is what we actually are. It doesn't introduce new gifts and qualities, just helps us to expand and make use of what was there in the first place.

Very much love,
Sister Wendy

––––––––––––

I had described for Sister Wendy an exhausting dream in which I was invited to give a lecture, and discovered, only upon arriving, that it was on a topic with which I was barely familiar. I did my best to extemporize, but with questionable results.

February 11, 2017

Dearest Robert,

Your nights seem rather stressed, as if you're having lecture anxiety. I must admit that speaking without a text is dangerous, but I think it's the best way to communicate. You can look directly at people and modify your remarks in response to their response. The first talk I ever gave was when I was made a reverend mother and had to face the community to give a spiritual conference. This community had not elected me. The very popular superior had come to the end of her term and the mother general who'd met me had taken it into her dear little head that I was what was needed. The community did not agree. I was very tempted to write out a conference: oh, the safety of a text! But I knew that if I did it once I would go on doing it. So I made myself think through what I wanted to say, make clear in my mind the points on which this talk would hang, and accept the horror of the whole situation as a gift from God.

When it came to television this stood me in good stead, and I've never felt the slightest fear of the camera. In fact, I'm happy to talk to the camera. There's a man there operating it, and I can watch his face and see how he likes what I'm saying. But it was a constant strain. I never liked it and am so grateful to have been released. I suppose it's the only apostolic work I've ever done for the Lord, so I can't regret it. Also, like the bliss of pain when it stops, my lovely silence is all the more precious now that it won't be broken again.

I shall look forward to reading Dorothy's granddaughter's book. Would that every saint had a granddaughter or a sister or a parent spilling the beans about them. Then people would realize how holiness is meant to be deeply human, non-perfectionist, part of a world in which people have to scrub floors and sweep drives and make foolish mistakes, irritate their best friends quite unwittingly, and be a nuisance generally. So, well done, Kate.

Lovingly,
Sister Wendy

————

February 15, 2017

Dearest Robert,

I am still watching for the full moon which is slowly coming into being. I can't tell you how lovely it is in my room to open my eyes and find the whole room alight with a golden brightness. One would think it was supernatural if one did not know the power of created nature. No snow here, no ice storms, just a calm, mellow light. I would like to nail it in place for when you come. But one of the wonderful things about nature is its unpredictability. God gives us so many ways of entering into our vulnerability and contingency. If we don't get it from the natural world, we can get it as we age from the physical world, and all the time for everybody from the emotional world. Only the spiritual world, the world of the Father and His Son and our sharing in their life through the Holy Spirit, is utterly safe and true and dependable.

Thinking about the approaching season of Lent makes me realize how infinitely deep and beautiful this season is. It's the time of year when every Christian has to face the sincerity of their desire for God. If we truly want Him, then surely it follows that we must spend some time each day in prayer. How can you love somebody if you don't want to be with them? So I think of all the millions of Catholics turning, perhaps shamefacedly, to Our Blessed Lord during this season and giving Him the great joy of His being able to give Himself to them. It's so obvious that we can't give anything. But since we live in Him, we don't have to.

Somehow I can't get over the weariness that has blanketed me for some time. Wouldn't it be a great happiness, dear Robert, if this was an indication of the blessed end to which we all move at our own pace? Yet I somehow feel that I'll be here when you come to offer a retreat for the sisters.

Now I come to think of it, it must be forty-seven years since I last made a retreat and have not felt the want of one. Of course my whole life is a retreat with the only non-retreat periods when I was out with the BBC, and I suppose when I was writing a book. But thank God few books took me more than a week. The two exceptions were my big books, *Story of Painting* and *1000 Masterpieces*.[5] All my other books are small. What a very great relief not to have to write any more.

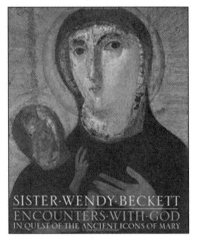

One of Sister Wendy's small books
(Orbis, 2009)

I'm beginning to ramble so good-bye, dearest Robert, and God bless, Sister Wendy

P.S. Therese and Dorothy: don't you think that essentially they're very alike? Strong, simple, self-sacrificing women who understand joy and who can bear everything because they look at Jesus. But perhaps that's just a definition of holiness.[6]

———

February 15, 2017

Dearest Sister Wendy,

Your letter offered many points for reflection. Thank you. "God gives us so many ways of entering into our vulnerability and contingency." This is a subject I think about a lot. So often we measure ourselves by our strengths and accomplishments (not you, I realize!)—but we are really being shaped by the things that are stripped from us. And perhaps all our life is getting ready to let go with perfect abandonment.

———

5. Wendy Beckett, *Sister Wendy's Story of Painting* (London: Dorling Kindersley, 1997); *Sister Wendy's 1000 Masterpieces* (London: Dorling Kindersley, 1999).

6. Dorothy actually wrote a book about St. Therese of Lisieux (her favorite saint): *Therese* (Notre Dame, IN: Ave Maria Press, 2016 [reprint]). I wrote an introduction to this edition, which I shared with Sister Wendy.

I had described a dream in which I was compelled to deliver a speech in Spanish.

February 23, 2017

Dearest Robert,

My heart aches for you with your labor-intensive dreaming. I have lovely helpful dreams in which supernatural truths are pointed out to me, often in pictorial manner. But they're very difficult to talk about, and I'd imagine very uninteresting to anybody but me [*This is untrue! says Sr. Lesley*], whereas your dreams have a macabre fascination. It worries me though that you work so hard by night as well as by day. May I suggest again, timidly, that you make a determined effort to calm your mind down before you go to bed?

I found in the end that I couldn't wait until Saturday to start Kate's book. I'm about three quarters through, sinking deeper and deeper into the whirlpool in which Dorothy swam so bravely. Oh Robert, the disorder of her life! It makes her heroism even clearer—that she didn't give up in despair or disgust. I agree with you on the completely new perspective this book provides. Instead of looking from a distance at Dorothy's completed life, we are actually in it, smaller than Dorothy, smaller than Tamar, looking up, both bewildered and impressed. I feel the book is almost as much about Tamar [Dorothy's daughter]—that noble and suffering heroine. Dorothy's mistakes and misunderstandings make her infinitely more accessible.

I've just passed the point when Tamar loses her faith. It's always been my contention that anyone who loses the faith never really had it. Once you fully understand what Jesus teaches it's like two and two making four, you can't lose that awareness of love, sacrificial love that is completely personal and overwhelming. But when you look at the trajectory of Tamar's Catholic life it would be very easy to conclude that in fact she was living on Dorothy's convictions and not her own. I'm longing to get to the end and find out if Tamar comes back to the faith and if Kate is a believer. But although this is such a wonderful book, it's saddening and challenging, in fact heart-breaking often, and I'm so glad I didn't keep it for my birthday. I want that to be a day of pure gratitude.

———

March 6, 2017

Dearest Sister Wendy,

I dreamed last night that I had invited Princess Diana to speak at Maryknoll. Knowing that we could not possibly accommodate all who would throng to her talk, I had done only very minimal advertising. Nevertheless, the chapel, which I had reserved, was nearly full hours before the scheduled talk. Then I was left to wait nervously, as the time approached—with no sign of our speaker!

Thus I spend my restless nights.

The situation with the Trump regime is reaching a point of feverish chaos—in just six weeks. Hard to believe he can keep this up for even a year. At five in the morning on Saturday he sent out a series of "tweets" accusing President Obama—"a bad (or sick) guy"— of illegally wiretapping his phone, claiming (with no evidence) that this was the greatest scandal since Watergate. The next minute he was complaining that Arnold Schwarzenegger, the actor who replaced him as star of "Celebrity Apprentice" on TV, has "pathetic ratings." All this from his resort in Florida, where he has spent the last four weekends playing golf. He has the attention span (and temperament) of a child.

———————

March 7, 2017

Dearest Robert,

When you write it's like touching electricity. You are alive and flashing and gleaming through so many different spheres of important activity. All the same I regret your doing this at night. How will you have the mental energy to irradiate your day with meaningful activity if you're fooling around with lectures by poor Princess Diana at night? May I make for the third time a gentle plea that you really try to quiet your mind before you go to sleep. If you just lay it peacefully before Our Blessed Lord for just ten minutes, it might be enough to snatch you off the treadmill. Here's where Monica could really help you because this kind of prayer is something she understands well.

I pray that God sustains you and that you use common sense about resting, dearest Robert.

Sister Wendy

———————

March 7, 2017

Dearest Sister Wendy,

I am TRYING to quiet my mind before sleeping. You are quite right that Monica is very disciplined about this kind of prayer. She often wakes in the night to meditate, and always begins and ends each day with very deep meditation.

Last night I dreamed that someone asked me about the history of the Maryknoll Sisters and I gave a lecture about Mother Mary Rogers, their wonderful founder. But I also dreamed my way into how I want to talk about Dan Berrigan in the lecture I am supposed to give shortly at a conference in San Antonio. Unlike many of my dreams, which are rubbish on consideration in the light of day, this one seemed very practical.

I want to start by talking about St. Martin of Tours.[7] Everyone knows his story about cutting his cloak in half to clothe a beggar, etc. I will use several paintings and icons of this. But much less well remembered is what happened next: how he laid down his sword and refused any longer to be a soldier. I want to talk about the way that certain saints picked up and remembered the peace message of Jesus—which of course was quite forgotten after Constantine's vision of conquering under the sign of the cross. But then I will talk about later figures who picked up and recalled this memory: Franz Jägerstätter, Ben Salmon[8], Dorothy Day, Thomas Merton—all people who were part of the cloud of witnesses who surrounded Dan Berrigan. He is another link in that chain—those who have been entrusted with the sacred fire of the gospel, nurturing it and passing it along. It gives me a chance to talk about this power of saints to ignite our conscience and moral imagination, to allow us to find new ways of faithful living, to "see and interpret reality in new ways," as Pope Francis says.

Other exciting news: It was announced today that Stephen Spielberg, who is probably the world's most successful Hollywood director, is going to make a movie [*The Post*] about the publication of the Pentagon Papers (the secret study of Vietnam that my father leaked to the press). It will focus on the story of the *Washington Post*, and star Tom Hanks and Meryl Streep—the two most popular actors. So it is bound to find a huge audience.

I will try to quiet my mind. I promise. But so much happening!

———

7. St. Martin of Tours (d. 397) was a Roman soldier in Gaul. One day he was moved to share his cloak with a shivering beggar, and that night dreamed he saw Jesus wearing that part of the cloak he had given away. Upon waking, he declared himself a Christian, and simultaneously refused to serve in the army any longer.

8. Ben Salmon (d. 1932) was a lay Catholic from Colorado whose witness as a conscientious objector in World War I in some ways anticipated the sacrifice of Franz Jägerstätter in World War II. Salmon was imprisoned and subjected to tremendous abuse for refusing to serve in the army. While imprisoned he wrote an impressive critique of Catholic teaching on "just war."

Along with everything else that was happening, I was able to share the good news of a letter from the prioress of Quidenham, inviting me to lead a retreat in November.

March 13, 2017

Dearest Robert,

Of course I'm absolutely thrilled that it looks as though you are going to be able to come, where you will make more friends. The sisters will respond immediately to you and the rich sacred fare you offer, and you'll respond to them. Here is a community of great diversity, with many very gifted sisters, but what makes them so precious is that every single one, even the odd-bods are really trying with all their heart to love Our Blessed Lord. There's not one sister of whom one could use that dreadful word "mediocre."

Your lectures sound of the greatest interest and what makes them so delightful is your own great interest in what you are saying. I think even dull material comes to life when the speaker is greatly enthused by it, just as the most entrancing of narratives can begin to drag with a lack-luster delivery. Once you've taken the terrifying plunge of speaking without a text, you won't want to go back. It's painful, as I know well, but it means you can communicate with an immediacy.

I'll pray for your nights dear Robert, that that great dynamo of a mind slows down and lets the tranquil water of sleep wash over it.

Oh, it will be good to have you here!

Lovingly,
Sister Wendy

March 14, 2017

Dearest Robert,

I can't tell you how pleased I am that you're coming. Remember I won't be at your talks. Somebody I know who was giving a talk here and to whom I said the same thing, replied, "Thank God!"

I have read another nasty article that speaks as if Pope Francis is destroying the very nature of the Church—trampling down its dogmas and flouting its wisdom. Whereas of course he is merely suggesting a modification to the Church's practical law on divorce. Nothing has changed more in the centuries than our understanding of marriage, and one can't imagine that Our Lord would remain imprisoned in a first-century mentality. It makes me very sad and yet what can one expect? Just as all your heroic fighters for non-violence—for the refusal to kill or damage or wound another—have fought against the church as much as against the state. There is no way of understanding these things. The only answer is to look into one's own heart and pray.

Very much love from sunny Norfolk,
Sister Wendy

————

March 15, 2017

Dearest Sister Wendy,

Forgive me for sharing another curious dream: There was some kind of nefarious organization that was trying to track down a group of men who had the assignment of saving the world. The latter were a curious group of agents, operating undercover out in the field. Their task was to turn a special key that would reset history in some way. Most of the agents had been captured. Hopes rested on one particular agent, who was thought to be dead. He was a master of disguise—often, for instance, appearing as a Jewish Hasid. With time escaping, he knocked on an office door and said, "Where is your Dell computer?" They pointed it out and he rushed there, inserted his key, turned it precisely thirty-five times, and there was a great flash indicating success.

I was reminded of the novel by André Schwarz-Bart, *The Last of the Just*—and perhaps my father, with his Jewish roots, trying to finish his book, with the hope that this will prevent the great conflagration.

————

March 16, 2017

Dearest Robert,

That is another most extraordinary dream. I thought your interpretation was valid, but I had another take on it. Despite all the difficulties, there was a clear simple solution for the salvation of the world—just turn that key. I think it's a rather wish-fulfilment dream, because your non-dreaming self knows all too painfully that there isn't any key and there's no certainty whatsoever as to what God is calling upon us to do. Every moment we just have to look at Him and respond in love. It will never end. That's both its pain and its hope. The end will be when Jesus comes in His glory. But how wonderful that there was a key and a way. One would suffer anything, wouldn't one, to turn that key?

I don't know if I told you about my great Jubilee delight in being permitted by the prioress, kind Sister Stephanie, to make a big donation to my favorite charity: Aid to the Church in Need. Do you know this charity?[9] It supports the persecuted church throughout the world and the poor church, the church that in some suffering countries is people's only source of health care and advice and schooling, let alone the Mass. This church that acts truly as the mystical body of Jesus, working without thought of self for all people who need help, moves me very deeply.

That is Dorothy Day's church isn't it?—wounded and dirty and hungry but looking always at the Father. She grows and grows in my mind as the saint of the century. As you know, I've a deep sense of Flannery O'Connor's holiness but her compass was small as God willed it to be. Dorothy though takes the whole world into her fragile arms. I feel so blessed that I am in correspondence with a man who knew Dorothy. It's like that old song, "I Danced with a Man—Who Danced with a Girl—Who Danced with the Prince of Wales."

I was interested that you spoke about your father's Jewish roots. I've often wondered but hesitated to seem intrusive. You have never given me a feeling that he's a man who sees "God plain," as it were. That he does see Him is evident from his actions—a man of such goodness and courage is just the kind of man who'll appear one day in your Lives.

Tomorrow is St. Patrick's Day, and though I have never seen, far less participated in, any of these ridiculous green-striped, beer-fueled, shamrock-waving festivals, I still feel a kind of grudging need to mark it somehow. But no, my St. Patrick's Day celebration will be a slice of cheese bread and a crumpet for breakfast. This is very high-powered celebration—Christmas, Easter, Pentecost level—but I don't actually have anything else on which to feast.

  With love and prayer and gratitude, dear Robert,
  Sister Wendy

————

March 16, 2017

Dearest Sister Wendy,

We had a wonderful time with Sister Helen Prejean last night. She is a great treasure. We went over her book and the most recent chapters I have

————

9. Aid to the Church in Need: www.churchinneed.org.

edited and talked about what is to come. She is supposed to moderate a panel discussion this evening at the enormous Cathedral of St. John the Divine (Episcopal) in New York on the topic "How can one reasonably believe in God?" She has no idea how this discussion will work, since those she is moderating include a Slovenian atheist and a strange performance artist. But she was eager to hear our thoughts on the subject.

I said that first we have to talk about what we mean by God, since there are all kinds of images and concepts that are not worth believing in, reasonably or not. Then I think before that question there are so many prior questions: Do we believe there is any larger meaning to existence, or is it all meaningless? Do we believe there is such a thing as a spiritual dimension to life? Is the appropriate response to life one of trusting openness or one of cynicism and fear? If life has some meaning, is it a beneficent meaning, or is it something hostile (or indifferent) to our wellbeing and happiness? I think our response to these questions is not entirely on the "reasonable" level—it is in some ways an aesthetic question, I sometimes think. The way some people respond to music, or nature. Sometimes it takes a big whack to knock us off the circle of reasonable everydayness.

I like your response to my dream—and the idea that the key is always in our hands. It reminded me of an experience I had when I first visited the Abbey of Gethsemani, many years ago (1979). I was at that time exploring my attraction to the Catholic Church, and of course my mind was filled with Merton. It was suggested to those on retreat that we reflect on a verse from scripture as we went to sleep, so I flipped open the Bible and let my finger fall at random. The verse was: "Lord, it is good for us to be here." I thought that was appropriate. But then the next day I did the same and my finger fell *on the same verse in a different gospel!*

Well, Sister Wendy, what is one to do with that?! Did it mean I was supposed to become a Trappist (which I did not do)? Did it mean, yes, I should become a Catholic (which I did do)? Perhaps it had a deeper Zen meaning—as in: It is good to be here—wherever here is, in the present moment. It is good.

Thinking of your response to my "key dream"—it reminds me also of Merton's reflection on "Fourth and Walnut" where he concludes: "There are no strangers. The gate of heaven is everywhere." And the key to that gate is always in our hand![10]

Last night my father was actually talking about growing old: "One minute you are holding your keys in your hand—while the next minute, as if

---

10. See the letter of June 20, 2016, when this pivotal experience of Thomas Merton was first discussed.

by magic, the key is nowhere to be found!" (Imagine if that is the key to save the world.)

My father has a deep resistance to organized religion. But there is no doubt that he is one of those Just, a bearer of the key—who carries on his conscience a sense of responsibility to warn and save the world from oblivion. (He identifies with Cassandra, who has the gift of seeing what will happen, but the curse that nobody will believe her.)

I wish you a happy St. Patrick's Day. The basis of Monica's devotion to him is that he drove the snakes out of Ireland, and she has a deep, primitive fear of snakes.

———————

Sister Wendy offered a deep explanation for her writing: "All my early books I wrote for people to understand that they could meet that Something in art, and of course my prayer was that then they would be stirred to turn their implicit awareness into explicit, and learn His name."

March 17, 2017

Dearest Robert,

I remember an issue of the *National Geographic* that had a wonderful article on snakes, which I would love Monica to be able to see. Robert, they are so beautiful! I don't think I have ever seen anything more visually appealing, more luminous with the Creator's ingenuity, than those baskets of snakes. I have touched a snake and they have the gentlest, softest feel to them. I also feel very sorry that they are so often destroyed in fear and ignorance, whereas so few of them, relatively speaking, are dangerous. Please urge dear Monica to cultivate her inner snake.

I've been to the Cathedral of St. John the Divine, but I'm sorry they're wasting such an opportunity as having Sr. Helen by presenting such a loose amorphous question with members of the panel who do not seem likely to understand its dimensions. Your questions that you gave her are excellent, but even one of them would consume a whole evening in discussion. I would love to know how it turns out, but can't feel very hopeful.

How wonderful to remember a saint like St. Patrick, a man absolutely conscious of his need for God on every single level. Living like that makes that question that poor Sr. Helen will have to monitor seem so frivolous. Doesn't everybody know in their hearts that there is a "Something"? If we haven't been fortunate enough to be taught, we may not be able to name that something, but in art and music and literature, in all the beauty of nature, and in the tenderness of human relationships, we touch or glimpse or catch a scent of that Something. All my early books I wrote for people to understand that they could meet that Something in art, and of course my prayer was that then they would be stirred to turn their implicit awareness into explicit, and learn His name.

Tell your dear papa that if he drops his key he should be able to pick it up pretty quickly. Anyhow, as you and he know well, material keys are for the losing anyhow. They're trivial. It's the spiritual key that matters, irreducibly singular and not within our control or for us to wield. God holds the key. What a comfort!

Very much love, dear Robert,
Sister Wendy

————

March 18, 2017

Dearest Sister Wendy,

Our backyard slopes up a hill, providing a wonderful stage effect with foreground and background. Right now it is still covered with a thick blanket of snow from the blizzard last month. Although it is starting to melt, it is a beautiful scene, and we love to watch the birds and squirrels frolicking about. I would love to put on a play—perhaps "Midsummer Night's Dream." It would be a perfect setting. Soon the leaves will return, and then the buildings now visible in the distance will once again disappear.

As for dreams—nothing special. I dreamed that I was in England and remembered an invitation to visit the bishop of Wexham (sic). I was going to take a train from King's Cross to Ixby (also sic) and then transfer to the train to Wexham, but I wasn't sure that I had got on the right train. Other passengers kept assuring me that it didn't really matter—there were countless ways to get there if I was patient. But I was skeptical and anxious—and not entirely sure of my welcome, even if I were to make it.

It is snowing again. May we all find our way to Wexham.

————

March 21, 2017

Dearest Robert,

I look through your eyes out of your window and rejoice in the space that your home provides. The only thing I would like to share with you in my space is a wonderful present that one of the sisters has somehow found to give me: orchids. I have never dreamt that orchids would come my way, with their extreme romantic beauty and grace. It's almost as if God said you can't have the trees and the grass and the sky and the little wildflowers but look! I am giving you the most beautiful things I ever created. I can't imagine where Sister Veronica got them from, but she's given me two, both pinky purple, and she hints at having other colors. I can hardly wait. The best thing is that once a week Sister Lesley hands them out to her so we don't have to worry about not caring for them properly.

The only real sacrifice I ever made in living in solitude was to be without music. But I made it very gladly and I have never felt any temptation to seek this form of prayer. When I speak of music of course I'm speaking of using the gramophone, all other forms of transmission never having come my way. I don't think I could have music in my life because it engrosses, it captures. It's a need for me to be free even though I know that for those captivated they are drawn into the presence of God, but somehow for me this would not be right. I'm sorry this is such an inadequate description.

Very much love,
Sister Wendy

Sister Wendy had described a small "mini-disaster," involving a fall that left her with an "an enormous lump on my behind"—but fortunately required no trip to the hospital.

March 26, 2017

Dearest Robert,

The unimportant pain and impairment of ability caused by my fall is such a grace. It surrenders me to Him in my human contingency, in an inescapable way, and reminds me so powerfully of Our Lord's taking upon Himself that same defenselessness, especially in His passion. To be joined in the teeniest way to such a redemptive act of trust in His Father's love is a great grace.

Anyhow this mini-disaster has shaken out of my mind any interesting things I might have been storing up to tell you. I'm sure the dear Holy Father will be deeply touched by your [most recent] letter. [*I had shared with Sister Wendy my latest letter to Pope Francis.*] In fact knowing the quality of his mind, you know in advance that he would have been touched even if by some misfortune it doesn't reach him. In some mystical way I can't but feel that the love with which you wrote and the quality of the writing will bring him happiness just in itself—seen or unseen.

Does Monica understand orchids? I feel, as of course a good Thomist should (not that I can claim that honor), that love always demands understanding. But also that understanding isn't necessarily limited by what we are.

———————

March 26, 2017

Dearest Sister Wendy,

I am so sorry to hear about your mishap. Fortunately, you are not a sporty type, so I doubt that this imposes a radical change in your physical routine. But it is amazing how any pain pins us down to our physical being.

I edited a book of writings by Thich Nhat Hanh, a great Vietnamese Zen master (whom I was fortunate to meet when I was 17). He writes about how, when we have a toothache, all we can think about is our toothache. But when we don't have a toothache, we don't think to be grateful about our non-toothache! We should be rejoicing all the time in the wonderful provision God has made for our embodied existence. In this case, I am glad that you are able to rejoice at not going to the hospital.

Yes, to answer your question, I would say that Monica understands orchids, and all living things—trees, butterflies, dogs—on a much deeper level than I am capable, though I am trying to learn.

———————

The subject of Thomas Merton was always a sore point for Sister Wendy. I was glad to hear her wonder whether in this case she had been too narrow in her judgments, though this precipitated the closest thing to an argument between us.

March 27, 2017

Dearest Robert,

I had a revelation yesterday about dear Merton. I was reading what he said on the 10th of December 1964. He was expressing his great happiness, and he says something to the effect that he knows he is essentially called to the life of solitude. At the same time, he says, this is not in any conventional sense—"far from it"—but he says that to categorize is ludicrous. It struck me that that was my mistake. Somehow in God's providence this very unusual

man is both called to solitude and unable to live in solitude. He holds these
two opposing tendencies innocently
within himself. I was reminded of
Dame Julian's insight into "All shall
be well." She says that she knows the
Church teaches about hell and she
doesn't deny it, and yet...and yet...
"All manner of things shall be well."

I've often been grieved that Merton never seems contrite about his extraordinary breaches of the rule and
his very flexible interpretation of the
vows. But I can see that he doesn't
understand that he actually has gone

Thomas Merton

against God's will. He feels himself different. It's a strange interpretation of
"love and do what you will." But he so ardently wants to love that he can't
believe that he isn't wholly free from the restraints that bind all the other
monks. So I see that I am too narrow in categorizing him, and understanding
this makes me feel very much less grieved, because he is a wonderful man
and has influenced so many, as you say.

I think if one were outside today here in Norfolk there might be some
signs of spring because the sun is shining brightly. Sister Lesley interjects
that there are tons of signs of spring out there, which is good to know. We
had a real touch of our own inner community spring today, when the news
came that our Chinese postulant, who has been trying in vain for a residence
permit, has got her visa. She'll be such an asset—a well-balanced woman.
As you know, such creatures are very rare.

With love and prayer and gratitude,
Sister Wendy

March 27, 2017

Dearest Sister Wendy,

It is interesting that Merton devoted so much attention to the question of
the "true self," and the need to escape the masks we present to ourselves and
to the world. I think a certain amount of Merton's bad-boy posturing had to
do with the pressures of the image he had helped to create for himself—as
the Monk, the Contemplative who had left his ego behind to be silent with

God. It was a clever move for his abbot to encourage him to write *The Seven Storey Mountain*. But it carried a price for Merton.

I think his relationship to his monastic vocation was very complex. He was a man with one foot in a style of monastic life that had been stable for centuries, but with the other foot he was exploring a new paradigm for religious life. There is no doubt that he struggled and strained against the constraints of a system he had voluntarily joined. But at the same time, he was pointing toward a new model of contemplative life that was not nearly so fixated on an old style of ascetical holiness—what he called a false sense of separation from the world. His example enabled other contemplatives to engage with the outside world in a way that didn't involve so much doubleness and subterfuge.

I don't know if you will agree with me about this. But I am glad if your reflection has made you more understanding or forgiving of poor Merton. (I cannot fail to think of him as my senior, although he was much younger than I am when he died.)

I recall my previous, unwelcome invocation of the Enneagram in reference to Merton. I realize it doesn't appeal to you, but I think it does help understand the deep-seated differences in personality that mean that one size of spirituality does not necessarily work for everyone. I think this insight has made it a useful accessary to spiritual direction in many religious communities.

Anyway, I think Merton would be what is labelled a "4"—the artist. The artist has a strong sense of his own specialness (which may be justified in the case of a genius like Merton, or not)—a sense that rules don't really apply. He feels and experiences things at a very intense level, which can result in emotional highs and lows. His own creativity may make it possible for him to enjoy solitude, but at the same time it is hard to resist the desire to be noticed and appreciated.

The value of the Enneagram is that it shows how one is being called to holiness within the challenges presented by one's own nature. Obviously there are different callings—to marriage, to religious life, to contemplative life. But regardless of the condition, we bring our own distinctive personality. And the challenges in religious life are different for a Therese of Lisieux, a Teresa of Avila, or a Mother Teresa.

Merton's love affair was obviously a great violation of his monastic vows.[11] Probably many monastics have been so tempted, but they did not

---

11. In Merton's diaries he documented an episode in which he fell in love with a nurse whom he had met while hospitalized for surgery in Louisville. For several months he carried on a clandestine romance, involving secret assignations and communications, thereby obviously violating a number of monastic rules. Eventually, he determined that this "doubleness" was a violation of his integrity, and that he had to make a choice. He chose to recommit himself to his vocation. See *Learning to Love: The Journals of*

write it all down in their journals! (Others may be tempted to other kinds of violation.) With his having done so, it is easy to see how deluded he could be—what ridiculous self-justifications he could devise. I think it is remarkable that he did not burn all his diaries, because on some level he wanted to be honest; he ultimately knew the difference between his true self and the mask. And so we can also see him working his way through this crisis, striving for honesty, faithfulness, resolution—on a higher level that I think represents his ongoing *conversatio morum*,[12] not just a matter of self-repression and discipline, but of growth toward the deeper meaning of his vocation.

Forgive me if I am talking about things of which I have no understanding.

———

March 29, 2017

Dearest Robert,

I cannot agree with some of the things you said in your beautiful and spiritual letter. I have had them on my heart all night, wondering whether I should express my concerns or simply leave things as they are. I'm not a person who likes confrontation or argument and with spiritual things I don't know whether argument is in any way fruitful. My conclusion is that when it's opinion, everyone is free to think as they feel drawn. The Enneagram is an example. I know many people find these very helpful. I can't bear the thought of them and feel we should just look at God and forget ourselves. But this is really just opinion, and what works for one person need not work for another. For me looking at God is what matters. Others can look at God more completely if they understand themselves. In fact that is probably the majority position.

No, dearest Robert, my problem is about what I would call facts. Let me just take up two points where I think that factually you may not be completely secure. There are probably more than two: I felt quite distressed by

———

Thomas Merton, Volume Six 1966–1967, ed. Christine M. Bochen (San Francisco: HarperSanFrancisco, 1997).

12. *Conversatio morum*, or "conversion of manners," is one of the basic monastic vows, along with obedience and "stability" (a commitment to remain in one's monastery) prescribed in the Rule of St. Benedict. Merton called it the most essential vow. Essentially, it is a commitment to the ongoing effort to go deeper into the heart of one's monastic vocation.

parts of your letter because I couldn't agree, but these are two that stick out in my consciousness at present.

The first is when you say that Merton was tempted sexually, but so are many other monks. The point is that not many Trappists would be because they are enclosed. Enclosure removes you from the fascinations of the world, but in return it protects you from many temptations. Members of an enclosed order shut themselves up sacrificially to be completely free for God, or as completely free as is possible. Because our dear Merton flouted the rules of enclosure and as a hermit had ample opportunity to have intercourse with the world without the monastery knowing it, he was exposed to temptation, and I think it was inevitable that this lovable man who had so early lost his mother would sooner or later long for female affection. Incidentally I don't think his affair was the worst of his un-monkish experiences. I think he was far more unfaithful with regard to obedience. But he certainly didn't see it as unfaithfulness, and he writes very fully and powerfully about all these (to me) spiritual tragedies without ever feeling the need to express sorrow.

The other thing, which is far more important, is what you say about his seeing the way to a new kind of monastic life. Robert, I think there will always be a need for the pure Benedictine/Cistercian monastic severity—like the Carmelites here: these women so full of potential feel the true need to shut themselves up and deny much that would interest them for the sake of the deepest prayer that is open to those who love Him.

There are many other ways of being a monk, but that doesn't mean that monasticism as it is now is a dead end and a waste of time, as Merton was beginning to think. His own lack of fulfillment made him read an emptiness into the lives of his brothers and, though there may well have been poor and crippled monks at Gethsemani, that was not because of the life but because of their unfitness for it. I think he has done great disservice to monasticism by his later writings, but fortunately no one takes nearly as much notice of them as they do of the wonderful romantic stuff that has drawn so many people into religious life.

I don't think I put this well, dearest Robert, and at the moment I simply haven't got the energy to grapple with it. I console myself that you have a closeness to Our Blessed Lord that can override any conceptions that seem to me false. Sister Lesley and I were so struck this morning by your life of Moses with its deep combination of mysticism and political wisdom. Your own life has been so rich—all those aspects that keep popping up that one didn't know about, and I have thought that I wish you would write your own autobiography. Of course in writing about other people you are writing your autobiography, because the saints you choose and the ways you speak about them reveal the true Robert.

Whenever I came across enthusiasm for an artist whom I didn't care for, I was very careful not to make my disagreements plain, because all enthusiasm, all love, is a blessing. I sometimes have a feeling that I'm a kind of nagger about dear Merton, peevishly seeking to undo your love for him, which is not at all what I want, but I shrink from love that is not founded on truth.

With apologies and great affection,
Sister Wendy

March 29, 2017

Dearest Sister Wendy,

I don't mind your friendly correction on matters about which I am so unqualified to speak. Forgive my presumption. I didn't mean to suggest that other Trappist monks also strayed sexually, as Merton had the opportunity to do. But there are other ways of straying, surely—and of course it is the work of a religious superior to know when to pull on the rope. Merton's nature caused him constantly to be straining against the rope, yet in the end I get the feeling that he realized that he needed the rope (even as he muttered and rebelled against it). My sense, in talking to monks at Gethsemani, is that Merton's abbot realized he was in many ways a special case who needed a very special kind of handling, and that he was deft in knowing, for instance, that Merton's monastic vocation really required that he be allowed to write. And I think the abbot dealt with Merton's misuse of the privilege of his hermitage in a very compassionate and understanding way—helping Merton come to his own understanding that he couldn't have it both ways. (It was Merton who recovered the eremitic option in the Cistercian tradition, and in fact, his abbot followed him in becoming a hermit.)

I do think that the earlier restrictions on Merton's writing on war and peace were unfortunate. I don't blame Merton for grumbling about them. At the end of the day, however, he did submit in obedience to these restrictions, and he was ultimately vindicated by changes in church teaching. I didn't mean to celebrate his misbehavior or to suggest that he somehow proves that the old asceticism or strictly contemplative discipline is now overthrown. But I do think that he was more than a bad monk—that he was pointing in the direction of a church more open to dialogue and positive engagement with the world, as represented for instance by the heroic Trappist martyrs in Algeria, and reflected in Pope Francis's deliberate selection of Merton as one of his "four great Americans"—highlighting, in fact, his role as an explorer of horizons, a voice of dialogue.

I would have said that stability, rather than obedience, was his great challenge.[13] His many years as novice master indicate the trust that was put in him (misguided as that may have been!). And I wouldn't dismiss all his later writing—much of it, like *Seeds of Destruction, Mystics and Zen Masters, Faith and Violence, Contemplation in a World of Action, The Wisdom of the Desert, Raids on the Unspeakable*, containing work of high spiritual value, I think.

I don't think for a minute that Merton had come to think that the monastic life was obsolete, a dead end, or waste of time! (If I thought this I would not find him nearly so interesting or worthy of attention.) I would be surprised if you could point to any of his writings that support such a conclusion.

I think on the contrary he felt it was an *essential, prophetic* vocation. I think his letters to Jean Leclerq make this very clear. I think this point, dear Sister Wendy, is a matter not of opinion but of fact. I think he was among those who helped to vindicate the meaning and relevance of such a vocation in the modern world—even if, as I will grant you, he was an ambivalent representative of the vocation he championed.

I should know better than to bring up the subject of Merton with you—a neuralgic subject—but I was encouraged by what sounded like a fresh note of sympathy and appreciation for him! I won't accuse you of trying to "undo my love" for him, but by the same token I don't want to disturb your sleep with my naïve interpretations. And no more about the Enneagram! (I hope I have not made you and Sister Lesley reconsider the encouragement to come to Quidenham!)

I am very glad to feel that you discern in me a closeness to Our Lord that makes up for some of my false conceptions. I agree with you that if you write about something you love, you are also painting a self-portrait. One's likes and aversions are so revealing.

Be well, and don't hesitate to tell me when you think I am mistaken about something! How else will I learn?

---

13. As noted, "stability," along with obedience, is one of the central monastic vows: the commitment of a monk to remain in the monastery in which he is professed. Merton was frequently beset by the desire to move to some different community, perhaps joining the more austere Carthusians, or becoming a hermit in Latin America, New Mexico, or Alaska. Ultimately, some of this restlessness was resolved by the abbot's giving him permission to move to a hermitage on the monastery grounds.

March 30, 2017

Dearest Robert,

Thank you for being so patient with me. As you know I love Merton very dearly and read him again and again. I think he is one of the great geniuses of our time. Something in me gets upset about anything I feel is false in a context where it matters. I say to myself if the false interpretation leads to greater love and service of God, does it matter? But this is means and ends isn't it? So I know that I will never be completely at ease with some of the things that are said with love and gratitude about dear Merton, but I think I must just silently offer this up.

(I had described a new film by Martin Scorsese based on Silence, *the great novel by Shusaku Endo about Jesuit missionaries in Japan. I asked her whether her interest in art ever extended to films.)*

My film director used to say that in some ways I was untouched by the modern world because I'd hardly seen any films or heard pop music, etc. So that's my only answer to your question about aesthetic pleasure in the cinema. In fact, when I entered it was still being called the bioscope, at least in southern Africa. And I feel quite up-to-date and daring even in using words like "cinema." I have never seen any plays either, except plays we took the children to, and these were amateur productions (this was in my twenty-odd years of teaching). I had never been to a symphony concert or heard an opera, but both those ambitions were fulfilled some years ago. A dear friend took me to "Il Trovatore" and I was absolutely enraptured. I also heard a concert of a piece by Beethoven, also overwhelming. But I have never felt I have space in my life for these experiences.

When you read, you're in control, you can *diminuendo* or not at will, rush the story forward, drop it, delay it. If you want to get caught up and immersed, you choose so to do. But plays, films, operas, concerts, you're not in control, you're taken up into an experience and held there, unless of course you actually get up and walk out. I have never wanted this because I hold my soul loosely in my hands and that is how it feels right to me. I can respond to His summons totally at any moment and never have to struggle free. Even when I'm reading a book that I'm really caught up in I know that I keep one foot always on the ground.

But I can see that for somebody whose vocation is different, film must be one of the great experiences of our times. Your father must have a dramatic streak, and perhaps it has transformed itself into this love of dramatic art in his grandchildren. You, I need hardly say, have enthralling drama in your nightly dreams.

Thank you, dearest Robert, for your true kindness to me and forgive me if I am irritating.

Lovingly,
Sister Wendy

P.S. I can't think of anything you could do or say that would in the slightest diminish my very great hope that you will be coming to Quidenham and sharing your wisdom and knowledge with the sisters.

March 30, 2017

Dearest Sister Wendy,

It is true that the love of movies runs deep in my family. Monica protects herself from thoughts and images that lead toward darkness—and it is a topic of occasional disagreement between us. I do see her point, and there are definitely films I wish I hadn't seen. She feels that this contributes to the taxing drama in my dream life. But mostly my dreams aren't disturbing—they are simply too interesting to me, so that I feel I have to hold onto them and bring them back with me to the surface of consciousness (though I will grant that it is usually not worth the effort).

April 1, 2017

Darling Robert,

I warm to Monica's avoidance of gloom because that's how I feel, though I sometimes think it is cowardice. It seems to me there is enough sorrow in the normal course of living, without searching it out in books and films. And yet, a film that goes through sadness into that deep catharsis that tragedy is intended to bring about: how diminished one would be if one always avoided it. I think for someone who lives alone as I do, one has to be careful though, because there's no human outlet and I think the same, relatively speaking, is true for the sisters. Dark threatening things need to be talked about so that the light of God can shine in the darkness.

Very much love,
Sister Wendy

April 2, 2017

Dearest Sister Wendy,

I have never had any interest in sports, but Monica is an avid fan and she has encouraged me to watch the playoffs of the college basketball league—the NCAA. This year one of the two contenders is the Jesuit school, Gonzaga, so of course I rooted for them, and they are going to the championship tomorrow. This prompted an article in the *New York Times* today about who St. Aloysius Gonzaga was, and noting that recently he has been claimed as a patron of those suffering from AIDS and those who care for them. Wonderful that basketball should be an occasion for people to learn more about a saint. (Perhaps in that spirit, you, or maybe Sister Lesley, will say a prayer for the "Zags" or "Bull Dogs" on Monday night. AMDG!)

———

April 3, 2017

Dearest Robert,

I have a great friend who has been a benefactor for many years, and she "owns" Norwich City Football Club in which I have therefore always taken an interest. I used to ask to see the papers on a Monday to find out how they were doing, but I stopped some time ago because it was getting me too worked up—something which I never want to be. I would never go to see a match of course, even if I was able, but I do like to think of them doing well.

So I enter completely into your feelings about St. Aloyisus Gonzaga's lads and their extraordinary elevation to the finals. Naturally as a devoted Washington Stater, let alone someone who has worked in a Jesuit University (Seattle University), Sister Lesley received your news with a flash of pride. I think she may well be praying for you this evening. I must confess that I will not be joining her because I can never bring myself to pray for things that Our Lord knows we would like but that are not essential. But I certainly would like them to return home dancing.

I find sports in the abstract very inspirational: such skill, such courage, such determination. When I was working for the BBC I always watched tennis matches, snooker, bowls, golf, and above all horse racing. Watching these supreme examples of energy and determination was a real and relaxing pleasure.

(In a previous letter I had written about a friend's disappointment in efforts to seek readmission to a religious community from which she had, some years previously, departed.)

I think it's a happy thing that your friend's request has been considered seriously and respectfully and sensible reasons given for suggesting that she stay as she is. The wonderful thing is that God always gives us what we truly want. We may not know that we want it, we may feel we need something else, but He understands us far better than we understand ourselves and what we long for He will give us always.

I send you my blessings and a virtual hug.

Sister Wendy

April 3, 2017

Dearest Sister Wendy,

I was very glad to have your letter waiting for me this morning, since I woke to a dream that was puzzling. I read somewhere that you have enjoyed watching "Star Trek" while staying in hotels. Well, this was a very Star Trek sort of scenario.

I was part of a delegation from Earth on a spaceship that was trying to receive permission to enter some distant galaxy. The authorities in this galaxy were obviously very advanced, and they had denied us entry for reasons that were probably beyond our comprehension. However, they had graciously allowed us to make a personal appeal, though I had the feeling this really wasn't going to alter their decision. For some reason, my delegation decided that I should do the talking. We were ushered into a kind of flight deck and offered comfortable seats. It was more informal than I had expected. They said, "We understand that you prefer to speak English," and I gratefully agreed. They said, "So, you are the ones who are always trying to expand into other galaxies." I said, "Well, that is not really the way we see it." They asked me a lot of friendly questions. I noticed that somehow I was not able to speak properly—just sort of gasp out words from the back of my throat. I attributed this to nerves.

I said, "Since you speak English, I wonder if your opinion of our race would be affected if you could read Shakespeare, Gerard Manley Hopkins, Flannery O'Connor, the King James Bible." They swept this aside with a little condescension: "We have read those."

There was more back and forth, but it was all in vain. Evidently the judgment was predetermined. No, we were not to enter the galaxy. Afterward (in my dream) I was overcome with exhaustion and fell into tears, but my companions reassured me that I had done as well as could be expected, and that probably there was a very good reason why our petition was not accepted.

Upon waking I found your letter, in which you say: "The wonderful thing is that God always gives us what we truly want. We may not know that we want it, we may feel we need something else, but He understands us far better than we understand ourselves and what we long for He will give us always."

I was certain that the dream brought to mind some experience of making an appeal that was fruitless—the decision having already been made for reasons I could not possibly understand. But I could not remember any such actual experience.

In fact, I wonder if my dream was really about trying to talk my way into Heaven—the books I have read, my eloquence of no account. (My voice reduced to a croak.) The message being, no, I am not ready or worthy of entrance. But perhaps it was not a closed door after all—but more of a "not yet." Perhaps with your prayers—since this would fall under the category of things not simply that we want but that are essential.

I too will not be praying for the Bull Dogs tonight. (They already got St. Aloysius into the *New York Times*, so God's work is done! The rest is up to them.)

––––––––

April 4, 2017

Dearest Robert,

We were both fascinated and amused by your dream, but as you yourself suggest, it was deeper than it seemed. I think your final comment of "not yet" is a very true one. It is clearly all about seeking through your own powers to obtain what is closed to you. Your powers, as you know, are great ones and I suppose all highly gifted men and women must grapple at times with what they can achieve through these powers and what can only come as a holy gift. There's all the difference in the world between the remarkable things we can do as human beings and the beauty that is quite independent of our achievement or even our understanding and that simply comes from God's love. Your fatigue and your initial dejection may be God's way of telling you that you put too much pressure on your own activity and personality. Maybe He says, "Just be, dear Robert. Let me love you and achieve in you what you could never do yourself." This doesn't let one off hard work and hard thinking, but it takes away the weight.

Every community has weaknesses. Every person has weakness, even the holiest, but in a good community these weaknesses are fought against, grieved over, apologized for, offered to God. In a strange way they strengthen a community because everybody in it is frail and dependent on the mercy and love of the others. I remember years ago a visiting priest saying to me how wonderful to be here at Quidenham where there was a community of such sanctity. He went on in this strain for quite a bit. I then disconcerted and disillusioned him by saying that the wonder here was not that the sisters were saints, but that they were frail women who longed to be holy and to live in a love that was not at the moment in their power. As Dorothy used to say, you really dispose of people by calling them saints. You assure yourself that their example is not meant to be followed.

Our work time is up, dearest Robert and I send you and Monica a kiss.

Lovingly,
Sister Wendy

––––––––––

April 4, 2017

Dearest Sister Wendy,

I stayed up late to watch the basketball game. As all the world knows, Gonzaga lost in the last two minutes. But St. Aloysius was still glorified, and I was a winner either way, since North Carolina (a little known fact about me) is where I was born.

Thank you very much for your sharp insights about my dream. It is hard not to believe that God is speaking to me through such dreams. No doubt, God also speaks to me through your commentary on my dreams.

A short message—but what a joy it is to wake up to a letter from you in the morning.

––––––––––

April 5, 2017

Dearest Robert,

I am touched by what you say about being refreshed by my letters and find it hard to believe. Thank you though for the sweetness and generosity with which you always reply to me. [*In a previous letter I had referred to a critical comment Sister Wendy had made about one of my authors.*] I had been thinking after your previous letter that your remark about my insight was certainly meant kindly but could indicate objectively that I had something of which to repent. It's always seemed to me that judgmentalism is one of the great barriers against God's love; well of course, judge not that you shall be not judged. I suppose it's difficult to find the line between trying to see people in the truth, which of course means in God, and being judgmental. I am certain we should revere and cherish everybody—those glorious creatures for whom, as St. Paul said, Christ died. But any false idealism bothers me, perhaps wrongly, perhaps I should just leave it. I always try to keep the balance when I'm talking about somebody, but when I think about it, you and Sr. Lesley are probably the only ones to whom I do talk. I know she would always tell me if I become uncharitable and I trust that you will too.

We are getting so close to Holy Week. The nearness of it overwhelms me at times with both joy and grief. It's always a physical struggle for me, this blessed week. But I can't think of anything less important than "my physical struggle." The real world in which we live, which is God's reality, His infinite closeness and His infinite otherness, is one we can never comprehend. Enveloped by it, seized by it, taken out of ourselves and into His Heaven by it: that's where we are, even those who don't know it.

Not much of a letter, dear Robert, but it comes with my love and prayer.

Sister Wendy

––––––––––

April 5, 2017

Dearest Sister Wendy,

I would not have charged you with being uncharitable or judgmental. There is no doubt, however, that Dorothy was prone to being judgmental—a fault she acknowledged in herself, and for which she was constantly moved to repentance. She felt that it was her own sins that made her so acutely aware of the failings of others. The sacrifices she had made for her vocation also caused her to set very high standards for others. Her sacrifice of her beloved Forster, for instance.

Thank you for your indulgence in listening to my dreams. I know that most people immediately glaze over when you say, "I had a most interesting dream last night...." As if you were about to tell them what the postman had for breakfast.

I had written about a visit with Jim Forest,[14] *my oldest friend, and now my author, whose books included biographies of Dorothy Day and Thomas Mer-*

––––––––––

14. Jim Forest died in 2022. At Orbis I published over a dozen of his books, including biographies of Dorothy Day, Thomas Merton, and Daniel Berrigan. See Biographical Glossary.

ton. Like me, he had been a young managing editor of The Catholic Worker, *and in fact it was through him that I made my way to working with Dorothy Day. We had stayed up late one night discussing the curious signs and synchronicities in our lives. This prompted Sister Wendy to reflect again on Val, her one childhood friend, whose name had come up before.*

Jim Forest

April 6, 2017

Dearest Robert,

How sustaining it must be to have a friend like Jim. When I was 14 and met Val I realized with almost incredulous happiness that God had given me a friend. I had never, I understood, expected to have a friend, knowing as I did that as soon as I was 16 I would be entering religious life, where I thought at that time the absoluteness of God's love expressed in the vow of chastity ruled out friendships. It certainly ruled out much contact, but Val was always there for me. She had polio as a child and the doctors had said she'd never walk. Her mother was a very vigorous, determined woman, and she forced Val back into normality, so that she ended up playing tennis well and with only a limp and a shrunken leg to remind her of what might have been.

All this tough energy meant that she didn't get much tenderness from her mother and when she came to stay with me and my mother came in to kiss us both good night, Val was absolutely overwhelmed. So all the time I was in the convent I knew she was keeping an eye on and visiting my mother, which was a great consolation to me. I never felt my dear mother quite approved of me, and I think she must have grumbled about me to Val because she said to me once, "Val is a real friend to you, she's always on your side."

Val died suddenly from a brain hemorrhage some years ago. I loved her husband too, who has recently died. I only say all this because it makes me understand what Jim Forest is to you.

I'm so glad you're resting and playing because sometimes I think you press yourself too hard. As for the dreams I assure you there's no virtue in listening to your accounts. I wish you could see Sr. Lesley's face as she reads your letter and hear her exclamations—well I hope you'll soon have both these experiences and you may even have a dream while you're here and have the pleasure of recounting it to her.

I can't think God minds our mistakes as long as we make them looking at Him. It's what we want that matters and we may not find the right forms in which to live it. But I agree with your general point about the wonder of these little linkages that can run throughout a life.

Our Saturday time is over, dear Robert, and I send you love and gratitude.

Sister Wendy

––––––––––

April 6, 2017

Dearest Sister Wendy,

You had mentioned your friend Val before. What a comfort she must have been to your mother, after you left for the convent, and it sounds as if your friend also found some maternal affection she was lacking from her own mother. But so hard to believe that your mother did not "approve" of you. Did she support your religious vocation—or perhaps did she feel that you were rejecting her example?

I remember Sister Joan Chittister[15] describing how as a very young child she attended her father's wake. There were some Benedictine nuns standing by the coffin and she asked her mother who they were. Her mother replied, "Those are special friends of God, and they are helping your father go to heaven." She knew right at that moment that she wanted to be one of them. Later, when she was about 15, I think, she begged the convent to accept her, and they said no, because she was her mother's only child, and it would fall on her to care for her mother. Her mother didn't especially encourage her daughter's vocation, but she knew her determination. So she went to see the mother superior and said you had better take her or she will just go some-where else: "I didn't give birth to her so she could be my social security."

Of course a loving parent wants only happiness for her child—and if your mother knew what happiness your vocation has brought you, she could only rejoice.

Last night we had the most wonderful conversation over dinner with Jim Forest about how we are meant to be ourselves—our best selves, not imitations of someone else. He was talking about how he judged himself in the past about not being as hospitable as Dorothy, or as contemplative as Merton—the two great figures in his life. Merton had urged him not to be-

––––––––––

15. Sister Joan Chittister (b. 1936), is a renowned and prophetic Benedictine nun, well known and widely read beyond Catholic circles, for her writings on peace, the role of women, and spirituality. I had published several volumes of her writings as well as a biography, which Sister Wendy would later read with interest not long before her death.

come a monk, as he had contemplated, judging that his "true vocation" was in the struggle for peace.

I said how confirmed Merton would be in that judgment. And Dorothy, too. I thought of your beautiful response to my dream, that God was telling me "Just be, dear Robert." This reminded me of the story of Sheila Cassidy— whom you and Sister Lesley may know; I think she is quite well known in England. As a young doctor she went to work in Chile. After the coup there she was arrested and tortured and only survived because of international pressure. Before this, and through this, she found herself recovering her faith in a deep way. When she got back to England she thought this meant she should become a nun, so she joined a Benedictine abbey, but it wasn't going well. Finally, the superior asked her what made her join the convent. She said she felt that God was calling her to serve Him. "Don't you think you can serve God as a doctor?" the superior asked. Instead of trying to live up to some image she had of a saint, "Why don't you just try being Sheila?"

————

From further reflections on Thomas Merton, Sister Wendy shifted her attention to memories of her childhood and of her early sense of vocation: "I could see no other way of belonging completely to God.... I truly think I needed to be bound to Him, held in the straight-jacket of religious consecration."

April 8, 2017

Dearest Robert,

To go back to the subject of judgmentalism, there's a narrow line between this and judging, or perhaps I should say there are several kinds of judging. In practice we are making judgments all the time, making choices and expressing preferences, and one cannot live in society without making practical judgments about whom to trust and whom to ask advice from, etc. But judgmentalism I think involves two ugly things. One is a sense of superiority: I am good and you are bad, I judge you. The second is that I know what is in your heart (which of course I cannot judge) as opposed to what you do. All the judgments we make of people, if we make them in Our Blessed Lord, are made not looking down as a superior, but looking up with love and reverence.

You know how much I have to say about Thomas Merton, and I think what I say is true, but never for one moment would I think that I was better than he; far from it. I look up to this gigantic figure in the Church with wonder and joy. It is because I so admire him that I grieve. I think much of this grief is foolish because as that 1964 quotation made clear to me, he accepted that he was a living contradiction. I can't believe that in this sense Dorothy was really judgmental. She made wrong decisions and misjudgments, as we all do, but she never lost her sense of the other as being Jesus—beautiful and precious.

Young Wendy Beckett

We are all so mysterious to one another that I feel I was wrong to tell you that my mother didn't approve of me. I felt she didn't, and I remember vividly her saying to me that I would enter and everyone would think I was a saint and only she would know what a difficult child I had been. When I'd got over this I asked her rather forlornly how I was difficult. She said I was very self-willed, which I take to mean both selfish and obstinate—a very displeasing combination.

But I never doubted that my parents loved me, not because I was good or nice, but because that was just what happened; parents loved their children and children loved their parents. Without any overt signs of this I would have been certain that she would have made any sacrifice for my happiness. What she actually thought of me, I really do not know. After her death my sister remarked casually that of course she was terribly proud of me. I was absolutely flabbergasted, having never seen the slightest signs of pride or even pleasure in me. She was a very private woman, and only God knows what was going on in her beloved heart.

I know she was pleased with my vocation, as was my father. They were very good Catholics and regarded a vocation as an honor. I can remember overhearing my father telling my mother that he would like me to do my degree first, and her saying something along the lines of: "She's a very awkward child, Aubrey, and she's wanted this always. I think we should just let her do what she likes."

This incidentally answers your question about when I knew. I love the beautiful story about Sr. Joan, but I had no luminous moment, or rather I lived in a luminous moment. I can't remember a time when I wasn't absolutely set on being a nun. I could see no other way of belonging completely to God, although I know and possibly knew, though not as clearly as I do at present, that any way of life can be one of total surrender. I think this may not have been true of me. I truly think I needed to be bound to Him, held in the straight-jacket of religious consecration. I don't need it now, but I'm sure I needed it when I was young—needed it and wanted it, longed for it. The holy vows were like the nails keeping me on the cross with Him.

Incidentally, April the 8th is the feast of St. Julie Billiart, who founded the Notre Dame de Namur nuns. I knew quite early on that I did not want to teach, but feared I was evading the rigors of a penitential life and did not feel I could take back my surrender unless specifically permitted by the order. Year after year they told me no, they needed me in the schools and there was a happiness in this because I was doing what God wanted and not what I would have chosen.

The Mass has always been central to me, but when I was young I simply wanted to be silent and lost in Our Lord's sacrifice. All this is long before your time and Sister Lesley's time, but I found it very difficult when the dialogue Mass was introduced. It seemed to me that we were losing that blessed silence in which one could truly give oneself. I remember saying something about this in community and a sister said to me sarcastically, "Oh poor priest, I suppose." To which I had to answer that yes, I would never have wanted to be a priest because of all their liturgical activity.

It took me years to see that the Mass is not a solitary experience, it's the Mystical Body expressed here and now by this congregation, all one in their acceptance of the Self-giving of Jesus. The dialogue part of Mass both expresses this and helps us to enter into it. I now see how powerful it is in breaking open the shell of our selfhood, which may seem deeply satisfying but is actually not what God wills for His human children. You could say that any time we pray we are within mental reach of a Mass being said somewhere, but actual attendance at Mass is a specific form of contemplation, quite different from our solitary prayer. I feel this more and more strongly as I age.

Our Saturday time is over, dear Robert, and I send you love and gratitude.

Sister Wendy

———

April 11, 2017

Dearest Sister Wendy,

It is funny how much we are marked, in early childhood, by the experience of our mother's love, or its absence. I was most fortunate in this area. Monica too. And such an experience makes one feel that life is essentially safe and friendly to our happiness.

My home for many years was not really a place of peace. One looks back and asks, well, could all that have been avoided? And then you reflect on all the ways that even suffering and hardship were part of what made you who you are. I think of St. Augustine's reflection on his life, and the realization that God was with him not only in the moments of exaltation and happiness but also in the experiences when the thought of Him was farthest away.

————

April 13, 2017

Dearest Sister Wendy,

The woes of an unhappy marriage! This was the background, I realize, in the experience of five years I spent writing my book, *The Saints' Guide to Happiness*. I took on a subject much larger than me and tried to grow into it. Each chapter was a pilgrimage; the last chapters, on love, suffering, and death, were truly written with tears and blood. I was trying to work out a spiritual framework for my existence—deep loneliness, stress, anxiety, and fear, and to find where God's will was present in this.

I would work on it every night, after everyone had gone to sleep, from about 11 p.m. to 1 a.m. After months of this, I would throw away what I had written and start again. I wanted to learn from the saints the truth that our happiness does not depend on outward circumstances—that there is a path to God in every situation. As Dorothy used to like to quote St. John of the Cross, "Where there is no love, put love, and you will find love." This is very true.

Of course I was working with the assumption that there was nothing I could do to change my circumstances. Thus, it is hard to find any basis in my book to justify the decision I ultimately made, many years later, to leave my marriage. And for a long time this left me feeling confused and lost. But I was not wrong to believe that God is in all things. The Indian Jesuit Anthony de Mello has written about sadhana—the particular spiritual path that lies in the circumstances of our own lives. We must find God in our own struggles, or nowhere at all. And the blessings I have received are so great.

I hope I am not imposing with such personal information.

Yes, I agree with your comment that Merton needed to write, and his abbot was very wise in realizing that Merton needed this outlet—that it was essential to his religious vocation. On one of my first meetings with Dorothy she gave me a book to read, *Prayer Is a Hunger*, in which the author, she noted, wrote that "writing is a form of prayer."

I realize that my writing to you is a form of prayer.

————

Sister Wendy shared her own dreams.

April 18, 2017

Dearest Robert,

I had a dream, too, but it's a short one so perhaps I can just get it in the deadline. I dreamt I was in a hospital in a big dark room all my own and a nurse knocked at the door and said they had a little child who'd been abused, could I help her? As she spoke another nurse was moving down the corridor with a bunch of babies—dear little round heads. I called to her, have you got twins there? And she said triplets! And then in a hushed voice, "They're the little brothers of the abused child." So I felt a great uprush of joy that the little boys at least had not been hurt. And I sat down and waited. The nurse came in with a very young child, not much more than two, I think, wearing just a little smock—a chubby baby with a round wounded face. Oh, it broke my heart, and before I thought that the touch of a stranger might be frightening, I had swept her up onto my lap in the position of a pieta. And I spent a long time in the dream just holding her and saying, "Oh my darling, my darling." It seemed to me that this is what Jesus does with the world and what He calls us to do.

Not like your dreams with their interest, Robert, but it's left me very moved and the image is very clear, although this happened two days ago. Holy Week takes us into that state of holding the crucified Jesus in our arms like Mary, and when we hold Him, we hold the world.

Time up beloved Robert! And may joy abound!

Lovingly,
Sister Wendy

———

April 18, 2017

Dearest Sister Wendy,

Your dream was a great consolation, and I am sure it will leave you with a warm afterglow. Like St. Robert Southwell's poem, "The Burning Babe"—that abused child, born to bear the grief and sorrows of the world. What a privilege to hold and comfort him. "My darling!" Thank you for sharing such a beautiful dream.

———

April 20, 2017

Dearest Robert,

Did you get my Easter card of St. Catherine of Siena in prayer? Jesus crucified has become more and more central to my life, which is normally a sort of resurrection life. But the resurrected Jesus was still Jesus crucified. As He said in today's Gospel, look at my hands and my feet. I think I might have been too lost in the heaven of Jesus and not fully accepted that He is always aware of suffering. Every Easter these last few years has brought a new insight to me. It doesn't come in one stupendous moment, but after prayer I find that I just have a new dimension to me. So much to thank Him for—our Eucharist.

St. Catherine of Siena

Very much love as always,
Sister Wendy

———

April 21, 2017

Dearest Sister Wendy,

I certainly received your beautiful Easter card. I agree with you that it is most important to remember that the resurrected Jesus still bore the marks of the crucifixion. It is wonderful to know that with each Easter you are still receiving new insights.

I think sometimes during the Paschal season we can get the idea that we have to coordinate our emotions each day: Good Friday, now this is a very sad day. But not to worry: A Happy Day is just around the corner. Whereas the whole paschal mystery is woven into the daily life of faith. Always dying to receive new life.

I had dinner last night with my friend Fr. Larry Murphy, the oldest Maryknoll priest (100!). He said he was very struck by the story of the disciples on the road to Emmaus. When they said to Jesus, "The day is almost over, and night is approaching"—that struck him very personally. He feels that his day is almost over, night is approaching. All the more reason to invite Jesus to stay with him.

———

April 22, 2017

Dearest Robert,

There seem to be so many mansions in your soul. But you and Monica live in the central mansion with its backyard and its happy permanence.

I have never managed to work up a mood for any religious occasion, but I find, don't you, that a sense of gravity or gaiety just settles upon one. I think I've not been all that receptive to the gravity and that entering in my small way into the Passion has been one of the great graces of old age, and yet even there, what joy. You remember the hymn, "There is joy for all the members / in the sorrows of the Head." That's why He suffered, didn't He? So that we would have His joy in us.

Words seem so false when speaking of such mysteries. You remember how our dear Merton says that saying that he loves God doesn't necessarily mean that it's true? I feel a growing distrust of words, at least my words. Your words and the words of other people come across with a truthfulness that I don't recognize in myself. Please God it is there though, unrecognized.

Our time is up dear Robert, so with an Easter kiss, I say Alleluia!

Lovingly,
Sister Wendy

April 22, 2017

Dearest Sister Wendy,

I am pleased that from the recesses of your Interior Castle my little world seems to contain so many mansions.

Last night we entertained my longtime friend, colleague, and one-time boss, Mike Leach. He was the publisher of Crossroad, which published *All Saints*. Then he became the publisher of Orbis. And when he retired ten years ago I took over his job.

Mike is 78, but he truly has not aged at all in the thirty years I have known him. He was a priest in Chicago, but left to marry Vickie, the great love of his life, and he went into Catholic publishing, becoming really the dean of Catholic publishers. He brought lots of joy to our office. He came in not just with big ideas and energy but with a big heart. I never could have taken on this job without his example. Soon after he came to work with us he worried that something was wrong with his wife. She seemed to be forgetting things. Before long she had to quit her job as a school principal and she was diagnosed with early-onset Alzheimer's.

His desire to care for her was Mike's chief reason for stepping down as publisher. For some years he used to bring her along to meetings, but eventually she was beyond that. Now all these years he has been caring for her. She is beyond words or recognizing anything. But it gives him pleasure to care for her. He is a great example of "everyday holiness."

He spoke last night about the stages of love: "First comes falling in love, which is the easy part. Then comes learning to love, which is the hard work. And then there is living in love, which is the best part." I assume this applies to other vocations, as well.

You cannot truly believe that your words don't convey truthfulness. We are not the best judge of our own words, or about anything about ourselves.

––––––––

I had sent Sister Wendy notes I submitted for my fortieth college reunion.

April 24, 2017

Dearest Robert,

I enjoyed your Harvard newsletter (so did Sister Lesley!), a nice succinct account of where-you-are-now. Have you ever been to one of these reunions? My Oxford college keeps me well up to date with their goings on and, although I know in practice I would absolutely loathe going back, ideally the thought of doing so is very appealing.

The great difference for me would be that I had a very young superior when I was at Oxford, very frightened of the worldly influence of the university, and she told me the rule of silence applied. The other two Notre Dame nuns thought this was ridiculous, which of course it was, but I was determined to obey to the last drop of my heart's blood and so I went through Oxford talking to nobody. I've read again and again that the great benefit of a university education is the discussions that undergrads hold among themselves, thrashing out all the great problems of life. I missed out on all this and yet can't say I miss it, if you know what I mean. It means that I have no university friends and my love is for Oxford itself. You and I who have been to great universities know what a sense of security this can give. I have never felt ill at ease or overpowered in any situation. Mind you, this may be just natural conceit.

I'm sorry this is such a bitty and dull letter but it brings you very much love and gratitude,

Sister Wendy

––––––––

April 24, 2017

Dearest Sister Wendy,

Yesterday we visited the Frick Museum with some cousins of Monica. I had not been there in many years. Honestly, it left me cold. I presume you know it. There are a couple of fine Duccios, Vermeers, and such—but otherwise I found it dreary, and I can't escape thinking about Henry Clay Frick, and the blood of all those striking steelworkers who paid for his wealth. (It is perhaps the same with other great museums, but I am not familiar with their provenance.) Perhaps someday visitors will ooh and ah over the luxurious treasures in Trump Tower.

I was rewarded with a strange dream: I was walking down the street and looked up to see that the moon was fractured into peculiar shapes, like a Picasso painting. Then a rumbling cloud of brown smoke seemed to unfold in the shape of various writhing faces—I figured it was some kind of effect created by anti-war demonstrators. Then suddenly I heard a voice say "Robert." It was my father—as he was in the 1970s. He was walking along with his close friend Howard Zinn, a famous radical historian who died some years ago. I told Howard (in my dream) that we were publishing a biography of Dan Berrigan. (In 1968 he had traveled to Hanoi with Dan Berrigan to receive some POWs.) He said, "That is long overdue." I asked if I could photograph him and he said sure, and sat on a post by the road. I had some bags hanging from my shoulders and was trying desperately to reach the phone in my pocket but just couldn't manage to get my hands on it.

It was a strange experience of time travel—witnessing the past, incapable of crossing the space-time-continuum (as they say in the movies) to retrieve some souvenir. How I wish I had paid more attention to my father in my dream; I have never dreamed of him when he was so young (so much younger than I am now). I woke up very shaken.

———

April 25, 2017

Dearest Robert,

I think you need many days in which you don't need to think about accomplishing anything and can just live. Your dream is fascinating but it's a pressured dream. The face in the moon that becomes obscured, and then the inability to find and use your camera and the implicit sense that you were losing forever an opportunity to be with your young father. Don't you think this might indicate the need to slow down a bit?

I smiled at your reaction to the wonderful Frick, but only because it re-minded me of my first time there very many years ago. I had a cousin living in New York at the time whom I barely knew but we met at the Frick and sat on the stone surrounding the pool. I was awed by the art I had seen but Brendan, like you, was gravely worried about the source of that art. He more or less said to me that he was horrified that I could take pleasure in work bought with the blood of the innocent. I realized with a sinking feeling that I was able to completely disassociate the tainted source of such trans-parently lovely objects. I console myself by thinking of Mother Teresa who, if you remember, was much criticized for accepting money that was ill-gotten. Other saints have refused such money. She just saw the use to which it could be put. I feel in myself it indicates a certain coarseness of soul, but one cannot say this of her.

Very much love to you and Monica, to the dogs and the grass and the trees and the flowers.

Sister Wendy

With my father in the 1970s

April 25, 2017

Dearest Sister Wendy,

It was funny to have that dream about my father in the 1970s, and then last night on television there was a showing of a documentary by Marcel Ophuls, "Memory of Justice," which is about war crimes, from Nuremberg to Vietnam. And he interviewed my father in 1975—there he was, young and in-tense, just as I had pictured him in my dream! And what is more, I remember that actual interview. I was in the very room (off camera!) at Kent State Uni-versity, the site of a demonstration in 1970 that left four students killed by National Guard troops—a notorious in-cident. I joined my father there in 1975 to commemorate the fifth anniver-sary of the shootings. Another surprising link in this chain is that my daughter Catherine wrote her thesis on French documentaries on the Holocaust, including Ophuls' "Sorrow and the Pity."

My father played an enormous role in my life, obviously—as he still does. But there is no doubt that much of my nature comes from my mother. It was she who took me to church, and who constantly reminded me that cleverness is not nearly as important as virtue.

But as I watched that documentary it brought me back to what it felt like to be following my father around to events like this—watching him be brilliant, and feeling inadequate. I am so blessed to have had the opportunity to develop a relationship with him that is so intimate and loving.

April 26, 2017

Dearest Robert,

There are so many little hares popping up in the meadow of your mind. But I can't quite complete this image because the last thing I want to do is shoot them. But I can't capture them and must just let most of your letter lie happily in my memory. Incidentally I think one comes to a time in life when one is living mostly on the books one has read and loved and these mean more than current literature. I'm in the re-reading stage, though I don't get enough of it.

Sister Lesley and I think you must be psychic to have had that dream about your young father, the very night before you saw him on television.

Dearest Robert, our time is up and it's just as well because I have nothing much to say today. I send you happiness though, since I can't send ideas. And I entrust it to my angel to pass on to your angel. Let me know if he does his duty.

Lovingly and gratefully,
Sister Wendy

May 1, 2017

Dearest Robert,

I've always sent at Easter a radiant image of the Resurrection, but this year it came to me very strongly that the image must be that of suffering. Perhaps I'm growing in an understanding of what it means to be baptized.

I've been thinking fruitfully about the self-knowledge of Jesus. We can't possibly know about this, and in fact I think every person is essentially a mystery. But it struck me this time that although that is broadly true, we can have some idea of what makes a person tick if they have an overriding preoccupation. An artist like Matisse, a musician like Mozart: one can imagine what was always present to them because their life revolved round it. There was no Matisse without art, Mozart's identity was his music. So I thought with Our Blessed Lord; the one absolute certainty we have about Him is His love for the Father. His awareness of the Father must have filled His mind from the earliest.

We are ready to say He is fully human, but He was also fully God. I think discovering His utter difference from everybody else must have been very painful for the young Jesus. This difference was not obvious in His home because His mother was also preoccupied with God, yet she was only human. Whereas for Him, wholly God and wholly man, it must have been difficult to distinguish the temporal from the eternal. Clearly He would not have had an intellectual concept of what He experienced, and I've always thought that the baptism must have brought Him immense relief, as well as happiness. Now He knew what His difference was. He was the "well-beloved Son." This would have given Him the confidence to decide what the Father's intent was because the clearest thing about Jesus was His total obedience: "I do nothing on my own, I do always what the Father tells me." This central passion never for a moment absent or diminished seems to me the one certainty that we can have about the inner life about our beautiful Lord.

Having written Sister Wendy a long account of a trip to Cambridge, Massachusetts, to attend a reunion at Harvard Divinity School, including descriptions of my encounters with old professors, fellow students, and friends going back for many decades, I had apologized for such a long letter with news of my comings and goings, "But all these people and encounters are part of the story of God in my life. And God has been so good to me."

Whenever you talk about a friend, I know we're going to be talking about God. I can't imagine anybody supported more by "a great cloud of witnesses." Whereas most people, I think, are very grateful to have met a few luminous others and even more so if these others have become part of the texture of their lives, you seem to have a richness that makes me smile with wonderment. And yet I can't help wondering, is it that you've been specially blessed with these holy and interesting friends or is it that you see people for what they truly are: holy and interesting. Maybe on a less prestigious level everybody is offered just the same support but they just don't see it. So I enjoyed every one of your encounters and thank God with you.

11.00 a.m. is striking from the church tower which makes us five minutes past our cut-off time.

With love and gratitude,
Sister Wendy

I had remarked to Sister Wendy: "I do get nervous when I contemplate my current happiness—thinking of Boethius and 'Fortuna's wheel.'"

May 5, 2017

Dearest Robert,

Having written a book on happiness you know that it's not dependent on circumstances. At the moment it's supported by circumstances, but you are in the blessed condition that is the birthright of all the baptized: lose everything and your happiness remains, however sorrowful you feel. Sister Lesley has just pointed out to me that you wrote that book on happiness at a most sorrowful time of your life. That bears out the truth of our joy being that of Jesus: "I have come that you may have joy and have it to the full." So I don't think one need ever be afraid and yet how deeply, deeply grateful one is when one hasn't to enshrine one's joy in sorrow, but can hold it up clear and bright like a monstrance.

I described a trip to Cornell University in Ithaca, New York, to research photos to use in Jim Forest's biography of Fr. Daniel Berrigan.[16]

May 6, 2017

Dearest Robert,

I'm looking forward to learning more about your friend Fr. Dan, because he's always been rather a background figure to me and my one closer

---

16. Jim Forest, *At Play in the Lions' Den: A Biography and Memoir of Daniel Berrigan* (Maryknoll, NY: Orbis Books, 2017).

look at him was meeting with his tortuous "poetry," to which I'm afraid I did not take. But this is quite irrelevant to the holiness and power of what he was. You have introduced Sr. Lesley and me to so many great figures, saintly people, selfless people, people who looked only at Our Blessed Lord and His little ones and I'm using little ones in a very broad sense to include the people your father fought for.

Sometimes we are puzzled as to why somebody whose life has stirred us to the depths doesn't seem to be canonized or beatified or even Servant of Godified. What amazes us both is that so many of these figures we have never heard of—like the two beatae in today's "Blessed Among Us" who are such outstanding women and from whom you quote statements of such absolutely fundamental truth.

Time is up, beloved Robert! Please rest and get over the strains of yesterday. Ask Monica to give you a glass of wine.

With very much love,
Sister Wendy

———

May 6, 2017

Dearest Sister Wendy,

You will learn more about Fr. Berrigan when his biography is published this fall. He was a complex person, but no doubt a prophet and a great peacemaker. It was probably his example that kept me connected to Christianity when I first learned about him in high school. Little could I have known that we would become good friends in later years. I found a letter from when I returned to college where he said, "I find it hard to put into words how much your friendship has meant to me." And yet there were also other letters that seared my fingers—excoriating me for letting one of his books go out of print or some other failing. In the end, though, love was the final word. He died a year ago last week.

———

May 16, 2017

Dearest Robert,

Lesley's family has left after a visit that was full of grace and joy for the four of them. It was such an exceptional time that we are making a novena of gratitude. I like this idea because we're not asking for anything—it's all been given, and we just want to say thank you. It's a novena to the Blessed Trinity, love itself.

Much love and joy in the Resurrection,
Sister Wendy

P.S. I love the Regina Coeli prayer three times a day which proclaims that through the Resurrection, "You have filled the world with joy." One looks round at our poor suffering smoke-filled world but yes, the deepest truth is that it is filled with His joy. We just have to see it.

––––––––––

May 17, 2017

Dearest Sister Wendy,

I smiled to read your novena of gratitude. Just today I had a letter from a friend, whom I have mentioned before, whose persistent illness has left him completely exhausted and feeling lost. He remarked on the years of darkness I endured and commented that my connection to God must be stronger than his. This alarmed me. I pointed out that there were many years when I could only utter a prayer consisting of one word: *Help.* I survived to the point that I could replace that with another one-word prayer: *Thanks!* I prayed that for him that day would also come. But I said I thought there was perhaps no harm in uttering that Thanks proleptically, even when the basis for gratitude was not yet in sight. I think that opens possibilities—if not in health or fortune, at least on the spiritual level.

––––––––––

May 17, 2017

Dearest Robert,

I am stricken with you by the state of your friend. We don't say thank you because we feel grateful, though it's very nice if we do. No, all the saints show that prayer is based upon choice, upon will, and that of course is the only genuine way that love works. I have never been able to enter into the Ignatian method of prayer with its great use of the imagination. Perhaps an over-reliance on the imagination disguises the lack of a hard-chosen commitment, which has no foundation in what one feels or imagines but lives in the bare truth of what God is and of what He has done for us. Your friend is the man for whom Jesus died, in whom His Father makes His home, who has the Spirit praying within him. Whether he feels this or not is unimportant. Might not this be the way back to health?

I hope above all your friend thinks about what you said to him about your own life—all those years when you could only say, Help. Can he see that you did say help, and the saying of it expressed your trust that help was there for you, whether you felt it or not? And so you never threw up your hands and sank to the ground. I rejoice so much that you eventually could say thank you, but even if that blessed day had never come, the hope and the love of "Help" is all that Our Lord needs to set Him free to transform us.

Anyhow I will pray very hard and hope there is good news.

With love and gratitude and joy,
Sister Wendy

I had passed along a fascinating essay by the great music teacher Nadia Boulanger on the subject of "attention," which reminded me of a profound essay by Simone Weil[17] on this subject and its relation to prayer.

May 23, 2017

Dearest Robert,

Thank you very much for that essay. I have referred many times in my life to Simone Weil's *Waiting on God* and of the overwhelming importance of this theme. What Boulanger doesn't actually say but which I will say is that all attention, if it is true attention, is attention to God. It's attention that makes us alive, not attention to ourselves, but to what is. If we look truly at creation we will see God reflected back to us. And if we look truly at God we will see Him reflected in creation. I don't like her dividing the human race into those who are real = attentive, and those who are just sleepers. Our Lord never gives up on people. I think you can teach attention even if it may not be of the quality that some people have naturally. Like many things we

---

17. Simone Weil (1909–1943) was a French philosopher, mystic, and activist. After her death the publication of her spiritual writings disclosed a deep and complex mystical life, in which she felt herself claimed by Christ, but hesitated to seek baptism, feeling called to live on the frontier between the Catholic Church and all those who remained excluded.

must practice it. Isn't that what growth in prayer is all about—learning painfully to be attentive?

With prayer and love,
Sister Wendy

May 23, 2017

Dearest Sister Wendy,

I agreed with you about the Boulanger essay—both what was appealing, and what in some ways gave me unease. Despite her tribute to the old woman pulling weeds, or the enlightened window washer, I couldn't help thinking there was a somewhat elitist viewpoint. Also a sense that some people are attentive from birth, while others are doomed to be dead fish. I think of the Buddha—who was asked to explain who he was and said, "I am one who is awake." Yet he wasn't awake from birth. Jesus didn't just come for those who are awake—but for the poor lost sheep of Israel. But does it require some modicum of wakefulness to be able to see the Messiah when he comes?

Yesterday I wrote a short foreword to a short biography of Sister Helen Prejean. I couldn't remember agreeing to do this, but they sent me the galleys with my name printed on the Contents page. I attach it for your interest, and you will see that I ended with that question—about how grace appears in our lives, and how it requires some response on our part.

I mentioned several weeks earlier that I was going to see my doctor about some mysterious chest pains. The next months were much taken up with a protracted investigation of my heart. When each test offered no conclusive answers, more tests were ordered. Sister Wendy followed these developments with maternal concern, urging me to slow down and get more rest.

May 25, 2017

Dearest Robert,

Well, dearest Robert, here is an opportunity to abandon yourself to the loving care of your heavenly Father. All He wants is for you to become what He created you to be and this painful passage in your journey is grace, however much it hurts. I know you'll refuse to let yourself get worried—that pointless activity. I know you will put this anxiety on the altar, and I will hold it there with you.

I wish I could make it easier, but of course one always wishes that for one's friends, even as one knows with complete certainty the beauty of being united to the crucified Jesus. No more time, dear Robert, but my heart is with you.

With much compassionate love,
Sister Wendy

––––––––

A prodigious reader, Sister Wendy often complained about her disappointment with some book she was reading—often one I had sent her. And yet she persisted.

May 26, 2017

Dearest Sister Wendy,

I counted it a great spiritual breakthrough when I realized that I didn't have to read a book to the end if I didn't enjoy it! You have evidently not achieved this level—or perhaps you have surpassed it. But I am always astonished how you stick with something to the end. I realize that sometimes you come to some appreciation that you might otherwise have missed. But please don't think that you have to read everything I send you. Life is short.

––––––––

Sister Lesley reminded Sister Wendy to share some thoughts about joy.

May 29, 2017

Dearest Robert,

No, I have no hesitation in leaving a book unfinished if I feel it is unprofitable. In fact when the county library van comes every month and Sister Lesley brings me a box of hopefuls, I sometimes discard book after book, having given them a fair chance to speak. But these are not spiritual books. With these I feel one should be more careful in case there is something as yet unrevealed.

I said something to Lesley and she said that I must be sure to tell you. It's not of great interest, but it was about the only thing I can remember being said to me that has had a serious effect. It was when I was barely professed and was sitting on the veranda with a very young Dominican priest. I don't know many priests, and I think this one must have been one of the young priests at Blackfriars at Oxford, who said Mass at our convent there. Because he was a passerby I must have spoken to him about myself, which is not something I usually did, and he said something to the effect that, what he missed was the note of joy. I can remember how this startled me because I had never heard any talk of joy. Love I knew about and hope and faith, but joy? I suppose I had subconsciously felt joy would be what God felt, nothing to do with me personally, as it were. But I realized that I was wrong. Joy was for here and now, joy was the atmosphere of Jesus. If we loved Him we lived in joy. And ever since then, over sixty-five years ago, it has been central to my life.

As I say, Robert, this seems to me rather commonplace, but Lesley likes it. What isn't commonplace is this frightening imperviousness to spiritual counsel. I'm sure I must have been influenced by people and helped. I can remember a few retreat anecdotes about things like self-pity and jealousy, but the only thing that really sank in and made a difference was young Fr. Dominic's comment. I hope he has had a joyful life himself. He may already be enjoying the fullness of joys in heaven for all I know. I still keep him in my grateful prayers.

With love and joy,
Sister Wendy

May 29, 2017

Dearest Sister Wendy,

Your comments on joy moved me deeply. It is striking that someone can offer us some spiritual advice that takes root and changes our life. In editing Dorothy's diaries I could see the genesis of certain phrases that stuck with her and truly made a difference. For instance, a priest who told her that it was ok to pray for a young man who had committed suicide, because "There is no time for God." (That is, for God, who is eternal, there is no time—the prayers we utter for that lost soul may have an efficacy that we can't imagine.) This was one of the most helpful spiritual utterances that was ever imparted to her. (In her last years she quoted this once in her column, and an angry subscriber scolded her: "Well, you must *make* time for God!")

How happy it makes me to think that you were encouraged to make time for joy! The gospels contains so many exhortations to rejoice!

There is, as I described in my book, a traditional way of thinking of happiness as only really applying to heaven, so that anything short of that is such a paltry and passing thing that it doesn't deserve the name. We are here "to love, know, and serve God in this life so as to be happy with him in the next." We are "poor banished children of Eve, weeping and mourning in this vale of tears," etc. And yet there is another way of thinking that stresses the continuity between happiness and joy in this life and the infinite fulfillment to come. Dorothy was more in this camp. Thus, she loved to quote St. Catherine of Siena: "All the Way to Heaven is Heaven, because He said, 'I am the Way.'" (Hence the title of my edition of her letters.)

I am very grateful to Sister Lesley for encouraging you to share that story with me. Who knows what happened to that Dominican priest who spoke the word you most needed to hear?—surely an angelic mission.

Anyway, I admire you for your ongoing reading and reflection. In your "room without a view" you are yet able to survey vast vistas.

Thank you for reminding me this day to rejoice!

––––––––––

May 30, 2017

Dearest Robert,

I was moved by Dorothy's wonder at being told there's no time with God, because this is something I've heard from babyhood—a Catholic cliché, as it were. But she saw the depth of that cliché, especially since it was new to her. Ever since young Fr. Dominic said that word "joy" to me, the reality of it has grown and expanded and filled my life. It coexists with that weeping and mourning in the vale of tears, but it transforms it and makes the sorrow into the glory of the Cross of Jesus.

I think sublimity is a very real thing and Dorothy, of all the women I know, deserves that epithet. I sometimes apply the word to those who demonstrate an empty word-sublimity, in other words not the sublimity of the life and love that we see in Dorothy, but great poetic words and cloudy concepts that really obscure a very simple biblical truth. One hears this occasionally in sermons. It's all so beautiful and lofty and when you come down to it, means nothing. I have to remind myself during these sermons that St. Teresa said she'd never heard a sermon from which she'd not drawn some good. Sometimes the only good I can find is to be compassionate and pray for the preacher who one feels must be hard-pressed interiorly to be forced to raise this screen of words. I also then pray for my poor self that Our Lord will save me from the need to disguise.

I'm sorry for rather a dull letter, dear Robert. Please take as much rest as you can while you wait for the doctor's diagnosis.

Lovingly always,
Sister Wendy

————

May 30, 2017

Dearest Sister Wendy,

I have a relative, a young man, who called today and surprised me by asking if I could recommend something to read to understand Christianity! (If you knew him you would truly understand how unexpected such a question was.) I suggested that he just read the Gospel of Mark to start with. "Which translation?" he asked. I said, any translation. But then he said he had looked at the King James Version and couldn't really understand it. So I said, "Anything but the King James Version"! Then I said—at the risk of self-promotion—that I had really intended my book, *The Saints' Guide*, as a kind of introduction to Christianity for people who don't know that much about it. He said he would take a look.

You never know what you say that makes an impression. Dorothy said that one time a man came up to her after a talk and said, "Miss Day, that was the most inspiring talk I've ever heard. In fact, I think you said something that has really changed my life." What was that? "That point where you said: It's never too late to turn over a new leaf."

————

June 2, 2017

Dearest Robert,

I can't help feeling that the young relative who called you sees in you the patient self-sacrificing love that comes from your faith. I think it's that that has drawn him to make inquiries about Christianity. Isn't this how most conversions come about? We meet somebody who so patently has something beautiful about them and we wonder why.

Of course there are others who are drawn by a sheer naked hunger for God and may know no Christians, but for the ordinary person I think a living example is such a summons toward belief. That's how Pope Francis appeals to his hearers—he so obviously lives in a certainty that fills him with joy and peace and makes all sacrifice welcome.

In the no-timelessness of God all the people you have met will be cheering you on, whether you've explicitly invited them or not.

Very much love and prayer, dearest Robert, with a private alleluia!

Sister Wendy

———————

June 4, 2017

Dearest Robert,

I'm convinced that we're not born human, we become so. Just as we become the kind of person that God intends us to be. Of course this isn't by any means automatic, but we who are in the Church, a living member of the Mystical Body of Jesus, are borne forward toward this completeness unless we actively resist it.

Over here it is sunny weather with the birdsong and brightness that seems so appropriate for Pentecost. Tomorrow, Whit Tuesday, is the day I came to Quidenham forty-six years ago. I am wordless in the face of such happiness as is mine.

Very much love, dear Robert,
Sister Wendy

———————

June 8, 2017

Dearest Robert,

I am now reading the large book you generously gave me of Thomas Merton's *Selected Essays*.[18] I'm about a quarter through. They are dense with intricate thought and reasoning—the kind of thing you say you have had very little of in your life. I have had very little, too, for which I am very grateful. The gift of life in Jesus seems to me too large and wonderful to need reasoning about. We are just called to live and be grateful, to receive His joy and give it to others. I'm afraid I am temperamentally averse to philosophical arguments and proofs and definitions.

———————

18. Thomas Merton, *Selected Essays*, ed. Patrick F. O'Connell (Maryknoll, NY: Orbis Books, 2013).

I think Merton needed this kind of thing because the great engine of his brain demanded activity. St. Teresa speaks about the "busy mill keeps clacking" as her way of describing the incessant activity of the mind. I think this is not sufficiently elevated a description for the intense workings of Merton's mind, but it is something for which I feel a genuine distaste. You seem to have escaped this need to scrutinize and rationalize as well. I don't think it's a sign at all of superficiality, but of a willingness to live quietly in the peace that His truth brings us. The whole mystery of God's love is so immense that thinking about it in any way is bewildering. Better surely just to be and receive, to allow Him to take us up into Himself, whether we are conscious of this or not. You are probably not very conscious of it, but that doesn't in the slightest diminish the reality of it.

When I first met Sister Rachel in the early '70s she was disturbed by the nothingness of her prayer. I pointed out that for her union with God was what I called "light off" and that this was to a greater or lesser extent, the state of most people. They are not consciously aware of Him. I was one of the few who, probably because of my weakness, needed "light on." But the light is showing me a state probably exactly the same as that of those who live in darkness. She wrote this up well in her first book, *Guidelines to Mystical Prayer*,[19] which you might find interesting for yourself.

To refer once again to dear Merton, it is when he writes about himself that he most makes clear his union with God and its availability as a support for other people.

With love and gratitude,
Sister Wendy

June 16, 2017

Dearest Sister Wendy,

"It has been quite a full week," I reported, in sending a long account of our trip to New Mexico for a theological conference. This included meetings with our friend Fr. Bill McNichols, and a description of his icon studio, with every surface crowded with icons, crucifixes, and holy cards; a visit with my good friend, Fr. John Dear, a brave peacemaker, who lives in a remote cabin; walks

---

19. Ruth Burrows, *Guidelines to Mystical Prayer* (New York: Paulist Press, 2017 [reprint]).

in the canyons of Georgia O'Keeffe country; the cathedral in Santa Fe, which features an enormous altar piece by the iconographer Robert Lentz; a visit with Fr. Richard Rohr in his community in Albuquerque. In Santa Fe I bought Monica a belated engagement ring: gold with blue-green opal and a dark rich amethyst at the center. "When she burst into tears, the Afghani salesman was moved to give us an additional discount." There was also news of the death of Fr. Miguel D'Escoto, the founder of Orbis Books, a meeting by phone of the Dorothy Day Guild, and finally, following our return, an account of my "nuclear stress test," which involved the injection of radioactive dye.

I am sorry this is just a letter to catch you up on this whirlwind of activity, without any deeper content. But as I traveled in New Mexico I kept wishing that I could show you everything: the beautiful little country churches; the Rio Grande river; the gorgeous adobe houses with their mysterious shapes; the turquoise colors; the dramatic clouds that emerge out of nowhere in the afternoon, the deep reaches of the desert; the deer, rabbits, eagles, and vultures one encounters. All very mystical.

Always, Merton was hovering in the background.

June 17, 2017

Dearest Robert,

It's astonishing that a man with so much to do, so many anxieties pressing on him, and with physical strain as well, should still have the kindness to send me such a long account of his fascinating visit to New Mexico. Everything in your letter was of interest. I don't want to go anywhere or see more of God's world, but your letter made me aware of it. That beautiful countryside held in His hands and that interesting human world also held in His hands: all came alive for me as you wrote. But I feel I mustn't encourage you! I wonder if you can afford to spend such time and energy? Anyway in this instance you have done it and it is much appreciated.

I'm getting toward the end of the Merton essays, and I must admit I find them highly entertaining. They are such an effusion of his need to communicate, to elaborate, to investigate, to stretch his intellectual limbs and dance a little. They are meant to be taken seriously, and of course there are serious though obvious things behind many of them. But I find it difficult to see them as other than free-wheeling expressions of his inability to be silent. The strange thing is that when he talks about solitude, which he does with unique power, he sees quite clearly that the solitary must be still and without entertainment. Yet, without expressly saying so, he persists in seeing himself as a solitary and in a way he is perfectly correct. We can only give God what we are, and what he was was an instinctive writer who could not exist without this outpouring. Underneath the words, though, and the speculations, and the drama, one is aware of a union with God. It was not according to the insights that he himself had, as to what a contemplative life should be, but I think it was true.

Oh, how much pleasure he gives me! How much irritation, too, but I think this is salutary. It widens my view of what is and what should be and what can be.

Very much love to you and Monica, very much hope that God gives you strength for what lies ahead, very much confidence that He will give you the strength.

Sister Wendy

––––––––––

June 19, 2017

Dearest Robert,

Lesley is having an eight-day retreat so I will not have access to her machine until Tuesday, the 27th. In these days of silence between us, will you think seriously as to whether you should carry on this correspondence with me? Of course I love your interesting and thoughtful letters, but you have very much work to do. Can you afford to spend the time that your messages to me take? Let me know what you feel.

With love and prayer and joy and gratitude,

Sister Wendy

––––––––––

During this interregnum in our correspondence, I wondered whether Sister Wendy was trying to send me a gentle message.

June 27, 2017

Dearest Sister Wendy,

I welcome back Sister Lesley and her omnipotent machine after this Great Silence. I hope it has been a time for peace and renewal for her. And I hope you too are rested and well.

When I received your note last week, with the question about whether I should spend so much time writing you, I wondered if this was a gentle way for you to express the feeling that I have intruded too much on your call to solitude. Perhaps I have become too familiar, imposing myself with tales of my dreams, my colleagues' troubles, my rambling and random reflections. If this is the case, please don't worry about my feelings, and let me know if you would prefer that I scale back or ration my urge to communicate. For one thing, I know that you rely on Sister Lesley's limited time, and I am surely claiming far more than my share of your availability.

If, on the other hand, your concern is really about whether I have the time or energy for this correspondence, I hope to reassure you of what a precious gift it has been. In writing you I feel that I gather up all the threads and material of my daily life and you lay it on the altar and bless it—if that makes any sense.

I stand ready to abide by your wishes, but my wish is that I might continue to write you. If I have your permission that will make me very happy.

I provided merely a bullet-point listing of all the notable events she had missed. I noted that the next station on my adventures in cardiology would be an angiogram—a small camera inserted in an artery to take a look at my heart from the inside.

And I leave you with a final dream: I was writing an article about a great fire, and I realized that I was able to understand a dog, who was telling me all about what happened from her perspective.

———

The angiogram did not go as planned!

June 27, 2017

Dearest Sister Wendy,

I want to give you an update and ask you to keep me in your prayers. During my angiogram today something went wrong—an electrical misfire in my heart, apparently, which caused it to stop. I was revived with a defibrillator and missed all the excitement. I had no sensation at all; the lights simply went off. There could be no better place for this to happen than in a cardiac unit. But as a result they made me spend the night for observation.

Monica came quickly, and I am feeling quite fine apart from painful swelling in my arm.

As far as they can tell, this was merely a very unlikely and unlucky fluke. But a reminder of how precious and vulnerable life is. Each day we should give thanks!

––––––––––

June 30, 2017

Dearest Robert,

Sister Lesley has just been able to read me your messages and we are both aghast. Clearly God is sending you a message, a joyful message, but a serious one. Your life lies like a trembling leaf in His loving Hands. From what you say, if your heart actually stopped, then for one moment you were dead, and His love called you back almost immediately to life. But it is a new life, a Lazarus life, given for His joy and yours too.

It must have been harrowing for Monica and the family. It just occurs to me that this may be very meaningful for your children. They can see how fragile our hold on life is, in fact we have no hold, it's God who holds and as St. Paul says, whether we live or die we are the Lord's. Well, He wants you to live and I'm very grateful that He does. You are a beacon of His care for the world, His warmth and His generosity. So many lives would be impoverished without Robert in them.

So you can see that my answer to your question about our correspondence is that I love and value all you write. You bring new worlds into my little room. My question was solely for your sake. I must also add that my response to your rich full letters is often, I feel, meager and maybe even more so as my energies dwindle. But my heart is open to receive everything you write and to rejoice in it and grieve with it and wonder at it and hold it all up to Our Blessed Lord.

I'll be praying especially after this strange cardiac arrest and wish they could give you some logical explanation. A "fluke" sounds unlikely somehow, but who am I to know. I know after this shock Monica will take great care of you, perhaps I should say even greater care of you. But you must do your part and not overwork.

With love and a great sisterly embrace,
Sister Wendy

––––––––––

July 1, 2017

Dearest Sister Wendy,

It cheers me greatly to hear from you. I am feeling rather battered and blue after this week. Yesterday, when my doctor called to see how I was feeling, and I said not so great, he had me come in for another checkup. He decided that there was one last stone to overturn—a CT scan of my aorta, which meant a trip to the emergency room, and many more hours of being poked and pressed. I must say all the nurses and doctors were so kind, efficient, and professional. The result is that there definitively seems to be nothing the matter with my heart, which should be cause for rejoicing. They remain mystified by my heart stopping, except that it is a possible but very rare outcome of the procedure. My doctor said he had only seen it once in twenty years of practice.

I told him that I felt like a boy who cried out "smoke" and set off a four-alarm response. Everything followed from my initial report of symptoms, which remain unexplained.

———————

July 3, 2017

Dearest Robert,

Are you making changes in your lifestyle after this summons that God sent you? I realize that your experience was almost perfunctory. You only know it happened because of what you were told and of the effects of the resuscitation. Obviously you didn't pass through death, you entered into it, and then God put His arms round you and drew you out. But it was a very serious experience, even though it was in a way a non-experience.

If Lazarus is only a few minutes in the tomb instead of three days, he has still passed into another dimension whether he realizes it or not. Robert, when one thinks of your great work on your father's book, your pressing anxieties about your friends, your lectures, your writing, and on top of that your job at Orbis. . . . Don't you think all this is too much for your body, and in the gentlest way possible, trying not to frighten the horses, God is telling you to cut down? Your dreams are wonderful and I love hearing about them, but they do suggest that even at night you're busy at work.

Might I suggest that you look at how much silent prayer you are giving yourself. It is there that our spirit is renewed in a way that we can't do of ourselves. It also struck me about your dreams that when you think of the Pope you are really looking at your own function to be a pontiff, a bridgemaker, between that completely dedicated world where you are so at home and that is exemplified in your friends and authors, and the world of your readers. I rejoice that you should have this function, but bridges need repairing sometimes, you know?

I'm sorry if this is a dull letter. Your letters are always so rich in thought and story and event. I have an almost one-tone life but that tone is multi-layered. I think I'm getting mixed up in metaphors, but I think also that you understand what I'm trying to say.

Much love and apologies, dearest Robert,
Sister Wendy

July 3, 2017

Dearest Sister Wendy,

I did have a very deep dream this morning. This concerns the Vietnamese Zen monk Thich Nhat Hanh, who in the past decades has become internationally renowned. I was fortunate to know him before he became famous. Exiled from his country during the war, he was living in Paris and serving as an ambassador of peace. When I was a 17-year-old schoolboy in England, I was inspired, after read-

In Paris, playing the guitar for Thich Nhat Hanh in 1974

ing an essay that Jim Forest had written about him, to travel to Paris and knock on his door. That afternoon made a huge impression on me, and it was in a later visit that I really got to know Jim Forest and so to begin our lifelong friendship. Jim took a picture of me playing the guitar for him. Though we did not meet again, many years later I secured Nhat Hanh's permission to edit an anthology of his essential writings for the Modern Spiritual Masters Series. Since then, his influence has only increased. A few years ago he had a stroke. Though he remains alive, now living in his old monastery in Hue, he is apparently unable to speak—only to communicate through gestures. All this by way of background.

I dreamed that Jim and I had gone to France to see him. It was like a Tibetan monastery that Monica and I recently visited in upstate New York. I could see in the great hall a lot of people silently meditating. And in the back I could see that Thay (as they call him) was also sitting there, as a succession of people were stepping up to bow before him.

Jim was making inquiries at some sort of kiosk, and finally they said that we could present ourselves, though there was no certainty of whether he would make any acknowledgment.

We went into a dark waiting area and stood in line. As we approached him it seemed that it was not his full body, but only an illuminated face that seemed to hover there in a half-immaterial form, almost like the face of the moon.

As Jim approached him, he responded with a slight Buddha-like half-smile. When I approached I looked deeply into his eyes, trying to communicate deep love. He showed a very deep response and somehow beckoned me to come forward and speak. I reminded him who I was, told him what a gift it had been to meet him at such a young age, how I have never forgotten him, and carry him in my heart. He didn't speak, but seemed to nod enthusiastically and communicated much love. Then I woke up.

This was a great gift, and left me feeling very cheerful about the capacity to communicate on a level beyond words, beyond physical presence.[20]

In my few seconds of in-between existence in the hospital, I didn't get to experience any deep "near-death" experience. It was just as if a switch had been turned off and then I was back again. I think I had time to say, "Gosh, that hurts!" and then the next minute they were waking me up. I wouldn't like to think that death is like that. But I am amazed in my dreams about the other worlds I visit, and all the experiences in my life that I carry with me.

Do we get the dreams—as well as the friends—that we "deserve"? I believe I have been blessed beyond anything I have deserved—including your precious friendship.

Yesterday, though I was too exhausted to go outdoors, I spent the day reviewing Dorothy's writings in preparation for the course I will be teaching next week in Boston. It is always moving for me to return to her work. Monica referred to me as one of her close friends, and I had to correct her—not in false modesty—to say that I really didn't know her all that well when she was alive. Many people spent much more time with her. But how to explain the feeling that I received some commission from her in my

---

20. Jim Forest's last book was a memoir of his friendship with Thich Nhat Hanh, *Eyes of Compassion* (Maryknoll, NY: Orbis Books, 2021). Jim died at the age of eighty on January 13, 2022. Thich Nhat Hanh died a week later, on January 22, at the age of ninety-five.

youth—something that has been the foundation of my life and my own mission?

I was very pleased by your naming this mission as bridge-building!

———————

July 4, 2017

Dearest Robert,

I find it hard at the moment to separate real life from dream life because all you told me of your encounters with Thich Nhat Hanh in your temporal life merge imperceptibly into your dream encounter. Once again I discover almost by accident another figure of giant spiritual proportions who has been in your life for many years, influencing it and taking it into new dimensions. One would think it would have been enough for one person to have had Dorothy, and I do agree that she was the launching pad. Yet, having said that, I look at your chronology and this great Buddhist preceded her by quite a few years. Maybe he was your John the Baptist figure, so that when you met Dorothy, or perhaps more truly when she met you, the flower blossomed.

I had gathered already that you were not as close to Dorothy as your superb editions of her diaries and letters and your deep, deep subsequent knowledge of her would lead one to think. But I think she was close to you; she saw you, saw your potential, and it was to that potential that she entrusted herself. These areas of luminous wisdom in your life seem to surround you on all sides. I wonder if you know how extraordinarily blessed you have been?

I hope your bridge-building life brings you another papal dream. This morning Sister Lesley read me one of Pope Francis's weekday sermons in St. Martha's Guest House. It was for the feast of the Sacred Heart where the Pope speaks about God singing us a lullaby and caressing His little one. He points out that to hear this loving song and to be held in those loving arms we have first of all to accept that we are little and to allow ourselves to be astonished. It's the astonishment that's so typically Francis, a child-like wonder at the magnificence of God's love. You have that astonishment—His gift.

Because you did not go through death, or so it seems to me, but just went into it and were drawn out by the Fatherly love of Him who sings a lullaby, there was no occasion for lights or insights or the various near-death experience stories. You just got your feet wet and were back on solid earth again. I must say I was consoled to know that your physician, who impresses me very much as a truly caring and intelligent doctor, has known a previous occasion of the heart stopping during an angiogram. This removes it from an undiagnosed weakness into a statistical probability (regardless of how improbable). Still all these things leave one very washed-out, which in itself is an occasion for grace. So much goes on in your life, dearest Robert, that it is good to be forced physically to slow down and let God just love you.

With very much love and a kiss to Monica, who must be so relieved to have you within her care again,

Sister Wendy

————

July 7, 2017

Dearest Sister Wendy,

The last days have been very full. But today was quite significant. I was asked to serve on the "Historical Commission" for the cause of Dorothy's beatification. I had been given to believe that this just meant looking over the assembled writings and certifying that it all seems comprehensive and in good order. Patrick Jordan, a former editor of the CW who was very close to Dorothy, and who has written a short biography, was appointed along with me.

So we went down to the Tribunal office at the Archdiocese to be "sworn in" and to meet the assistant to the Roman Postulator. Well, it turned out to be a much bigger deal. Pat and I will essentially oversee and give our approval to the material that will be assembled and presented to Rome, and we will be responsible for preparing her official biography.

I was quite stunned by this awesome responsibility.

By the way, on the subject of slowing down, I often share your counsel for me with Monica, who invariably shouts out, "Exactly! Good for you, Sister Wendy!"

————

July 9, 2017

Dearest Robert,

I am especially glad to know that you are appointed to work on Dorothy's cause for canonization. I can't think of any way to make God's goodness shine forth than to show people Dorothy's relationship with Him. Even her human flaws, the occasional impatience or injustice or misjudgments make her holiness even brighter, I think. It is all so real—a real fallible human creature coming to know Him and to understand the wonder of His love.

Oh Robert, what a privilege. It was a very great honor to be chosen to bring your father's book to maturity and here is a very much greater honor bestowed by the Church which will affect millions. I hope your father's book has millions of readers, too, but by definition they'd have to be intelligent. Even the most stupid and least educated can be uplifted by Dorothy.

Although it isn't in your league, I had a dream early this week, but I hesitate to talk about it, thinking of your great narratives. My dreams are so passive and I'm usually looking at pictures, though occasionally thank God, I'm looking at an angel. However, this was a picture dream and the point was that the pictures were paired. I was being shown that every longing of the heart has its response from God. I can't remember all the images though I do remember the wonderful feeling of astonishment and joy when I saw the first picture each time and couldn't imagine what God's answer would be. Unfortunately, I only remember the more obvious examples. There was the young Virgin Mary, and the image was from that great early icon of the Annunciation. She was longing to know what God wanted her to do with her life. And of course the matching picture was the Angel Gabriel telling her. There was another one of Our Blessed Lady, too, not concerned with her vocation, but just with her great longing to love God, her arms outstretched. The matching picture was the little baby in the manger, stretching out His small arms. And then there was Psyche and of course matching her, the human spirit was Eros, love itself.

One little picture that puzzled me came from a book I loved as a child, *Flower Fairies*—I don't know if you had it in America, but it was a delicately painted little volume of flowers with an imagined and ethereal child-fairy. When I saw this I couldn't imagine what the response could be—what was the flower and its spirit longing for? Then I recalled how St. Paul tells us that the whole creation yearns in eager longing for the revelation of the children of God and when I turned to the pair, the other picture was of the Blessed Sacrament, that great Ingres image of Our Lady holding up the Eucharist. As I looked at it I realized that the host is formed from the growing wheat, vegetation like the flowers, and the longing of the natural world to receive what it can of Him is so beautifully and overwhelming fulfilled in the transformation of the bread into the Holy Body of Our Lord. So you see I had a beautiful night, but no Robertian drama.

Very much love,
Sister Wendy

I found it fascinating how often Sister Wendy's dreams offered deep expressions of her vocation and of the function of art.

July 9, 2017

Dearest Sister Wendy,

I loved your dream! It seems to me that your wonderful dream of "call and response" between great works of art is a perfect depiction of your own response to art—and your capacity to see in all things an implicit question that is answered by God. It reminded me of Origen's typological reading of scripture, in which Adam's tree is answered by the Cross, Noah's ark by the Church, etc.

This seemed to me a most satisfying dream, and I'm sure it left a lovely glow.

Interestingly, I had just had a dream the same night that included you. I was getting on a train in Cambridge. It was some kind of local train and I knew I would have to switch to get to London. But I couldn't tell where this train was going. I asked a conductor who was very friendly, and I struck up a rapport when I told him that I had gone to school in Cambridge many years before. He explained where I could switch—an unfamiliar town. I got off the train to buy a ticket but there was no ticket office. Just then the train started to leave so I jumped aboard but had to sit in some strange outer deck. A new conductor came to me and asked for my ticket. I said I hoped I could buy a ticket on the train but he said no. I told him I couldn't find the office, and he was very skeptical and accusatory.

At this point my friendly conductor showed up and assured him that I was a good bloke, and he should give me a break. They then conferred privately and afterward they presented me with a rare "Golden Ticket"—which entitled me to travel anywhere I wanted for free!

I asked them whether this train could also take me to Norfolk as well as London—thinking that I might visit you! But then I considered that it would not be polite for me to show up without warning.

Well, I also did feel very consoled by this dream—and the thought that in my life I have received so many blessings beyond anything I have earned or merited.

Meanwhile, I feel just fine, and have no concerns about my imminent demise. I have so much to do!

July 10, 2017

Dearest Robert,

Perhaps "so much to do" and "imminent demise" have a connection! But at least I'm glad that you're feeling fine and that there are such grace-filled meetings in your life.

I loved your dream, especially since Cambridge is so close to Quidenham and your dream train could have been coming in our direction. But oh, it's that golden ticket that I think is so significant! Your good angel and your bad angel both conferred about this and agreed that this entrance into the Kingdom of Heaven was to be freely given you. I think something within you must know that He is lavishing enormous grace on you—symbolized by the ticket. And just as to use the ticket you have to go to the trouble of taking trains and choosing destinations, so for this extraordinary grace to be fruitful you have to work and suffer. But all difficulties and sorrows are joy when we know they are His way for us. If that's how He comes, welcome always.

Very much love, dearest Robert, and rejoicings with you and Monica on your beautiful moon,

Sister Wendy

————

July 15, 2017

Dearest Sister Wendy,

I wrote about the experience over the past week of teaching a course on Dorothy Day at Boston College, beginning with an overview of her life and the story of her conversion, her spiritual influences, her social and political ideas, and her place in the peace tradition of the Church.

. . . On the fourth day I talked about the role of saints in the church, the process of canonization and how that applies to Dorothy. There were lots of questions. One woman asked me if I would be willing to talk more about my personal relationship with Dorothy. I did so, but very quickly it went into a very deep place, as I truly relived and experienced so many memories, struggling to hold back tears. I have never given such a presentation—you can't do this in a one-hour session. But this came at the end of 12 hours, and I felt I had earned the right to get a little emotional. I think it was more like a retreat than a class, as I really delved deeply into the paths in my life that my early encounter with Dorothy opened up.

I described at length the people we had met, the reunions with old friends, visits to the Museum of Fine Arts and to the Isabella Stewart Gardner Museum, one of Sister Wendy's favorites, though I found it dark and cluttered.

July 17, 2017

Dearest Robert,

I'd agree that the MFA is one of the greatest museums in the world. I filmed there and know it relatively well. I had a mini-revelation there, in secular terms, of the beauty and artistic importance of furniture. I had never understood its sculptural dignity and charm. I am referring specifically to American furniture. I was in the American wing to film very early Indian pottery, but then we moved on to the seventeenth- and eighteenth-century furniture and the love, knowledge, and enthusiasm of the curator opened a whole new field of art for me. I didn't film at the Isabella Stewart Gardner, but I examined it in case I might. I love its smallness and the head curator, Hilliard Goldfarb, became a real friend.

But the museum remains in my mind as a place of enchantment and I wonder if it might have gone downhill over the years. Certainly I don't remember any darkness and I found the miscellany fascinating. Here was the mind of Mrs. Stewart made visible. It has never to be altered from her arrangements, and there is such a variety.

I'm sorry it didn't work for you. There's nothing for it, Robert, but for me to up sticks, cross the waters, take you by the hand, and Monica by the other hand, and walk you through that dear little museum. If it has degenerated since my day I will rely on your expostulations to bring them to their senses.

Please forgive this uninspired but affectionate letter.

Lovingly,
Sister Wendy

July 17, 2017

Dearest Sister Wendy,

Monica's niece is named Isabel (whom she calls Isabella) and she was thrilled that the museum offers free admission to anyone named Isabella— though not to their aunts.

If only we could take you up on your offer to walk us hand in hand through the museum we would gladly offer you an all-expenses paid excursion! Alas, that does not seem likely in this lifetime.

Tomorrow I fly to Cincinnati where I will spend two days reading aloud from my book of Franciscan saints for an audio edition.[21] How I wish they could use your voice instead! I am only nervous about mispronouncing all the difficult Polish, German, Italian, Portuguese, etc. names. In preparing my talk my mind went back to tenth grade when I first discovered *The Little Flowers of St. Francis*—my first encounter with the saints. How this changed my life I couldn't say. I remember enthusiastically telling my teacher about this and he said (I remember this so clearly), "You don't believe all that stuff do you?" I don't know whether I had the courage to reply, but my heart was saying YES!

Many years later: after getting out of jail, Dorothy presented me with a beautiful little hardbound copy of *The Little Flowers*. She signed it to me: "To Robert Ellsberg, one of our editors, with gratitude for his courage, for his next stint in jail."

———————

July 20, 2017

Dearest Robert,

I'm reading a book by a Fr. Buckley, SJ, based on the questions Our Lord asks in the gospels. I think this a brilliant idea and he certainly treats the first one very powerfully: What are you seeking? You remember he put this question to Andrew and Philip after the baptism.

The beloved and beautiful girl who looks after my worldly affairs came recently and although I hadn't the energy to stay long with her I wanted to put this question which I had found so moving. She answered that she wanted to find a man who would complement her and with whom she could have a family. I hadn't the energy to take this up with the dear girl but of course that is not what I meant or what the Lord was asking. The question is about the meaning we seek for in our lives, what we're for, which is far deeper and more integral than the happiness of a settled life with a partner. I realize that I have always asked myself: what do I want? And of course the answer has always been that I want God and only Him. But the subsequent question is less easy to answer: how do I set about this? I remember the feeling of intense joy I felt years ago when I realized I didn't have to set about it. God was doing it. He was the one who wants. We have just to let ourselves be loved.

---

21. *The Franciscan Saints* (Cincinnati: Franciscan Media, 2017).

Today is the anniversary of my consecration to a solitary life in 1972, but perhaps I've told you that? The value of the consecration was that it gave me an official place within the church hierarchy, one of the consecrated of whom there are as you know very few. It also gave me stability in my relationship with the community here. But spiritually I have never felt that these ceremonies matter.

Dearest Robert, I really feel too weary to continue. I would not want to be a correspondent who received so much and gave very little, but I may well bound back in great vigor very soon, watch this space!

Very much love,
Sister Wendy

July 21, 2017

Dearest Sister Wendy,

It makes me so happy to hear from you. You must never imagine that you "take so much and give so little."

I did not know of the anniversary of your consecration to a solitary life! Although I know you have not exactly been sealed into an anchor hold, that is a very long time spent as a solitary. I am sure you have found exactly the place where God wants you to be.

I mentioned that I had been an exchange student in Cambridge in 1972, the same year she was receiving her consecration as a solitary in Norfolk, not so far away.

July 22, 2017

Dearest Robert,

As I write I can see vividly the photograph of you and Dorothy—the old saint hollowed out by love and sacrifice, concealing her face, and the young ardent disciple who has the whole course of apostolic sacrifice to go through and yet embraces it in trust; where Dorothy has arrived, there he too wants to be. That was a very moving picture of a beginning and an ending.

We must have been only few miles apart in 1972. I had come the previous year unhesitatingly committed to the certainty that this was my life. The sisters, on the other hand, quite reasonably, wanted to make certain that I was balanced enough to lead a life of solitude. I remember Sister Rachel, the Prioress, saying to me anxiously, "You won't have ecstasies in public will you?" She also urged me to make certain that I washed and kept clean. She says she didn't but she did! I had no hesitation in assuring her that I would wash because that was within my power. All the rest was up to God, but I don't think I have ever embarrassed the community in public, please God.

With Dorothy Day in the late 1970s

My hermitage life was not exactly disrupted, but interrupted for short periods by the strange vocation to talk about art. The only decision I made in this was the decision to ask the Prioress (Rachel) if I could have a rest from my translating work [of Latin texts] because I was feeling unwell and just look at art until I recovered. Feeling this might be rather self-indulgent, I offered to write a book about the art. From that book all sprang—more books, magazine articles, interviews, the interest of the television people, journeys, time away from my hermitage. If I had known that this would happen I would not have written the book, which probably means that I would not have asked to stop my translating work. Yet, I can't but feel that God wanted all I did because there are so many people who seem to have learnt something from it. I recently received a book on England and reading through it I found a quotation from me in which I say that God comes to people not just through religion but through beauty, through the transforming power of art and music. That is why I wrote, not for the Christian but for the clueless people who didn't know that art would show them Jesus, even if completely anonymously.

Lovingly and gratefully,
Sister Wendy

July 22, 2017

Dearest Sister Wendy,

This morning from our window I could see that the flowers that Monica planted have burst into bloom, looking like a Monet painting. There is also a ripening raspberry bush, though I fear that squirrels have been making off with the first fruits. Monica is a deep believer in what you say about beauty leading us to God. She has trained me to be more attentive to such signs—in clouds, flowers, trees, moonlight.

I talked in my class about this quality that Dorothy also shared—this sacramental imagination that made her keenly attentive to signs of beauty everywhere. (Like St. Francis, with his hymn to Brother Sun and Sister Moon.) I pointed out that this also applied to moral beauty: an act of kindness, someone sharing bread with a neighbor (the literal meaning of "companion-ship"). I recalled the card that she sent me when I was fasting in prison: an aerial picture of Cape Cod with the inscription: "I hope this card refreshes and does not tantalize you." I noted that that was Dorothy: the recollection of beauty, while sitting in a slum or jail cell, could inspire you to greater courage, hope, faith. And I said that is also why I write about the saints: because the thought of such spiritual beauty can refresh and ennoble us.

Your anniversary made me think back to 1972. My father was on trial for his life (facing 115 years in prison) in Los Angeles, where I had helped him copy the Pentagon Papers. My mother was appalled when she learned that he had got me mixed up in this. My mother had a very hard time, and her only desperate concern was to keep my sister and me safe and far from the hordes of ravening reporters. This was not easy since the trial was in Los Angeles, where we lived. Of course I was torn between wanting to attend his trial and my mother's determination that we have nothing to do with it. It was tearing me apart.

In the midst of that I applied for the opportunity to go to England, to be as far away from it all as I could. But that had its own stress. I felt the terri-ble fear that I would wake up to the news that my father had been killed.

So all that comes back to me as I recall where I was in 1972 as you were being consecrated as a solitary in Quidenham. We were at one point geographically close, but what a distance we would travel in the subsequent decades to be able to speak heart to heart!

I had a wonderful conversation with my father today. We have so much fun together, so many ways our minds work the same way. As he always likes to say, "You are one of the few people who think that I'm funny." And it is true.

Wishing you beautiful sights—or at least memories—of beauty.

July 23, 2017

Dearest Robert,

Time is very short on a Sunday and I only have ten minutes. Let me use them in thanking you for your beautiful letter and rejoicing in your relationship with your father. It seems to me that what we love best in those we love is that they share our sense of humor. It's a great privilege to have that joy with one's parents and I don't think it's all that common.

Thank you for sharing your homily for your mother, which counterbalances the account of your relationship with your father. Both are so deep and so blessed. Obviously you needed them both. Without her tenderness, your father's ruthlessness would have been damaging. Without that steely intensity in him, her sweetness might have softened you. As it is you have been well-tempered in the fire of parental love and were ready to receive the impress of Dorothy's extraordinary surrender to the will of God. And now you have gentle Monica who sees the beauty of God in all around.

Well, dearest Robert, the ten minutes is up, there'll be no machine tomorrow, which may be just as well because my energies are still low. But who knows what Tuesday will bring to both of us?

Very much love,
Sister Wendy

Another rare disagreement was occasioned by my admiration for Princess Diana.

July 25, 2017

Dearest Sister Wendy,

I watched a very moving documentary about Princess Diana, featuring her two boys interviewing people who knew her. On the one hand, her loss was like a meteor in their young lives; yet they didn't know her all that well. Still they carry her love in their hearts, and they have tried in some ways to carry out her legacy, keeping up with the charities she supported.

July 27, 2017

Dearest Robert,

I have strong feelings about Princess Diana but I am unwilling to share them with you. When I was talking and writing about art I never spoke about anything about which I might be critical.

Sr. Lesley is tired but thank God, and I say this purely selfishly, she's well. I'm better than I seem to be, if you know what I mean. We are both certainly much better than you, dear Robert. I hope you listen to Monica. She has the wisdom to see when you are being a Big Brave Man and when you need to give in. But since this is her and your business, not mine, I peacefully leave it to God.

Very much love and prayer,
Sister Wendy

––––––––––

July 27, 2017

Dearest Sister Wendy,

I believe strongly that friends need not agree on everything. It would be very tedious if we all shared exactly the same opinions and tastes. One time I did recommend a rather low-brow comedy to a friend, and afterward she said she hated it so much that she worried that it had affected her judgment about me. As long as my warm spot for Princess Diana doesn't lower me in your esteem, that is fine. Like you, I don't wish to trample on other people's enthusiasms, as long as they are harmless.

I am so glad to hear that you are "better than you seem to be." I think I will use that as the title for my memoir, if I ever write it. I hope that Sister Lesley gets some rest—and not only for selfish reasons!

––––––––––

August 2, 2017

Dearest Robert,

Some time ago I had two or three small heart attacks, very small, and on Monday I had another one. They leave one feeling depleted and very weary. But I hope to be able to answer your letter tomorrow. This is just to explain the delay. One is also left feeling the joy of total dependence on God.

Lovingly,
Sister Wendy

––––––––––

August 2, 2017

Dearest Sister Wendy,

It was kind of you to let me know of your condition, but please don't worry about replying until you feel better. Meanwhile I will be praying for you. Please rest up and feel better. If memory serves, a nice cup of tea is the English remedy for all conditions.

———————

August 3, 2017

Dearest Robert,

I truly am better.

One of the sisters who likes owls got a most beautiful birthday card—a picture of a tawny owl which, when opened, has the owl's call. She has lent it to me for the day with strict instructions to return it! I'm going to see if I can get something of the same kind because I really miss my birds. They were quite active at the caravan where I had a little bird table. I never had any food to put out for them, but I had a soup plate that I kept filled with water, from which they all drank and in which the little birds used to swim, or rather lie on the plate and flap their wings. Some nights ago I heard the owls in the wood crying to one another. There seemed to be a whole range of these cards, so if they're not too expensive I might have a substitute.

Very much love dearest Robert,
Sister Wendy

———————

August 3, 2017

Dearest Sister Wendy,

I couldn't be happier to hear from you if your email came with an owl call or a dog's bark.

This morning my father FINISHED his book. He had put in a couple of secretive days of industrious work on it and pronounced himself very happy with the results. But when he sent it to me yesterday I said NO—he must remove all the new material he had added, which really didn't work. Thankfully, he accepted my judgment, and so after another night of last-minute details he was ready to let it go at last.

I have been writing short reflections on the daily lectionary readings for a *Bible Diary* that is published in the Philippines. I have been enjoying it. You can really say quite a lot in just a couple of hundred words, when you don't have to do all the fleshing-out that would be required for a homily. The extraordinary thing is really how simple and clear the gospel message is—repeated over and over from one text to another. And it astonishes me that so many Catholics (including Pope Francis's adversaries) don't recognize the obvious message of Jesus: that God's love and mercy are so much greater than the law. Jesus constantly confronts the tendency of good religious people to think that they are God's special friends—not like all that riff-raff, the sinners, the pagans, the unclean, the outsiders. Christians of course have projected all this onto the Pharisees—when it is clear that this was all written in the early church as a warning against adopting such attitudes.

Well, obviously I read the gospels through a Pope Francis lens.

I pray that you are feeling better, with the reassuring echo of owls to keep you company.

————————

Were Sister Wendy's small heart attacks a signal "of that great encounter for which we so long"—or simply signs of a steady diminution of the quality of life? Either way, as she observed, "If heaven is here already, as I firmly believe, then there is not all that difference living or dying."

August 5, 2017

Dearest Robert,

I have no idea as to whether these small attacks are signals of that great encounter for which we so long. If they are just diminutions of the quality of life, they are blessed in that too. I can scarcely encompass the joy of being in Jesus and receiving His love; in fact, I can't encompass it, I am speechless and conceptless, and yet aware. So if heaven is here already, as I firmly believe, then there is not all that difference living or dying, as St. Paul says, whether we live or we die, we are the Lord's.

Happy feast [of the Transfiguration] tomorrow when we celebrate that Truth in its fullness! I think that Jesus was probably transfigured whenever He prayed, which may be why He prayed in solitude. This time He brought three apostles with Him and they saw the luminous presence of His divinity. How hard it must have been for Him not to show the transfiguring presence always of His closeness to the Father in the Holy Spirit.

Much love, dearest Robert, and love to your precious Monica,
Sister Wendy

————————

August 6, 2017

Dearest Sister Wendy,

I am of course moved by the peace and equanimity with which you face the future. It would be a surprising shame if one who had spent her whole life preparing for union with Christ were apprehensive as the encounter approached. Nevertheless, it is strange that we can believe deeply in something that is beyond our comprehension. To me I think it comes down to a certain trust. I have had such experience of God's presence in my life that it seems reasonable to believe that this will continue even in death. In my book I wrote about Henri Nouwen's observations from studying the circus acrobats, especially the trust that the flying trapeze artists place in their "catcher"—the one who really does the hard work. "Dying," he wrote, is "trusting the Catcher."

Or I think of my mother, who was not learned about theology but spent much time reflecting on things she heard in Sunday sermons, such as the priest who said that when he works up in the attic his dog waits expectantly at the door. He is not allowed to go to the attic. He has never been there. But he desires to go there, "just because he knows that I am there." My mother had a great love for her dogs, and she could relate to this story.

———

Sister Wendy continued making the effort to "use words and thoughts" as long as I wanted to hear them.

August 8, 2017

Dearest Robert,

I was thinking today how nothing seems to matter except the total inner centrality of God. That's true life, as it were. Outside this inner depth are the other things in my life—reading about God and thinking about Him. But they're peripheral, and I was feeling I really do not want to bother with words and thoughts anymore. Then I remembered the Mass. Here we have words and thoughts and a disturbance of my solitude because I have to get there. Even if Mass were said in my room, there would still be this invasion; and yet the holiness of the Mass, its mystical power, is so infinitely greater than my own personal union with God. In fact, I would not be able to live in this union were it not for the mystical power of the Mass. So if words and thoughts are inescapable there, I have no right to let my human weakness withdraw from this outer protection, as it were, of reading and thinking. We must make the effort.

I think in old age one feels too weary to take trouble, and yet taking trouble, as you know, was what the Curé d'Ars [St. John Vianney] thought of as the essence of our response to God. I'm sure he was right. And that the distinction between fatigue and laziness is tenuous. So, my conclusion, dear Robert, is that I'll go on using words and thoughts as long as you want to hear them.

Lovingly,
Sister Wendy

I sent Sister Wendy a copy of a very impressive document, including Latin headings and official stamps, representing my appointment to the "Historical Commission" charged with preparing Dorothy Day's cause for canonization. As I noted, "It is exciting to have such an impressive document. All it lacks is some sealing wax and a ribbon, and that is easily rectified."

August 12, 2017

Dearest Robert,

I am in awe. When the religious awe has slightly receded I think my main emotion would be of great sympathy. You're unfortunate in that your own special Servant of God wrote so much and was written to so much and written about so much. Dearest Robert, where will you find the time to do all this searching? I hope the other three on the committee are gentlemen of leisure and can take most of the burden off your all-too-willing shoulders. Tell Monica she must prevent you from volunteering, by force if necessary. Should she buy handcuffs? But of course I am very happy for the honor and for what it will lead to. It doesn't matter for Dorothy herself all that much, but it will bring her powerfully before the world and she has so much to give.

Lovingly,
Sister Wendy

Sister Wendy described a particularly remarkable dream of her own.

August 25, 2017

Dearest Robert,

I don't have the exciting narrative dreams that you have, but I did have a beautiful dream early this week. It was really in three parts. First I was looking at magnificent pictures of lakes, then I was actually walking beside these lakes, seeing them in their full reality, and then the lakes were inside me. I was containing the lakes. But the significant point is that when I was walking beside the lakes I realized that there was something wrong. The lakes were being damaged, poisoned perhaps, and it was my great sorrow over this and my desire to purify them that carried me into the third stage. Because in my own self the lakes were being changed and purified. I suppose this is an image of what being a Christian means. In Jesus we take the whole wounded world into ourselves and suffer with it, holding it out all the time to His holiness. So you see this was a deep and beautiful dream, a dream that enlarged me and made me feel a part of His redemptive suffering, which of course is true of all of us. That's why we live still and don't flit off to heaven: His lakes need us.

So dearest Robert, with my love and prayer,
Sister Wendy

————

August 25, 2017

Dearest Sister Wendy,

The account of your dream is truly extraordinary. It would be wonderful if it were just the transition from seeing a painting of a lake, to seeing the actual lake, to realizing that the lake is inside of you. That would appear to describe the powers of insight, imagination, and compassionate empathy that you have brought to your apostolate of beauty. But then you take it to a completely different level when your contemplative eye becomes a kind of healing filter, purifying the pollution and healing the suffering of the earth. As you say, this could not be a more profound description of the Christian vocation. If it were appropriate to award points for a dream, I would say, "Well played, Sister Wendy!" I am speechless with admiration!

I am feeling reasonably well. Although it is true, as you say, that I am older than I was ten years ago (as are we all!), I actually feel that there is little comparison with my actual vitality and enjoyment of life. Ten years ago I felt more like King Lear—"bound upon a wheel of fire, on which my own tears doth scald me." I remember an occasion in which, following a trip to the emergency room with my daughter, a nurse asked me if I felt suicidal, and I said, "No, not literally. I just feel that if I died right now that would be ok." At the time, I was writing a book about happiness! That is probably what kept me going.

I could not have imagined that I had such peace and happiness to look forward to. God is so good.

———————

August 26, 2017

Dearest Robert,

Thank you for so sensitively and powerfully entering into the mystery of my dream. I think the player here was not me but God, don't you?

I can see how relatively blissful your life is, despite health and work troubles, compared with ten years ago. Those agonizing years must have been a time of great grace; after all, it was then that you really understood what happiness is. As long as we think that happiness depends upon everything going well with us, we are living in a state of illusion. Once we grasp that Jesus is our happiness and He burns on irrespective of all that occurs, or rather burns brighter for all that occurs, then we can never be truly sad again.

I am reading a biography of Dietrich Bonhoeffer,[22] and I am at the point where he is beginning his real struggles with his church and his country. But I was astonished this morning to see that, with all his enlightenment, his first reaction, which he sustained for quite a bit, was to defend the Jewish Christian, not the Jew as such. I find it so helpful to discover how slowly grace percolates through the Spirit. We don't see all the implications of our faith in one glance, we suffer into it. Another thing that struck me this morning in Bonhoeffer was that he speaks in one place of the essentials being word, sacrament, and suffering. Not long afterwards he speaks of word, sacrament, and community. I know that suffering has infinite forms, but I think community will always bring suffering, even if it is low grade. We are such mysteries to one another, and to love and be loved is so important that no one can exist in truth without suffering from the presence of others. But we grow this way, we enter into the reality of Jesus this way, so it's all fruitful.

———————

22. Dietrich Bonhoeffer (d. 1945), a German Lutheran pastor and theologian, was executed by the Nazis for his part in an underground conspiracy against Hitler. His *Letters and Papers from Prison*, edited by his friend Eberhard Bethge, had an enormous influence on post-war theology.

I have of course read Bonhoeffer before, but this new and well-written biography reminds me (which I had quite forgotten) that I don't really take to him as a person. It makes me wonder with such love and awe at how God works patiently away at each of us, using our very weaknesses to get close to our hearts.

Time is up, dearest Robert, and energy is fading, but love remains as ever.

Sister Wendy

August 31, 2017

Dearest Sister Wendy,

I spent a couple of years long ago reading my way through Bonhoeffer. I agree that I never found him all that personally appealing. But he has always stood out as one of those paradigmatic religious figures of the twentieth century that interest me—those who struggled with the challenge of being faithful, when so many of the props and certitudes of the past seemed inadequate or suspect. I think the problem that Bonhoeffer was wrestling with is not so far removed from the challenge now in this age of Trump.

You write: "We are such mysteries to one another, and to love and be loved is so important that no one can exist in truth without suffering from the presence of others." I am thinking about this a lot as I try to write a review of Kate Hennessy's biography of Dorothy Day. We scarcely know one another, even those we love the most; we scarcely know ourselves.

While driving my daughter Catherine to the airport on her way back to Paris, we had a very deep conversation, reflecting on all the "chances" or interventions of grace that have guided our lives, both mine and hers. She is finally more open to recognizing this. In the past she tended to focus more on the failures, the things that didn't come through as planned, the sufferings she has experienced. Now she sees more clearly how all these things were guiding her on her path, opening up new possibilities—and all the people who helped her along the way, whether she recognized it at the time or not. I hope that she might come to be more trusting about life, and open to the presence of the Spirit.

I have been thinking about what you told me before, about the lessons in true happiness I learned while working on my book. As you note, I learned that happiness does not depend on circumstances. And that is a wonderful thing to contemplate, especially when you have no choice over your circumstances. Yes, you can be truly happy in a hospital, or a prison, or a difficult marriage. But here is what I have never known how to answer: How do you know when the right thing to do is to change your circumstances? There came a time when it seemed like the right thing for me to do—a matter of survival, really. And I tried to do that with as much integrity and care for the wellbeing of others as I could manage. I felt as if I was moving in the direction of truthfulness and authenticity, and I don't know anyone who didn't urge me to do that. But even though I feel deeply that this was the right thing to do, I didn't know exactly how to square it with the principles in my book.

I have been reading about "virtue ethics"—which distinguishes between a moral system that is all mathematical and precise—and one that allows for greater ambiguity, as one stumbles in the dark, trying to move in the direction of greater freedom, truth, goodness. (Bonhoeffer, of course, was trying to struggle with this in his *Ethics*, as he wrestled with participation in a plot to kill Hitler, even though this utterly violated his understanding of Jesus' moral teaching.)

I saw a movie called *Locke*. The whole thing takes place in a car on a motorway in England where the protagonist is driving all night to get to the hospital in London where a woman he slept with one night is about to have a baby. He has no particular connection with her—it was a very regrettable lapse. But now she is having a baby. He had promised her that he would be there when she gave birth, and now she has gone into premature labor. He is a very important contractor, and the next day he is supposed to be in charge of a huge construction project, a massive pouring of concrete. He spends the whole drive on the phone: with his boss, explaining that he won't be there (of course he is fired); his assistant (talking him through what needs to be done); his wife (with whom he must share the grave news about his transgression); his son; various other municipal authorities whose help he needs to arrange for the concrete delivery in the morning; the hysterical woman in the hospital and her doctors (to whom he must explain that no, he is not her husband, but yes, he is the father of the child). Within this completely fraught situation you see him trying to thread a needle, trying to do what seems like the right thing in relation to all the competing obligations he faces. And he also is contending with the ghost of his own terrible father, who was not there for him as a child—a memory that is goading him to try to do the right thing.

The old manuals don't really address such moral complexity.

And yet in the gospels, as I am writing my little reflections, I constantly see Jesus calling people out of their own morally ambiguous circumstances—not to condemn them, but to call them to grow in the direction of greater love, truth, freedom. And having to contend with the carping criticism of those who see everything in narrow legal boxes.

Well, I am still seeing things through a glass darkly. But soon I will at least see you face to face!

———————

Once again, Sister Wendy's wise support and understanding were deeply encouraging.

September 1, 2017

Dearest Robert,

Your gripping account of the film and your personal reflections on your marriage and your choices highlight for me the uniqueness and, I feel, the simplicity of these moral choices. It is so clear that Our Lord wants to free us from rules and complexities, while of course drawing us to a high standard of goodness. To me the answer has always been that if we pray and look at Him we need not fear our choices. Even if we look back and think that technically we made a bad choice, it was good in that we tried to do good. I think our body is a great ally here. You knew you had to get out of your marriage from the very pressures psychologically that were becoming overwhelming. I could say the same thing about my leaving Notre Dame for a life of prayer. I asked repeatedly, pleading that I actually needed more prayer. When I was refused, I was content, happy, because I was doing what God wanted.

It has been said to me that I must have been wretched when I had to struggle so hard to cope—a comment I heard with surprise. I always felt happy. But when it was obviously becoming too much physically, with fits and heart trouble, the doctor's verdict to my superiors freed me to come to Quidenham. If I had just walked out because I felt I needed it, I would always have been uneasy about selfishness. As it happened, I clung on happily to God until the permission came.

You didn't have a superior's permission, but your body and mind played the same part. You knew for survival what you had to do. I think these decisions are always basically of that simplicity. They may be painful and we may desire greater clarity, but both circumstances and emotions put before us the choice of action that God wants. I don't think one can rely on this security unless one prays and wants to please God. The happy freedom, the deep, wise hilaritas of the Gospels (a term that Bonhoeffer likes), is what Our Lord teaches us—not a network of rules and prohibitions. Your man in the film is in an impossible position with so many conflicting claims. But there's a simple heroism in his attempt to meet them, and it's that attempt that God makes possible. He makes it possible even for the implicit anonymous Christian. It's the grace that comes to all of good will.

I find that I am degenerating quite appreciably, especially with regard to hearing. So when you come and we have a few minutes together, don't be surprised if I have to use sign language. This deafness is very new and it's especially inhibiting when it's a person I don't know and a voice I don't know. If I concentrate I can hear Lesley, but I don't always concentrate. When you come I will promise to concentrate, but I can't promise that the sounds proceeding from your lips reach me with any meaningful content. Perhaps we're just meant to wave at each other, who knows?

Very much love dear Robert,
Sister Wendy

September 1, 2017

Dearest Sister Wendy,

Please don't worry about your encroaching deafness. Through our letters we have been able to understand one another perfectly well. I would be happy to sit quietly in your presence and look out the window together, or look at the pictures I would like to share with you.

My daughter Catherine today sent me a video of a father and daughter (in England) talking about what it was like for their family to go through the terrible ordeal of anorexia. I was deeply moved, because of course it brought back vivid memories. I asked Catherine if some day she might feel comfortable with me writing about this experience, and she said yes.

Twice I have spoken about it when I was giving retreats, and both times people came up to me in tears to tell me that they had been through this with a sister or daughter. The film ends with their meeting with Prince William. I know you are not a fan of his mother, but they talked about her bravery in speaking about her own experience with an eating disorder, and the importance of bringing such things out of the shadows and into the light. I don't think anyone who has not been through this can really understand what it is like. The only comparable thing I can point to is the stories in the gospels where Jesus encounters people possessed by evil spirits.

Thank you for listening so attentively, and your ability to hear everything so clearly.

I had shared excerpts from the book I was compiling of Pope Francis's words to young people, The Courage to Be Happy.[23] *I also described an article by conservative Cardinal Robert Sarah, condemning the work of my friend Fr. James Martin for his efforts to build a bridge between the church and the LGBTQ community.*

September 4, 2017

Dearest Robert,

I start this email immediately after reading your email, so I am still awed and rejoiced by the deep-felt sincerity and love of the Truth that our beloved Holy Father so communicates. We may well have had popes as holy as he, but none have come anywhere near his power of communication.

I'm quite distressed about poor Cardinal Sarah's tunnel vision. Wouldn't you agree that the great need of the contemporary church is to rethink and go far more deeply into the theology of sexuality? The official attitudes are still those of past centuries when the mystery of what it means to be a sexual creature was not understood.

It is bliss to be in my own chair with fresh air from the window blowing gently on me, and no extraordinary exertions called upon until a small exertion crops up on Monday. Our doctor is coming to see me but only, I think, about the absence in my body of potassium which seems to worry her. One only has to mention lack of potassium and everybody shouts out "bananas!" I find this a difficult fruit to eat because it is so bulky. Fortunately the National Health list of potassium-rich foods, gives ten, with "banana" at the bottom. At the top are foods much easier to eat, at least for me, like white mushrooms and spinach and salmon—not all that easy to get these things, of course, but Sister Lesley is trying. Your own physical tribulations are far more significant.

Very much love from a depleted but still surviving,
Sister Wendy

———

September 4, 2017

Dearest Sister Wendy,

By this time I hope you have survived your doctor's visit. If she has prescribed you nothing more than a good diet of spinach, salmon, and

---

23. Pope Francis, *The Courage to Be Happy: The Pope Speaks to the Youth of the World*, ed. Robert Ellsberg (Maryknoll, NY: Orbis Books, 2018).

mushrooms (and the occasional banana!), then you will pretty much conform to my ideal diet. Monica would hasten to add cabbage and kale,
which she eats every day for breakfast.

Dorothy Day also had low potassium—so you share that debility. She
too rebelled against the bananas everybody tried to foist on her.

I read a most beautiful article in the paper today. Young people are
drawn to the desire to be famous, to leave a great mark on the world, to per-
form extraordinary deeds. But this was about how it is possible to have a life
full of meaning, even if it leaves a mark on only a small number of people
around us. It focused in particular on George Eliot's *Middlemarch*, and how
Dorothea Brooke emerges as a true heroine—not fulfilling all the grand
dreams she had once envisioned, but in her quiet acts of friendship, service,
and devotion. It quoted the passage: "For the growing good of the world is
partly dependent on unhistoric acts; and that things are not so ill with you
and me as they might have been, is half owing to the number who lived
faithfully a hidden life, and rest in unvisited tombs."

I quoted that passage at the end of *The Saints' Guide*. And it is actually
the passage that inspired the title of a forthcoming film about Franz Jägerstätter, *A Hidden Life*.

I have the example of my father, of course, who has left such a great
mark on the world—and yet who always reproaches himself for not having
done more. And then there was my mother, who seemed to occupy a very
circumscribed world. And yet it was astonishing to see the love she inspired
in so many people: the mailman, for whom she always saved the sports section from the paper; her dog walker; the Mexican gardener who was so worried that she would be alone on Christmas that he brought his whole family
to deliver tamales.

It is much harder to write about people like that, unless you know them
very well—and we all know such people. I worry that in writing so much
about extraordinary figures it can make people feel that they could never be
like that, any more than they could paint like Cezanne. Reading the Gospels
is helpful, because it is clear we are not called to be prodigies or geniuses,
whether in the spiritual life or any other realm. Just to be merciful and forgiving: such ordinary virtues! With opportunities at hand every day to exercise them. Or as Micah says, "to act justly, love tenderly, and walk humbly
with God."

———————

September 5, 2017

Dearest Robert,

The thing about the diet of spinach, mushrooms, and salmon is where it's going to come from. I get my vegetables from the community dinner, and I can't ask the busy sister-cook to do special things for me. Bananas, unfortunately, I can acquire. Even more unfortunately, when the doctor told me about this potassium problem, she said she didn't want to give me medication because it had such very unpleasant side-effects. I'm hoping that she hasn't got to backtrack on this but we'll see.

Meanwhile your state of health does not fill me with confidence. Quite apart from these tests you keep having to have, there's your feeling of fatigue, which would be unknown to a vigorous young man like you. Well, we are both in God's hands and happy so to be. I'm very encouraged to share anything with Dorothy, even a potassium deficiency!

I should have opened this letter by telling you of my great joy and gratitude in receiving your Franciscan book on Saturday. It has a lovely cover and still more lovely contents, it's a beautiful book. I particularly like the last entrances, those modern and contemporary saints who have lived the life that we are living. Many of them are not people of extraordinary achievement; in fact I think one of your gifts is to highlight people like your mother, quiet people who loved.

I think it's a certain lightness of spirit that characterizes the Franciscans, a charm that the wonderful Mother Teresa doesn't have, though of course she has her own quality of very great spiritual beauty. I also noticed that some of your saints are intimately shaped by their Franciscan vocation whereas with others it seems more a shelter in which they developed. A fascinating book.

Very much love, dearest Robert, and a sigh of sympathy at the thought of Monica's breakfasts,

Sister Wendy

––––––––

As the date of our trip to Quidenham approached, Sister Wendy repeatedly tried to curb my expectations, warning me of her deafness and lack of energy, the disappointing landscape, her own general dullness.

September 7, 2017

Dearest Robert,

When you come to Quidenham I'm afraid you will find the walks rather disappointing. You clearly live in an area of great natural beauty. I think Quidenham is beautiful too but it's green and calm and uneventful—a good setting for a contemplative convent, but with no great views. Not long now until you come!

The doctor has been and will be coming again and the nurse is coming this week to take more blood. It's the effect that lack of potassium has on the heart that is important, I gather. She heard creaking in the lungs which could be the fibrosis or could be the effect of the weakening heart, but I don't myself think there's any dramatic change. I expect to be completely here when you come. Though whether I'll be completely here in terms of energy is another matter.

More and more I can see the centrality of the cross in our lives, and how the very symbol of the cross is barren unless we see it as the suffering Jesus. And that image of Jesus crucified is so fundamental to our Christian lives and so antipathetic to our natural instincts that we cannot love it and cleave to it enough.

I think in my youth I took Jesus crucified for granted, the prelude to Jesus risen. I looked more at what He had done for us on the cross than what it actually meant personally and psychologically. But there's no holiness without it, is there? A taking up of His cross is the only way to follow Him. How well and how simply Dorothy knew this—all the saints, I suppose, but her letters and her diaries involve us in the reality of what this means. We owe these precious volumes to you, dearest Robert. Your lives of the saints are magnificent, but perhaps your editing of Dorothy's work is even more significant.

Much love,
Sister Wendy

———

I had described for Sister Wendy my growing awareness of the spiritual dimensions of editorial work: "Lots of people can effectively wield a red pencil. But the challenge of working effectively with a range of authors—with all their sensitivities, neuroses, fragile egos—is something one must learn." Lessons I was still learning.

September 9, 2017

Dearest Robert,

Your vocation, such a unique but profound one, is all the more beautiful if you did not in fact have a natural attrait to this sort of creative sensitivity. I have seen from your letters the way in which you take command, so subtly and sweetly that it is imperceptible. I just wish that your God-given gift could reach a wider readership. It really hurts me when you say that so and so wrote a wonderful book but it didn't sell. That seems to me all part of the world as it is; after all, Our Blessed Lord had no outside advantages in getting His message across. It could well be also that some of your greatest books have a long future ahead of them and may come to be seen for what they are long after our own time.

I write to you with another sixth of a banana sitting heavily within me. I have a great appetite in theory and can get very excited about the thought of food; it's just that when it actually comes I can't eat much of it. Before I came to live here in the monastery itself I could get away with all this, but now Sister Lesley brings me the plate and takes away the plate, and I've no plant at hand into which I can drop what I can't get through. Mind you, she's a very non-critical sister and very rarely makes comments. This is one of the things I love her for. I feel I'm slowly dissolving and hope there will be enough left at least to wave at you when you come.

We had a great pleasure at the end of Mass today. One of the sisters has a friend who is an opera singer and he sang Schubert's "Ave Maria" in the sanctuary. This was a double treat because Schubert is my favorite composer and because this beautiful prayer was sung after Mass. It always grieves me when there is music and singing during Mass. The Mass takes up all our attention for what it is, and I feel we have to step out of the Mass, as it were, to listen to this praise of God that is so beautiful and yet apart from the great divine action of the Mass. But before or after is splendid.

Music is a rare delight for me and that is how I choose it to be. I have a lot of other little pleasures which I think God gives me, e.g., detective stories or a glass of wine. Music is a far deeper joy than these, but I have always felt that this was too great a pleasure to fit into my vocation. After all, asceticism means denying yourself what isn't necessary or would intrude, but when God gives the pleasure, as He did this morning, oh alleluia!

Very much love,
Sister Wendy

———————

September 10, 2017

Dearest Sister Wendy,

I heard a beautiful interview with the Irish poet John O'Donohue, where he talked about how marvelous it is to see someone who is ideally matched with the kind of work they are meant to do. Apropos of your comments on music, he also spoke of his love of music and its ability to convey beauty. He said, "I think music is what language would like to be."

Dorothy Day certainly lived a life of asceticism—in enduring the noise, dirt, chaos, and disorder that came with opening her home to the poor and so many hurt and broken people. But she had a great love of beauty, especially in nature. How she loved to get away to her little bungalow on the beach in Staten Island! And music: she loved opera. Every Saturday she listened to the opera broadcast on the radio.

Hoping that every day, in every way, bananas are making you better.

––––––––––

After describing a short-lived, but agonizing ailment, which had the benefit of causing me to cancel a trip to Chicago, I recounted a final drama with my father's memoir, involving, of all things, some misunderstanding regarding the acknowledgments. This had a very wonderful outcome.

September 14, 2017

Dearest Robert,

What vast halls of experience you have walked through in these last few days. First you had that intense and mysterious pain, which must have so undermined you, it even led you to cancel your plane trip to Chicago, and I don't think that withdrawing from work is characteristic of you, is it? It seems so typical of God to lead you into the profound experience with your father at a time when you were physically weakened. I think this made the encounter all the more significant because you did not have the usual defenses that the healthy body offers.

Your last email contained the beautiful recognition by several authors of what you had done for them; now the author who above all matters to you has been inspired to express a truly meaningful recognition. This is a kind of "rest in peace" moment for you both. You have done it, he has seen it, he has expressed his gratitude and affection, his need of you and your coming to meet that need with such generosity. Very few parents and children can have such an explicit statement as to what was needed and what was given. Usually it's the other way around: it's the parent who gives and the child who thanks. Well, that is still true here because he has given the fruit of an intense and sacrificial life and you have thanked him by helping him bring it into book form. But the emotional interchange is even lovelier in its humility and openness. So these have been wonderful days for you, dear Robert. And perhaps the pain opened the doors even wider than they would have been so that you could move through into this fulfillment.

So, I rejoice with you, dear Robert, and hope you will be better soon, physically.

Lovingly,
Sister Wendy

September 14, 2017

Dearest Sister Wendy,

As usual you state things with total clarity and such compassionate understanding. Thank you. I did have a great feeling of "rest in peace" yesterday.

It is true, as you say, that few parents and children have an opportunity to say what needs to be said—and after one has died, the survivor carries the burden of regret. Of course that is part of the value of faith, and the knowledge that our relationships can grow and heal.

I have no such regrets with my mother. We both were able to say everything that needed to be said. She, in particular, always felt that she had not been a good enough mother—which was ridiculous. But I was able to tell her that she was the best mother in the world, which was true. And I think she was able to let go and move on without any sense of unfinished business. What a great blessing!

September 15, 2017

Dearest Robert,

You made me think of my parents with whom I did not have a final expression of love. But it never seemed to me to matter. I did love them, and I knew that my parents would have made any sacrifice for the good of their children. I never felt the necessity to say any of this and still feel quite happy with the knowledge that in the love of God, Love itself, they now have complete awareness of my affection for them. But this is in the context of somebody called to the hermit life. For the normal human being, like everybody else, I think these explicit acknowledgments are very important, and I thank God for you.

　　With prayer and joy and love,
　　Sister Wendy

―――――

September 16, 2017

Dearest Robert,

　　First of all Sr. Lesley's absence: the English Carmels are in the process of voting in a new president of the Association and each Carmel is sending their prioress and an elected representative. I feel a reflected glory in that Lesley has been elected as our representative.

　　I am sure there are as many people consumed with love of God today as there have been at any time in history. It's so encouraging to get these little glimpses of what goes on in the secret of the heart. I know I'm often humbled and awed by what I see of the sisters here, and that could be multiplied many times throughout the world.

　　I have recently been made painfully aware of my limitations by my answer to an appeal for help by a sister in which I hurt her. I am still convinced that she needed to face up to a truth that she was smoothing over, but how badly I did it. If it had been done well this beautiful woman would have accepted what I said. Knowing that one has failed is a great grace I think, because it opens us up to our infinite need for Our Blessed Lord. The more He can give Himself to me, the more there is for other people, especially those I have failed. So this sorrow is a joy which I think should be true of all sorrows.

　　With love to you and Monica, and with respectful congratulations to your father on completing his book,

　　　Sister Wendy

―――――

October 10, 2017

Dearest Sister Wendy,

　　On Sunday I spoke at a program organized by Pax Christi, the Catholic peace organization, in New York. Martha Hennessy, one of Dorothy's granddaughters, and I were asked to speak about DD and peace. I woke up that day to see how many football players had joined a growing protest against racial injustice by dropping to one knee during the playing of the national anthem. Their numbers were swollen by Trump's having sent out a crude call for owners to have them thrown out of the game.

I spoke about how Dorothy used to kneel in church when the national anthem was played. I said there was more than one way to "take a knee"—as she did when she sat outdoors in protest of compulsory civil defense drills during the 1950s. Loving your country and loving your church means knowing when to kneel, when to stand, when to sit still, and when to march.

I offered an update on the campaign of vilification against Fr. Jim Martin, SJ, because of his efforts to promote dialogue between the church and the gay community.

October 3, 2017

Dearest Robert,

Thank you for encapsulating the state of play in your life at the moment. I can give you in return no summing up of my state because it's always the same. I'm not all that well but I'm functioning, and nothing really happens except the stray hornet or the stray spill or slight mishap. The big events or at least the ones one can talk about, are books, which is both your world and a pointer to more than your world. I shall certainly be here and alive when you come. Can it really be next month?! But please have the lowest possible ex-

Father James Martin, SJ

pectations about me. I shall certainly come to the parlor to see you, but it may not last long and you may be taken aback by how dull I am. I don't think these things matter very much, and I don't think a face-to-face encounter matters very much. Our friendship is in our exchange of letters where it is something real and deep and a great gift from God.

The thing that struck me most in your letter was what you said about Fr. Jim. His career has become such a progression of ever-escalating success that I have trembled a little for him. This upwelling of prejudice is a very great grace for him. It will hurt him and unsettle him because one can't but feel that behind his pleasure in his success is a great insecurity. But this is where the Lord is in His holy cross. Again and again, Jesus spells out that suffering, opposition, persecution, and grief are blessed. We find it so difficult to see the cross as anything but horrible. Indeed it is horrible, and Jesus was the first to show it as such, but it is by taking up that cross that we follow Him, and only by taking up that cross.

My beloved St. Elizabeth of the Trinity said that a Carmelite was one who gazed on Jesus crucified. I think that's true of all of us. Unless we open our arms to the suffering Jesus we can never live in the joy of the risen Jesus. To quote St. Elizabeth again, "In this life, joy and suffering go side by side." So this is a wonderful thing for Fr. Jim, and it has the great distinction of being a parallel to what's happening to our beloved Pope Francis. Isn't it baffling that these holy sticklers for the law can't see the close resemblance to Jesus' adversaries in the gospels? "They will not lift a finger" to remove the burdens.

I hope the Holy Father goes into print about all this. Obviously he can't help the hundreds of thousands who have escaped from a disastrous early marriage and are technically bound to refrain from the sacrament. I say he can't help them because it would clearly divide the church. But it will surely come now that there is the Pope and others who see that Jesus would never drive away from His table those who want Him, but are unable to discard obligations of love to other people. At least we've got a beginning of wisdom here. Thank God for the Pope. Thank God, too, that he will accept fully the pain of the criticism; and I hope seeing the Holy Father's love for our Blessed Lord will help Fr. Jim.

Very much love,
Sister Wendy

―――――――

October 7, 2017

Dearest Robert,

The effect of our lives on the lives of other people is something very real, though it is something that I cannot put into effective words. I suppose St. Paul comes the nearest to explaining this mystery when he speaks of the Church as a body, and that if one part hurts, all the body hurts. Equally bliss in part, think of sunlight shining on the skin or the joys of a good meal or a good sleep or a good read, and how the whole body rejoices in it. We are the goodness that God is giving His Body, the Church. It is His goodness not ours; but we have to be ever attentive to receive it from Him so that we don't deprive our fellow members of the joy that is their due.

How are you going to come to Quidenham, car or train? I hope your time here is one of great happiness, which will add to your lovely memories of England. I've no doubt that you will be impressed by, and drawn to, the community here. There are many strong minded individualists, but they are united in a genuine and sometimes painful desire to give God everything. As you say about the saints, different sisters are at different stages, but they're all moving.

I can hardly believe you'll be here next month, dearest Robert. Let's hope we get all our rain in October.

Lovingly,
Sister Wendy

_____

October 9, 2017

Dearest Robert,

One's heart aches for America with all these natural disasters seeming to underline the central political disaster. But I think to myself that the way towards integrity is often a way of suffering, and this may be the best thing for the country. Anyway it's in God's hands and we can only pray.

I'm reading a book about Merton, which includes reflections by Fr. John Eudes Bamberger, who of course knew Merton as a friend, as a fellow priest, and as a psychiatrist. Fr. John Eudes says that Merton was incapable of solitude, and, in fact, his living alone meant that his worst instincts went unfettered. He quotes a letter he wrote to Merton telling him that picnics and excursions were absolutely wrong for a monk. I would have liked more of a discussion of the internal conflict within this exceptional writer, because Merton seemed to have the need to think he wanted solitude, even if he couldn't cope with it when he got it.

I must say it's not an easy thing to be a genius, especially a genius in a religious order. I've never wanted to be an artist or a creator of any kind, though there is possibly laziness in that frame of mind as well as apprehension. But, fortunately, God gives us burdens that He enables us to carry. I love to think how often He tells us, do not be afraid. I say that to myself for you too, with your heavy burdens.

Very much love,
Sister Wendy

_____

October 18, 2017

Dearest Sister Wendy,

I have been out of touch, what with our trip to Boston for my fortieth class reunion at Harvard. Naturally, Monica, the extrovert, made many more new friends, with whom she is already exchanging messages.

I wonder if you have ever been to the Fogg Museum at Harvard? It has been beautifully refurbished since I was last there, and I was truly overwhelmed by the magnificence of their collection—especially their stunning medieval art. I was struck by a thirteenth-century painting of St. Dominic, a beautiful bust of Christ, a life-size Pietà carved from wood. There was a very striking apparition of the head of John the Baptist appearing to Salome, and some amazing pre-Raphaelite paintings, one of the "triumphant Holy Innocents"—a crowd of joyous infants capering around the Holy Family on their way to Egypt; baby Moses with shocks of fire flying from his head; beautiful Chinese screens; two Van Goghs—a self-portrait, and his painting of peasant boots....

We also visited the Harvard Museum of Natural History, which features the famous display of "glass flowers"—though not really my cup of tea.

It was a very beautiful drive through the changing New England foliage. But I was glad to get back Sunday night.

—————

A surprising turning point arrived in Sister Wendy's estimation of Thomas Merton!

October 19, 2017

Dearest Robert,

As I continue to reflect on Merton, I'm beginning to feel that my categories have been too limited, that Merton overflows all normal regulations and is a complete one-off. I still wish he could have toed the moral line more faithfully, even if it is only the morality of holiness as opposed to that of simple virtue. I'm not referring to his affair with "M," which was a kind of breakdown I think, but his criticism of the abbot and other monks. A lot is made of that great mystical breakthrough at the corner of Walnut Street when he saw all humanity luminous with God and felt complete reverence for everybody. He may well have felt that for the world, but he doesn't treat or speak of his brothers with that loving reverence. I think these and other unloving attitudes are just the detritus, the sparks flying off from his great involvement in God and His world, and I think I have made far too much of them. All the same, he has so much to give and he, in fact, gives so much that one longs for him to give everything.

Very much love to both of you,
Sister Wendy

In a P.S. from Sister Lesley, she informed me that "Sister Wendy had a painful 'heart event.' She chose not to have an ambulance called, but simply waited it out. She took some medication, but the pain was quite severe and the whole event has left her very tired and foggy. She is much better today, and I think she will continue to regain strength, but I wanted to let you know so you could keep her in your prayers. Thank you again for your correspondence with her; it helps her 'think' and perks her up a lot—but don't feel obligated!"

———

October 20, 2017

Dearest Sister Wendy,

I am very touched by your ongoing and ever-evolving relationship with Thomas Merton. Perhaps it is part of the monastic vocation to strive for simplicity—or perhaps purity of heart ("to will one thing"), and Merton was irreducibly complex. And yet it is hard to imagine another setting in which his particular gifts could have borne such great fruit. As a parish priest, a professor, an intellectual, a chaplain, a writer—as a husband? He struggled and chafed against the restrictions of his life, and yet this friction provided some of the energy that fueled his creative genius. Now, you could say, a monk has no business worrying about creative genius. Perhaps true enough—and so it is perhaps best, as you say, that he was a "one-off"—he was Merton. He himself rebelled against being made into a poster boy for the monastic life or for any other ideal. He was Jonah—being carried to his destination by the Providence of God, in a vehicle not entirely of his choosing. Anyway, it shows great humility on your part to suppose that "perhaps my categories have been too limited."

I loved what you said about the Body of Christ. A wonderful subject for meditation. I did not sleep well last night, and I hope that the rest of the Body was not unduly disturbed.

———

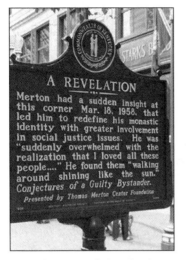

A REVELATION

Merton had a sudden insight at
this corner Mar. 18, 1958, that
led him to redefine his monastic
identity with greater involvement
in social justice issues. He was
"suddenly overwhelmed with the
realization that I loved all these
people...." He found them "walking
around shining like the sun."
Conjectures of a Guilty Bystander.
Presented by Thomas Merton Center Foundation

*Sign on the corner of 4th and Walnut
in Louisville, KY*

*Sister Wendy's new assessment of Thomas
Merton was no simple matter of changing
her mind. It seemed to reflect a deeper
reevaluation of her own long-standing
judgments and categories, an opening out
of her own "narrow and selfish mind."
Was it possible that in her own way she
was recapitulating Merton's famous insight
"at the corner of 4th and Walnut," which
he described as "waking from a dream of
separateness, of spurious isolation and
supposed holiness"? As she approached
the end of her life, it seemed as if Sister
Wendy was continuing to grow in self-
knowledge, in solidarity with humanity,
and trust in the mercy of God.*

October 22, 2017

Dearest Robert,

The rest of the Body was holding you up to God when you had your bad
night, and so it always will be. It's taken me a long time to understand that
there is no solitary Christian. For many years I could only see Our Blessed
Lord as my world and nobody else, not just the far-away nameless masses in
China and South America, but even the people I knew and loved didn't really
matter all that much. I prayed for them in the abstract, as it were. But over
the years Our Lord has taught me how united we all are in Him, that we
praise in Him in Holy Communion and pray in Him always. So through His
goodness He has opened out my narrow little selfish mind and made me
aware of what He has always been conscious of, the solidarity of humanity.

More and more I do see the paradox of Merton's needing Gethsemani
and the great wisdom of Abbot James' treatment of him and the impossibil-
ity of his living the life of an ordinary Cistercian monk. I'm wary of what he
says about not wanting fame or significance, because I think he did. He can
take one's breath away by his innocent assertions of his own extreme importance to monasticism, and, in fact, to ecumenism, let alone political wisdom
in the States. But there is a sense in which what he says is right, and why
should he not be conscious of this? Every now and again he feels that this is
unseemly and makes swatting movements, but they never last. It is his general thrust, his search for God on multiple levels of personality and experience that make him so riveting to read.

I feel it is only common sense for me to admit what I should have seen long ago, that I am just too small and conventional a person to understand how the wrongness of much of his activity was a sort of off-flow from the rightness. Strangely, I think to some extent the abbot did recognize this. I don't think he ever understood the extent to which Merton ignored his religious commitments, but there's a great truth in what Merton says towards the end: that he doesn't think the abbot minds what he does, as long as he stays in Gethsemani. I think it was meant as a disparaging remark but in actual fact it's a wise one. I think the abbot had understood that Merton simply overflowed all categories, but that as long as he had a stable base, he could be stabilized. It was a blessing that he died when he did, because the new abbot was far too unaware of Merton's innate incapacity to be confined within monasticism, however genuine his desire.

Lovingly,
Sister Wendy

––––––––

October 22, 2017

Dearest Sister Wendy,

I am very touched that you share such confidences about your own spiritual journey. Perhaps in your life you don't have a lot of people to share such thoughts with—and perhaps that is how you like it. Though I live in a very different world, it means a lot to me to be able to share so much about my inner and outer life with you. One of the things that draws me close to Monica is that she is one of the few people I have ever known who truly does strive to examine everyday events and encounters in terms of the spiritual life—trying to learn from experience and always striving to do better. This affords endless subjects for discussion, but also a capacity for silence.

What you say about the Body of Christ, and feeling more connected to the rest of the world, is an idea that was very dear to Dorothy Day. I wondered whether she got this, to some extent, from dear St. Therese, who believed so strongly that her little prayers, sacrifices, and acts of devotion, might literally hold up others in Indochina and around the globe. So Therese was named a patron of Mission. Dorothy believed strongly in this. And I think the progress you have made here has its own counterpart in Merton's capacity to see that Solitude ultimately led to Compassionate engagement with the rest of humanity. Maybe that increase in a sense of solidarity is linked to your own increasing capacity for compassionate understanding of dear Merton!

Holiness comes in so many forms—because I think our path to God has to contend with our very individual personalities, our strengths and particularly our weaknesses. I suppose a very deft abbot or spiritual director realizes this. And I wonder whether in the history of religious life there has too often been a "cookie cutter" approach that sees human nature as basically the same, and needing to be trimmed and shaped to match some predetermined pattern. Maybe I'm wrong.

But Merton was obviously a very special case, and a wise abbot knew when it was time to pull on the rope and when to relax it. For all their tussles, Abbot Fox obviously had great regard and respect for Merton; he made him his own confessor! And after his retirement, he imitated Merton in becoming a hermit. I heard that when he heard of Merton's death he was stricken, and said if he had known this would happen, he never would have resigned as abbot. I found that very poignant.

———

October 27, 2017

Dearest Sister Wendy,

As it turns out, in preparation for my talk next weekend at Yale on Merton and Nouwen, I was reading Nouwen's final journal, and the account of his fatal heart attack in Holland. He was only 64, but he took terrible care of himself. I chose as a title for this talk, "The home where I have never been"—from a line from Merton's *Asian Journal*, in which he wrote that he sensed that in undertaking this journey he was "going to the home where I have never been." Of course in his case, and for Nouwen—on his "sabbatical journey"—they were going toward their deaths, both from heart attacks. And this fills me with worry about you, which I know you will dismiss. Please eat your bananas, avoid riotous living, and conserve your energy until I get there!

I had a deep conversation with my daughter Christina last night. She is applying to Union Theological Seminary, as I may have told you—interested in ethics and particularly care for the animal world. In her application, which she shared with me, she said, "I love the saints, and I love my Pope." I was so touched that she said, "my Pope." She said that it was truly a life-changing experience when I got her a ticket to go with us to see Pope Francis at Madison Square Garden. She was so moved when he simply said, "Pray for me."

———

October 28, 2017

Dearest Robert,

Of course the high-point of your letter is Christina's "my Pope." A father must long to have his children live by the richness of what he has been given by God. So your letter has been a very great joy this morning.

My little heart attack, one of a small series, is nothing like the massive invasions that carried off Nouwen and, electrically, Merton. All they really do is give me a chance to accept some pain in union with Our Lord and the days of diminished energy. I hope very much that my energy levels will have risen before you come.

I love the very thought of a monastery, though I did not expect that I would end my days within one. It was life on the outskirts that I so cherished, able to walk up the drive to share in the liturgical riches, but then retreat to my little trailer in the woods. When I first came to Quidenham in 1970 I used to go to nearly all the offices until it struck me that actually all I really wanted was Holy Mass, and that I was far more drawn to praying in solitude and sharing emotionally in the liturgy than joining it physically. That, of course, is still true. I only leave my room in the wheelchair for Mass, though I am pumping up the energy for your visit in November.

Meanwhile, happy birthday to your beloved Monica.

Lovingly,
Sister Wendy

––––––––––

Perhaps to test her newfound appreciation for Merton, I offered critical remarks of my own. But she didn't take the bait. As she would reply: "The more I have come to see through the inconsistencies that are so frequent, and realize that he is not inconsistent in wanting God, the less upset I have become by his failures."

October 28, 2017

Dearest Sister Wendy,

I find myself reading Merton now with your eyes, and often feeling annoyed at him. For instance, when he writes a letter to the community (thinking "the touch was light enough"), insisting that under no circumstances must he be elected abbot. This causes a lot of resentment among the brothers, who say he was unkind and insulted the community. He says they were apparently hurt when he said the last thing he wanted to do was end up having to "spend the rest of my life 'arguing about trifles with 125 confused and anxiety ridden monks.' This evidently threw a lot of people into tailspins, thereby proving that I was right." Really? And yet the very next week he wonders whether perhaps he was too harsh on the community.

I have not spent much time inside monasteries—just my visits to Genesee and Gethsemani. The last time I visited they treated me very nicely, with a personal tour, including some time alone in Merton's hermitage, which has been preserved pretty much exactly as he left it. There are woods all around, and beautiful hills for hiking. The chapel is my favorite place, though there are many fewer monks than when I first visited forty years ago.

Stay well until I get there. And afterward too.

———

October 30, 2017

Dearest Robert,

One thing I must say is that you mustn't imagine that when people come to Quidenham I meet them. However, I'm determined that we'll have a meeting, even if it's brief. You will find me very dull but good-hearted.

I very much hope I haven't spoiled your delight in dear Merton. The more I have come to see through the inconsistencies that are so frequent and realize that he is not inconsistent in wanting God, the less upset I have become by his failures. He seems to have an almost preternatural unawareness of himself and his motives—at least at the time. It is almost amusing to find how sometime after he would diagnose with precision how wrong and foolish he has been.

I am glad that you have been in the holy precincts of those monasteries. In a women's monastery there is nowhere you can wander, as it were. The enclosure is barred to all but the sisters, and we have a very small lawn with a crucifix outside on the drive, and if you go far enough on the east you will come to the mere, which makes a little, though rather muddy, walk. Of course there are walks outside on our country roads, but it is not the same as wandering through the great expanses of the American Trappist houses. You seem to live in such extraordinarily beautiful surroundings. Quidenham to me is just right—not exceptionally beautiful and certainly not dramatically so, but quiet and, to me, lovely.

When I first came here I was asked to spend a year of probation (though I could never think of it as such, I was here to stay) in a little one-roomed apartment at the back of the guest house. When Rachel showed it to me she said, "I'm afraid the windows don't have a view," to which I replied in astonishment, "But I didn't want any view; anyhow I keep my eyes shut when I pray." She told me later she thought this was very odd, and of course I am very aware that beautiful scenery, like art and music, raises the spirit to God. But there are other more direct ways, aren't there?

Fr. Bill McNichols has sent me some beautiful images of icons and tells me that he takes me into his Mass every day—for which I am profoundly grateful. I think if people were only allowed to go to Mass once a year or perhaps once in a lifetime, near their death, it would be recognized as the great mystical grace that it is. I've read nothing in any saint's visions that is more profound than the daily encounter with Jesus in the Mass.

Very much love to you both,
Sister Wendy

———————

November 1, 2017
Feast of All Saints

Dearest Robert,

Lesley and I want to send our love on this day that is special to you. The saints have been your life-work and the truth and beauty of God made visible in Jesus, made visible in His saints, is at the heart of what you are. Thank you and God bless you.

With love and gratitude,
Sister Lesley and Sister Wendy

———————

November 7, 2017

Dearest Robert,

We'll be meeting tomorrow. Who would have thought I'd ever write that! Very much love, dear Robert, and be prepared for a great let-down when the wheelchair appears. I accept the humiliation in advance.

Lovingly and gratefully,
Sister Wendy

———————

November 8–11:
A Trip to Quidenham

Quidenham is a small rural village in Norfolk, not far from the city of Norwich, home in the fourteenth century to the famous anchoress and mystic Julian, who was one of Sister Wendy's favorites. The Carmelite monastery of Quidenham, where Sister Wendy lived, is situated in a great brick manor, acquired by the Carmelites in 1948, and expanded to include a chapel and other buildings. The sisters, who all live within the monastery enclosure, are rarely seen in public. Surrounding the monastery are sparse woods and fields populated by wild pheasants.

Monica and I arrived on November 8 and were warmly greeted by the prioress, Sister Stephanie, before being shown to our lodging in the well-named "Peace Cottage." That afternoon we were able to have a brief visit with Sister Wendy, who was conducted by wheelchair into the "parlor" by Sister Lesley. Sister Lesley had warned us that Sister Wendy found it difficult to lift her head and look at people eye to eye. She herself had warned us about her failing hearing. But we had no difficulty communicating. Greeting us both warmly with an embrace and a kiss, she was as lively and engaging in person as in her letters. She had gifts to share, including presents for my children. What we discussed was not of great significance, as we mostly basked in the joy of meeting face to face at last.

That evening I shared some brief introductory remarks with the community. We had to be personally escorted through several doors and hallways to arrive at the meeting room in the enclosure. Sister Stephanie had graciously made allowance for Monica to attend my presentations,

Entrance to the reception area

and she sat beside the sisters, who were arranged in a wide semi-circle around the room, while I sat before them at a little table in the middle. I don't know what I had expected this inner sanctum to look like, but I can report that it resembled nothing so much as an ordi- nary library.

We meet face to face at last

I had been told that for the sisters' part the retreat would be conducted in silence. And so I was surprised, but not unhappy, when on the first evening one of the sisters asked if she could make a comment. She said that they had been reading Kate Hennessy's book about her grandmother, Dorothy Day. "I think that many of us have the feeling that we don't really care for Dorothy," she said. That was the only intervention during the course of the retreat. Otherwise, I gave two talks per day, one in the morning and another in the afternoon, on the subject of saints and holy lives, and how in reading the spiritual text written in their lives we can learn to read the story that God is writing in our own lives.

In between I had a full schedule of "parlor" meetings with individual sisters, including Sister Lesley. The so-called parlor was a rather austere *room separated by a long table, at which I was seated on one side, while on the other, a door opened up from the enclosure. These sessions were invari- ably fascinating, some of them deeply per- sonal and moving. Each sister had some-*

The Quidenham Carmelite monastery "parlor"

thing very specific to

discuss—rarely connected to the topics I had discussed, except insofar as they shared their own journeys of faith. I learned that many of them had a particular passion for poetry, music, or art. While from a distance they were all quite uniform in their brown Carmelite habits, it was clear that there were no two alike, and for this many of them credited the forward-looking attitude of Sister Rachel (Ruth Burrows). In her influential term as prioress she—who had welcomed Sister Wendy to live on the grounds of Quidenham—had encouraged the sisters to cultivate and value their individual gifts. It seemed like a very happy community. I was honored to have a parlor session with Sister Rachel herself.

Between talks and sessions, Monica and I roamed the country roads and fields around the monastery and attended some of the monastic hours of prayer from a section of the chapel reserved for guests. Our section, which we had all to ourselves, faced the altar, and on the other side was the choir where the sisters gathered. Sister Wendy, who was not part of the monastic community, only attended Mass each day from an alcove overlooking the choir. On our last evening Sister Lesley asked us please to make sure to notice Sister Wendy during the "exchange of peace" as she wished to send us a special blessing. Sure enough, when the moment came, we saw Sister Wendy, sitting in her wheelchair, gazing at us with a great smile and with outstretched arms, like wings, raised up in the air.

We were able to see her again the next day before our departure. She happily posed with us for photos and chatted about my experience and impressions of the community. I have little recollection of what we said. Words were the least of it. But as we parted she grasped my arm and said, "You know, for me this is heaven."

Sister Lesley wrote on December 22, 2017:

> *Dear Ones,*
> *I'm sorry to tell you that our dear Sr. Wendy had a fall yesterday, early on Thursday morning. A medic came to see her and said she has badly bruised her leg, and unfortunately has broken or cracked her sternum and/or ribs. She's very grateful that the break cannot be healed by medical means and must be left to fuse itself. In fact, she's very grateful altogether for God's goodness in letting her have what she calls "a small share of the cross" and for the great kindness of the community. This has rather diminished her capacity to communicate because she needs all her energies to cope with the*

chest pain. So although she might be very glad to hear from you, please don't expect much from her. She's being brave and happy.

Love and gratitude for your love and prayers,
Sister Lesley

And on December 30, 2017, Sister Lesley sent out another general update on Sister Wendy's condition, noting that "Sister Wendy herself is grateful to have this small share in the passion of Jesus and doesn't want you to feel anxious in the slightest about her. She says that a few leaves have fallen but the tree, unfortunately, still stands firmly enough, and the time of very great joy has not yet come."

PART THREE

THE ART OF LETTING GO

I began the new year by bringing Sister Wendy up to date on various family and friends who visited over the Christmas holidays, while bemoaning the arrival of harsh weather—a so-called "bomb cyclone," with powerful wind and frigid cold.

January 5, 2018

Dearest Robert,

Here in Norfolk the weather is remarkably mild. If that were not boon enough, nuns don't have any live-in visitors, and of course I have no visitors at all. So apart from the struggle with Christmas cards, Christmas for me is a time of very great happiness. I think that's been deepened by the pain that the fall brought about. Things are much less painful now, though I am still getting periods of breathlessness; perhaps that will be how God opens the gates for me. "I rejoiced when I heard them say let us go to God's house," but as yet He has definitely not said it.

As you know I'm rereading for the third or fourth time over the years Thomas Merton's letters (I'm halfway through volume 3). It may be because I'm not feeling all that well but my reaction is not as in previous readings. I feel very conscious that actually these are not happy letters. They're the letters of an over-burdened man struggling to keep his path clear to God while pressured on all sides. The fact that he brought most of these pressures upon himself is beside the point, that's his nature. But I hadn't realized before what a stressful life he led in his monastery. There's humor all the time and occasional wild gaiety, but there's not much joy. I feel increasingly sorry for him, and I feel admiration too.

He's a strange phenomenon, and I believe with you that his search for God is profoundly inspiring. It's the orientation in itself that I love. I find actual quotations rather dicey because one knows that in a page or two he will demonstrate the opposite. For a man of words, as of course writers are, his words mean less than his naked longing for which there are no words. I think he'll always be a great enhancement in my life and a great bafflement, often a sorrow, often a joy, and I'm glad we share him. But I don't think anything I can say about Merton is usable for the kind of talks you are going to give. My reaction is so deeply nuanced, and one wants people to have more forthright encouragement.

One of the consequences of my small accident is that my powers of enjoyment have been diminished. I'm not reading anything with the pleasure I would have expected. This is humanly unwelcome but a great chance to receive some spiritual purification. I have always been certain that all pleasure is from God, but it's good to experience that so is all non-pleasure.

Now we are on the brink of the Epiphany, that extraordinary feast whose radiance exceeds any human comprehension.

Very much love,
Sister Wendy

———————

January 8, 2018

Dearest Sister Wendy,

It is a balmy twenty degrees below freezing today, and, following two weeks of polar temperatures, it feels like spring.

I am very interested in your deep response to Merton's letters. Clearly writing letters was a major part of his occupation, all the more remarkable when one considers how much else he was writing. When I worked on Dorothy's letters it occurred to me that letter-writing was one of her major apostolates—though little acknowledged. Whereas she spent a few minutes a day writing notes in her diary, she must have spent hours almost every day writing letters. In the case of Merton, who kept copies, he surely thought they would eventually be read by other people. (Not so, in Dorothy's case, I am sure.)

The best letter writers in my acquaintance are my friend Jim Forest and you (thanks to Sister Lesley!). But it is a dying art. I'm sure my children never write letters. (Or maybe they just don't write them to me!)

I feel like going into hibernation with all the other woodland creatures.

Wishing you steady improvement, and renewed "powers of enjoyment."

———————

January 14, 2018

Dearest Robert,

A nasty cold has been laying low the community, and since Lesley was one of the laid low there's not been an opportunity to answer your email. She says she's better but I'm not certain.

Letters have always interested me as a literary genre. It's in his letters that you see the full extent of C. S. Lewis' Christianity and of Dorothy Sayers' deep and intelligent commitment to the faith. What makes Dorothy Day's letters so outstanding is the conviction they convey of her holiness. The letters in a way are her life lived out before us. I don't think there's anything like them for simple beauty and power. Just to read them is to know what it means to love God.

Thomas Merton's letters don't do that. What they show is the incredibly diverse interests of this gifted and stressed man of God. It's the diversity that fascinates, a diversity that is always centered on a hunger for holiness. But I must confess that he does not give the impression of either happiness, as I said before, or of that peace that is inseparable from holiness. He is too stressed, too competitive, in a way too interested in too much. So many of his letters are not written in response to another but are his own response to achievements, mainly in literature and of course mainly in spiritual literature. All the same he is spread very wide and only a genius and a man of real spiritual hunger could maintain such a spread.

I don't want to tire Lesley, and I'm afraid my own energy levels are not all that brilliant, but I enwrap you in the warmth of my love and prayer,

Sister Wendy

————

January 14, 2018

Dearest Sister Wendy,

I find I am becoming something of a hermit myself. I am happiest just to stay indoors, and don't really feel like seeing other people, aside from Monica.

Right now my main task is to prepare another lecture on Henri Nouwen and his "counter-cultural spirituality." I want to talk about compassion, solidarity, and his attention to God's grace, disguised in weakness.

I wish you well in your happy reading project. I had never thought much about whether Merton was a "happy" man. He seems to have had a great capacity for whimsy, a sense of the absurd, and an ability to take interest and delight in many topics.

When I was writing my book about happiness, I said to a friend, "A truly happy person wouldn't write a book about happiness." She said: "A truly happy person wouldn't write a book about anything."

———————

Sister Wendy had always eschewed "elegant chit chat." I was honored that she put our correspondence in the category of "things that matter." Among the large difference between us, she observed, was her relative lack of interest in social questions. But I could only agree with her that this was hardly noticeable "because on so many levels we communicate with love and light."

January 15, 2018

Dearest Robert,

Now I have the cold and if it laid low Sister Lesley, that stalwart woman, imagine what it is doing to feeble Sister Wendy! It just has to be lived through with joy and gratitude. It's not a cold in the chest, so I can't expect it to be a real step toward eternity, as that would be; it does mean that my head is dizzy and foggy and this is not going to be much of a letter.

I've never understood why anybody should want to be anything but a hermit. So I could only feel at one with you. I remember once when I was still in community, people discussing their ideal afternoon, and several said to be talking with their friends. I think I kept my face impassive but I thought it was a hideous notion. Of this I am not proud.

This is also why I've never wanted to write letters or books for that matter. What is the point of elegant chit chat? With you it is different because we are really talking about things that matter to us.

One of the ways in which you and I are very different is that your wonderful father has brought you up to value social justice very highly. This is your big thing and I'm very grateful that the Church has you to speak for it. I don't want to shock you or alienate you, dearest Robert, but I cannot take much interest in this topic so dear to you and to Pope Francis and to all serious Christians. It all seems to me so obvious. Of course war is wrong; of course there should be social justice; of course we should love and revere one another; of course there is no happiness that does not include a desire for the happiness of all our brothers and sisters. But I feel that's a sort of given for me. I don't feel any call to fight for it or even to talk about it. I suppose this shows up my inadequacies, partly from my sheltered life and partly from my very uncombative intellect; but I can't change it and make myself interested. When I get to Merton getting rightfully worked up about these matters I tend to skip. If you feel that we should now cease correspondence, just say.

Of course, I can only write like that because we share so much, and although this central element of your life is not that of mine, one would hardly notice it, because on so many levels we communicate with love and light.

I think that's as much as I can do today, dearest Robert.

Lovingly,
Sister Wendy

_____

January 18, 2018

Dearest Sister Wendy,

I feel most remiss in not writing you at once—especially in reply to your suggestion (surely in jest) that I might want to cease correspondence because you are not interested in the subject of social justice. If I did that, who would take an interest in the following dream from last night?

I have arrived in a city in Asia, maybe in Thailand or Cambodia, on some kind of writing assignment. I check into a hotel, dressed in pajamas and a red silk smoking jacket. As I put down my bags an associate who has been waiting for me—I think a photographer with whom I am supposed to be collaborating—rushes down and insists that I come upstairs immediately. It will be obvious why this is so important. We go upstairs where he hands me a book and says, "First, read this poem by Rilke." Then he invites me to look out the window at a great Himalayan mountain. It is obvious that there is some kind of mystical connection between the poem and the mountain, and I thank him for bringing this to my attention. When I go downstairs to resume checking in, I ask the manager, "Where are my bags?" He looks around with embarrassment. Obviously they have been stolen.

_____

Sister Wendy's illness forced her to modify her usual ascetic regime. She worried that this might be the beginning of a slippery slope.

January 19, 2018

Dearest Robert,

The good thing about your dream is that there is poetry in it. The bad thing of course is that there is the darkness of loss. Perhaps the message is that it is the poetry that matters?

The thing about this chest infection is that it does indeed affect the breathing and life becomes a conscious struggle. But we who have the blessing of the faith know that this struggle is the cross of Our Lord and that it's a privilege to carry it and share in His redemptive suffering. Mine is a small share, and the offering I make is completely open-ended. When one thinks of the sorrows of the world, one can never know which is most in need of redemption, because some are completely hidden in the heart of the sufferer. So, by a sort of back road, I do share in your great passion for social justice, but in a very formless fashion, which I am grateful that you accept.

I have been given antibiotics for my chest infection and was faced with the problem that they have to be taken three times a day with a meal, but I only eat twice a day, morning and noon. Since I came here in 1970 I have not had supper (though when I'm not here in the monastery I am open to all sorts of enjoyments). Sister Lesley worked out that since I get up at the extraordinary hour of 8:00 p.m. I could have a little something then. (I used to rise at about 2:00 in the morning and the hour has gradually gone back. It used to be seven hours but now in old age I need far less sleep. I try for five but it's normally four or even three—just to explain why I get up at 8:00 in the evening…). So, for my 8:00 p.m. pill she put out a little supper: a half-slice of buttered bread and some crisps. Robert, I can't tell you how I'm enjoying this treat. The sheer pleasure and eagerness with which I attack my little meal makes me realize that when I made this decision nearly fifty years ago it must have been difficult.

I've never believed in penance for penance's sake, but I see the ascetic life as simplifying and leaving one free for God. So, I think I must have struggled back then not to eat anything after noon, but now it has become completely second nature and I don't miss my supper in the slightest. But I'll miss it now when my antibiotics are finished. I can see this as a wonderful chance to remake that original little sacrifice, uniting myself with the hungry of the world and offering my own slight hunger to God as a symbol of my soul's longing for Him. I'm really going to miss that little plate and thank God for it.

No more breath, dear Robert. Perhaps you should put Mr. Trump on the altar and sacrifice all your reactions to him. Where does it get you? He needs love as does everybody and he needs reverence as does everybody. God despises nothing "that He has made."

Lovingly,
Sister Wendy

January 19, 2018

Dearest Sister Wendy,

To hear you luxuriating over the pleasures of a half-slice of buttered bread makes me feel like an awful glutton. I am glad you are on antibiotics, however, and hope that your recovery is swift. It is also remarkable to hear of you rising at 8 p.m., an hour before I normally go to bed.

I spent much of the day today with a priest who has written a book about his eleven years as chaplain at Sing Sing prison, the maximum security prison here in Ossining. It is a very moving book and it is clear why he became beloved by the prisoners. So many of them wracked with guilt, a feeling of wretchedness, many having ended up in prison after a long lifetime of abuse and misery. While working in an AIDS unit, at a time when this was a certain death sentence, he describes how he asked the men to say something they were grateful for, and one of them said, "I am grateful that I got AIDS, because it made it possible for me to be in this faith sharing group and for the first time in my life to experience love."[1]

I hope you graciously accept all the bounty that Sister Lesley prepares for you, even if she slips in a little jam on your bread.

———————

January 20, 2018

Dearest Robert,

Although I'm sure I'm getting better, I still have very little breath, so this isn't really a letter, just a response. Please don't back Sister Lesley up in her attempts to continue my medicinally-induced suppers. She tends to say, "You're nearly 90, why shouldn't you have a little pleasure?" I feel that's a false argument. Surely the older one is, the more one should embrace the purification of sacrifice? (Sister Lesley says argument is welling up inside her. I sometimes think her role as amanuensis makes demands that I don't always recognize.)

Just thinking about the horrors of prison fills one with sorrow. I am so grateful that there are priests like your friend who can enter into the darkness and give it a meaning.

Much love, dearest Robert, from your breathless but very contented,
Sister Wendy

———————

———————

1. Ronald D. Lemmert, *Refuge in Hell: Finding God in Sing Sing* (Maryknoll, NY: Orbis Books, 2018).

January 20, 2018

Dearest Sister Wendy,

Please don't exhaust yourself in replying.

I assure you that I will not conspire with Sister Lesley to increase your pleasure. It seems to me, however, that it would be a great act of humility and a mortification of your will to accept whatever is given you, and this great sacrifice on your part might surely offset whatever pleasure you receive from what most people would consider an extremely *petit* (emphasis *petit*) *dejeuner.*

Sending you love—wishing that I could also send you some of the extra breath that I don't need.

———

January 21, 2018

Dearest Robert,

I'm using my little store of breath to thank you for a delightful but duplicitous letter. If you had seen Sister Lesley's holy triumph you would have realized that for her your words were a great success. I shall have to ponder them. I know how easy it is to be self-willed and to think one is pleasing God, when one is really just pandering to one's own fantasies of what sacrifice is. That doesn't mean, my dear friend, that you've convinced me, but I won't consider the subject completely closed. Sister Lesley pleads that it's not a half-slice, it's less; she says it's about a fourth of a slice, but it's the principle Robert, the principle! And incidentally, jam would destroy the exquisiteness of the experience, where the slight salt of the butter celebrates the rough texture of the bread. Anyhow, two more days before I have to align myself with the opposition or plough a lonely furrow.

I don't think you are really well Robert. You shouldn't be so tired, should you? Are you overworking? I think you have as much a duty to look this problem full in the face, in fact more of a duty, than I have with my miniscule asceticism. No more breath now.

Much love,
Sister Wendy

———

January 22, 2018

Dearest Sister Wendy,

The release of a new film, *The Post*, about the publication of the Pentagon Papers by the *Washington Post*, has stimulated new interest in my father's story, and by extension, in me. I had a very enjoyable interview with a reporter from the *NY Times* this morning. I thought he was simply going to want a few quotes to go with a story about an upcoming program at the Museum of the New York Historical Society (which is billed as "The Kid Who Helped Leak the Pentagon Papers"—in which I will be unveiled, as the unlikely "kid"!). But to my surprise, he wanted to write a whole column about my story, and we talked for an hour and a half.

After talking for a long while, I said that for many years I was reluctant or shy about discussing my part in this story. On the one hand, it was a burden growing up to be the son of a great man, and I wanted to establish my own name. Then, there was that voice of my mother, always a little nervous about the intentions of people who wanted to hear about it. As she would always say, "People will pretend to be interested in you just because of your father." And then there was the fact that this was not such a happy memory for me. People would say, "Wow, that must have been so exciting!" Well, not exactly —having my father on trial for his life, my mother suffering so much.

But time passes, and now I can own this part of my story, which happens to be part of history, and one of ongoing relevance. It has certainly helped shape my life, without determining it, and I am happy at the age of 62 to talk about it.

I think of you meanwhile in your ascetic redoubt. Much of what you have given up—traveling around the world, visiting museums, meeting interesting people—was not a great sacrifice, since you were happier in your hermitage. But I wonder why good food, moderately supplied and lovingly provided, can't be accepted with the same delectation that you bring to the libraries of books you devour, or the vast catalogs of beautiful images that you have consumed. It is all provided by the same loving Father. Remember that Jesus was accused of being a glutton and a drunkard!

Now in my case greater moderation in eating is definitely indicated, both from the standpoint of body and soul.

But just talking about meals brings me and Monica to the sweetest memories of our time at Quidenham, and the lovely meal that was delivered once a day, and the sweet discipline required of us to ration it.

Hoping you are able to fill your lungs with the sweetness of life.

———————

January 23, 2018

Dearest Robert,

My recovery has taken a backwards step. We hold on to Our Blessed Lord and wait for Him to draw us into the sunlight.

As to the little supper, you must remember that from the age of 16 I have led a very disciplined life: up at the same time, to bed at the same time, so many hours for this, so many hours for that, all meals eaten in the refectory.... Since I have established for so many years that I don't eat after midday, it's difficult to adjust. But I think you're right and Sister Lesley's right that there is some pride and self-will here. The world is full of God's beautiful gifts to us but that doesn't mean that we are meant to enjoy all of them. Think of the vows, which sacrifice the most precious gifts, so it's not just because I like the little supper that I feel drawn to sacrifice it; I'm just not sure what my motives are. However, the first course of antibiotics has not been successful so I've started with a much stronger pill which means, of course, another week of delicious bread and butter and crisps. I can postpone my GREAT DECISION.

No more breath dear Robert but much love,
Sister Wendy

I shared with Sister Wendy the sad story of a young man I had known since his birth who committed suicide after a lifetime of mental suffering. He left behind a moving document on the role of the artist in standing up for truth and goodness in an era of lies.

February 2, 2018

Dearest Robert,

The reflection you have sent me from your young friend is perhaps too sacred to be commented on. Of course, irrespective of the great courage and the great heart exhibited there, we can't help but feel wistful that he was not aware of the strength that comes from God. What we can't do *God will do.* There's such a security and a happiness in knowing that our weak desires for the goodness that James speaks about are turned into reality through the grace of God. I don't know how people manage when they think that it all depends upon them. But how nobly he takes up this burden.

I'm reminded of the perennial problem: can a bad man be a good artist? James is surely right in feeling that goodness is essential, and I think it follows that it is from this goodness that the wonder of art will spring. But of course sometimes a person is a mixture of goodness and badness—Caravaggio is the obvious example—and it's from the goodness in them that their art comes. The art is the goodness in a way; it's what they aspire to be.

It's tragic that doctors couldn't and can't make life viable for people suffering from bipolar disease. Surely one day there will be help. God's help never removes the suffering and the pain, but it binds it into the whole of one's being, and in uniting it to the sufferings of Jesus makes it all redemptive and meaningful.

Breath has given in, but love remains vigorous,
Sister Wendy

————

February 14, 2018

Dearest Sister Wendy,

I hope this finds you feeling better. Today is both Ash Wednesday and St. Valentine's Day. In that spirit I send love, but no chocolates.

Last weekend I was in San Diego to give a talk at a conference on Henri Nouwen—"A Revolution of the Heart: The Counter-Cultural Spirituality of Henri Nouwen." I suffered a lot over this talk. The night before I was to give it I realized that it was complete rubbish, and that I should start all over. I got up refreshed and inspired and it went all right—though in retrospect too long.

So Lent has begun. I hope this doesn't mean an end to your extra quarter slice of buttered bread. I wish you a happy journey toward Easter.

————

February 15, 2018

Dearest Robert,

I didn't have my little supper on Ash Wednesday and I felt the physical lack of it. I used to have no food at all this day but Lesley has begged me to have some soup for the past year or two and I can see it's more pleasing to God to accept her judgment than to insist on my own.

I love Lent, knowing that all over the world people are taking Our Lord more seriously than is their usual. I think that's the point of penance, not to make us suffer, but to remind us of God. So there really aren't many penances meaningful for me, because I am reminded of Him always. Perhaps I need to remember more the hungry of the world, which I am trying to do.

I'm still not recovered, though the cough is definitely better, but I'm weak and what Sister Lesley calls "squashed." However there's a special joy in praising the Lord from this lowly state and in living *ad laudem gloriae*. I really suffer very little but I don't think greatness or littleness matters very much, it's the *ad laudem* that matters.

> With love and joy,
> Sister Wendy

—————

February 16, 2018

Dearest Robert,

Your conference speech on Henri Nouwen is magnificent and I have passed it on to the community to appreciate. But reading it, I thought to myself that his essence, which you describe so well—lonely, bored, anxious, depressed—is something that I cannot empathize with. The desperate reiteration of his passionate emotions is not perhaps the reading I would choose. I know how he felt, though I don't understand it, and I revere greatly his courage and perseverance in seeking a response. Intellectually he knew all the answers but he could not live them. Yet one never doubts his almost frightening earnestness and desire, the truth of the man, which is precisely what one doesn't find in dear Merton. Nouwen sings one song, deeply and beautifully. Merton sings many songs beautifully, but without the inner truth of Nouwen.

So many people seem to come to holiness through damage. It's seeing that the damage is the way to be united to the crucified Jesus that's important

> Still not much breath, so I'll leave you with a Lenten kiss.
> Sister Wendy

—————

February 16, 2018

Dearest Sister Wendy,

Yesterday I had a great surprise. A friend of mine visited the Catholic Worker/Dorothy Day archives at Marquette University and evidently looked up my letters to DD. He found three, which he photographed and sent to me.

This one particularly touched me—written to her on her birthday on November 8, 1976 (I was twenty):

Dear Dorothy,

You write that "love is an exchange of gifts." I could think of nothing to give you that would signify adequately my gratitude to you for all that you have given freely and continue to give; so, may I use this occasion as a pretext for saying what so many must have said to you before: that my life has been inestimably enriched by your life—that if it had not been for certain accidents of Providence, I might have lived out my time at Harvard, unaware of the courage, wisdom, and goodness of which the human heart is capable; that it has been the great privilege of my life to share with so many countless others in knowing you and loving you.

Happy birthday to you always.

I started to read this aloud to Monica, but it brought back many emotions, and I couldn't get through it.

And there was more yesterday: my daughter Christina received news that she was accepted at Union Theological Seminary.

So you can see this was a wonderful day.

February 17, 2018

Dearest Robert,

I rejoice in your day of graces, crowned by this beautiful gift of your daughter's success. And it is success in the very area most dear to you, the understanding of the work of God.

I had described the opportunity to meet Cardinal "Chito" Tagle of Manila, one of my authors, and to hear him deliver a talk on hope. Still, my heart was burdened by a terrible school shooting in Florida. I reflected on how hard it was for me to let go of my anger. "Pray that I receive that grace."

I think the Cardinal chose well to speak on hope. Pope Francis calls it the "hidden virtue," but it is tremendously important. He says, you will remember, that it's not optimism; it's a spiritual clinging to a trust in God. That's where your anger has to go because it's a disturbing emotion. I will pray that you are able to put your anger and distress on the altar; after all, Jesus felt exactly the same helpless anger at the blind follies of the powerful. But He hoped, He gave it to the Father. May this be true for us all, dearest Robert.

Your letter to Dorothy was extraordinary for a 20-year-old. She wonderfully repaid your love for her and is still loving you and drawing you to God. I'm so happy about your work for her cause.

Much love dearest Robert,
Sister Wendy

_____

Sister Wendy received a new book featuring the icons of our mutual friend Fr. William Hart McNichols, and this inspired a surprising idea.

February 21, 2018

Dearest Robert,

I had a thought which may not be workable, but I wondered if it would be worthwhile my collecting the thirty or so of Fr. Bill's icons that I most love, writing a commentary on each and offering you this little book? I must point out that my energies may not be up to this and Lesley has limited time. But she says she would absolutely love to be part of it if it goes ahead. You may feel there is enough in print already, but I feel these icons are so profoundly beautiful that there is a need to make them available.

Lovingly always,
Sister Wendy

_____

February 22, 2018

Dearest Sister Wendy,

I am thrilled by your suggestion. How deeply Fr. Bill will be moved by your generous offer, as am I. Naturally, it depends on your energy, and you may find yourself putting your hand to the plow and feeling that you cannot continue. Even if that is the case, just your thought of doing this is a great gift.

Yesterday was a very deep day. I went down to see my author James Cone, the father of Black Liberation Theology, who confirmed that he is dying. They tell him he has six weeks to six months. (Monica thinks it is terrible to tell this to someone, but I think I would like to know realistically how much time I have.) We talked for about two hours about the memoir we have been working on and many other things. He was grateful and touched by the level of work I had done for him. He said, "There is no one else I would trust my book with." I told him that working with him for over thirty years had made me a better editor and a better man. I hope he has many more good days.

———

February 22, 2018

Dearest Robert,

I was moved by your time with James Cone. I am completely with you in the certainty that one would like to know [how much remaining time one has]. It is a solemn and a sacred moment when one realizes that the full vision of God is very close. But my father, a doctor, used to say that he always knew when a patient wanted to be told. Clearly James did want to and you and I would want to. When God comes with outstretched arms for Monica she will want to know how close He is or she will not. No one can tell in advance how one will react to this sacred and blessed moment. You must feel awed by the part you have played in so many great books, both by your skill in editing and by your supportive friendship.

I think it might be best if you were to make the suggestion to Fr. Bill, pointing out that I may have undertaken more than I can actually manage, but that you are honoring my desire. The first practical step would be to choose the images. What I will be doing in the next days or weeks is looking through the images I've got and seeing if I have enough for a book.

Also I'd need to feel confident that you would accept a commentary that was as short or as long as I felt right. But one never knows until one starts what one is drawn to say. I would also need to feel sure that you feel you could sell this book.

Lovingly,
Sister Wendy

———

February 23, 2018

Dearest Sister Wendy,

You can imagine how excited Fr. Bill was to hear of your idea. He called me right away and just said, "Please tell her she can do whatever she wants—any title, any selection, I leave it entirely in her hands!"

Last night I induced Monica to watch one of my favorite movies, "Goodbye Mr. Chips" with Robert Donat and Greer Garson. It is about a middle-aged schoolmaster, a lifelong bachelor, who has never been able to connect successfully with others, until he has a providential encounter with Greer Garson over a school holiday. They fall in love, get married, and return to the public school, where all his colleagues are absolutely astonished that he should have made such a catch! And the experience of love opens his heart so that he becomes capable of giving love and receiving the love of his students. Years go by and Chips becomes a beloved institution among generations of students. (Sadly his wife dies in childbirth—but the inestimable good in his life has already occurred.) Though this was not a test, it would be hard for me to love someone who could watch this with dry eyes. Of course, Monica was weeping buckets by the end. "That is the greatest movie ever!" she cried.

Of course I have always thought her entry into my life was something like that. You did not know me so much before, but so many old friends say I am like a different person.

———

February 24, 2018 *(Sister Wendy's 88th birthday)*

Dearest Sister Wendy,

I am so happy to send you birthday greetings! I hope you will receive a dispensation to enjoy yourself today—with an extra cup of tea, or a flower, or an especially happy memory.

I will be feasting in your honor—if not with cake, then with gratitude for all the gifts you have showered on me.

I shared with Sister Wendy a very great gift—an account of a healing reconciliation with a close family member. I had previously shared my sufferings with Sr. Wendy, and she had offered her prayers and much wise counsel.

Thank you for your prayers and encouragement. I am happy to report this news to you as a birthday gift.

———

February 25, 2018

My dearest Robert,

That was the best birthday present I could have. I join with you in thanking God for this new level of understanding and clarity. Now you have to build on it.

> With love and joy, your 88-year-old friend,
> Sister Wendy

———

March 10, 2018

Dearest Robert,

I'm so pleased that the Nouwen letters turned up [*Love, Henri: Letters on the Spiritual Life*]. He has a charm and a truthfulness that is moving. But if some friends are truly high-maintenance, Nouwen as a friend must have been bankrupting. I was interested this morning to see how his own need of exhibiting weakness and receiving support became elevated to a spiritual principle. I'm sure he is wrong here but with elements of rightness. The important thing is to be there for the other person and not be all that concerned whether they are there for you. But this suggests a strength which he felt was false. I would say that it is in this unselfish love that we live in the love of Jesus and give up relying on ourselves. Incidentally what a wonderful tribute the editor gave to you in the acknowledgments—well deserved, dearest Robert.

Ever since I broached the subject, I've been thinking about that book on Fr. Bill's icons. I started a rudimentary selection of the ones I love best and decided that as a sort of test case I'd work on John the Baptist. I told you that I saw, as the great difficulties, my own feebleness and Sister Lesley's lack of time. But I've discovered there's a greater difficulty, and not one that I expected. The thing is, dear Robert, these icons are profoundly full of the presence of God for me. To talk about them, I have to take some steps back, and I can't do this without pain.

If the icon of St. John was an ordinary Western painting, I would happily comment on the difference between the hands, for example and the use of blue. But as it is, it feels almost sacrilegious; it seems wrong to regard the icon as anything but an opening unto God. I can't make comments. When I look at it I fall into prayer, and that's it. I don't see any way out of this, Robert, because it goes to the very root of my love for icons. They're not "works of art" in the worldly sense but functional, living theology, uniting us to Our Lord as we look at them. The kind of distancing that is necessary for a book seems to be beyond me. So will you please admit my failure to our dear Father Bill? And I apologize to you as well.

Sister Lesley points out to me that I've written two icon books. But that was then. I've grown past that interest that had so much intellectual delight in it. Furthermore, these were all illustrations in books and there was not the embrace of encounter that I now experience. I hope this makes sense.

I saw a bird—a young hen pheasant fly into my window and wander about on the flat roof outside. But I became so anxious for her that I got little pleasure from the encounter. I think she stunned what little wit she had, poor lamb, by flying into my window. But thanks be to God she recovered when I was at Mass and I don't have to feel anxious about her anymore.

I'm on antibiotics again which consoles me in that it suggests God really wants me to have that supper.

March 10, 2018

Dearest Sister Wendy,

I wanted to share this dream with you. I was in Dorothy Day's old room in Maryhouse. She was very old. There were other people in the room but we were able to talk quietly. I was telling her about things I thought would interest her, including my editions of her diaries and letters. In my dream I wasn't conscious that I was telling her about her own diaries and letters—in fact, I said, "You would find the letters especially interesting, since I presume you know many of the people you wrote to."

By this time everyone else was gone. I was afraid that I might be boring her. We were sitting on the floor. I started to tell her about YOU—"you know, the nun who did all the programs about art?" She didn't seem to recognize you, so I was telling her all about your story, and about our correspondence. At this point I realized that Dorothy was growing very tired. She lay down and put her head in my lap, and I just started stroking her hair. Then I woke up.

I thought you would rejoice to share dream space with Dorothy.

As for Fr. Bill's icons: Please don't feel any regrets if you don't think this is something you can do. I was very moved by your explanation—that you find yourself so drawn into prayer that it seems unnatural to comment on the icon as you normally would a work of art. Still, I wonder if there is not a way of approaching this that wouldn't violate the nature of your response, but would, in fact, assist others in truly seeing more deeply the spiritual reality depicted in the icon.

In responding to, say, an icon of John the Baptist, would it not be possible to reflect on the mystery represented by the saint, and use that as an entry into prayer, rather than, say, commenting like an art critic on the placement of the hands and the other iconographic conventions?

But of course I will respect your decision. And I wouldn't want you to strain yourself or approach this as some kind of job or commitment.

Hoping a combination of antibiotics and extra rations of toast and grog will restore your health.

––––––––––

March 15, 2018

Dearest Robert,

I can see now why people hail you as a genius because your suggestion about Fr. Bill's icons is a doable one. I don't want to do it and don't know if it will actually be done, but I've been praying and thinking and here is what I would offer on the icon of St. John the Baptist:

St. John the Baptist

John the Baptist was the first person we know of to encounter the adult Jesus. He was overwhelmed by two insights. One was that this Jesus, who had come to him so unexpectedly, was the Lamb of God. This meant, of course, that he immediately saw that Jesus was a sacrifice, a victim. Right up to the Passion, despite all that Jesus taught them and spelled out for them, the apostles could not get their minds round this. John saw at once: Jesus was called to die for the sins of the world.

He also saw the immense, incomprehensible distance between himself and Jesus. He summed it up by saying that he

Fr. Bill's icon of John the Baptist

*baptized with water but Jesus would baptize with the Holy Spirit.
John was calling his countrymen to repentance, to sorrow for their
sins, and the baptism in the Jordan was a symbol of this. It showed
their good will and their desire, but it did not change them; it did not
take away their sins. Baptism with the Holy Spirit was sacramental,
no longer a symbol, but a reality. As the catechism says, it achieves
what it signifies.*

*Yet John did not follow Jesus, and Jesus did not call him. After
this one tremendous encounter, Jesus moved on into His mission and
John stayed by the Jordan baptizing until he was arrested and martyred. The comment Jesus makes about John (who had sent a message
from his prison in a state of doubt, wondering whether Jesus was truly
the Messiah or whether they still had to wait) is an illuminating one.
Jesus praises John as He praised nobody else, no one greater has
been born. He goes on to say that the "least in the Kingdom of God is
greater" than this towering saint who belongs really to the Old Testament. The difference between John and the "least" is that the least
has been baptized, and so lives in the Kingdom. The least, and which
of us does not feel that we are the least, can say, because of baptism,
"I live now not I but Christ lives in me." Baptism is a life-changing
event that no words can really describe. We are taken out of ourselves
and into the life of the Blessed Trinity. We can neglect to use what has
happened to us, but that is another matter. We are in the Kingdom.*

*It seems to me that this icon is really about baptism. John has
worn himself out with longing for the Kingdom, and he stretches out
painfully to the Holy Spirit. The Spirit is there, but enclosed in his own
heaven world, our world, the baptism world, which is not John's. It is
an orb which the Spirit completely fills. And of his own power, John
cannot reach it. Years later St. Paul would find people who believe
themselves to be Christians, but had never even "heard of the Holy
Spirit." They had only received John's baptism. Jesus' baptism was of
a different order, not a natural order, but one that brought us into the
heaven of the Spirit, and made us able to dwell in Him and He in us.*

*We cannot make ourselves temples of the Spirit; grace is pure
gift. But for each of us, God will give us what for us is best. For
John, it was the longing and the inability. Perhaps we who have the
ability through grace do not have the longing.*

I don't know if you think this would be acceptable. But dearest Robert,
this is a struggle for me. I can't think why I ever suggested writing those
commentaries. I'm hoping that you'll say that you like my effort, will send

it to Fr. Bill, and explain there's not going to be a book. But if you are set upon it I would try to produce four more.

I'm still smiling about your beautiful dream. Dorothy is part of you now, and I can't think of a saint who would be more wonderful to have intimately associated with oneself, perhaps St. Elizabeth of the Trinity. But Dorothy in her own way is as great and as beautiful. I'm not surprised she had no recollection of me, but I hope from heaven she looks at me with loving compassion.

I finished Nouwen's letters and must confess that once or twice I couldn't but smile at the innocence of his self-preoccupation. To lay down your life for your friends: he is right to see this as essential. But his reading of it is that you explain yourself fully, opening all your vulnerabilities to your friends. Who else has thought that? The normal reading is that it means that you forget yourself and take on fully the life of your friend. I don't think he could have understood that. Yet I am struck by a great similarity with Merton. Amidst all his frustrations, angers, fears and illusions, Merton struggled always toward God. In a less complex manner Nouwen struggled through his neediness always toward God. They're wonderful examples of how temperament can never stand in the way. Both were in a sense badly equipped to be holy, but their very weaknesses occasioned a longing and a love that the more balanced would not have.

Henri Nouwen

We've had Laetare Sunday[2] so are rejoicing in the wonder of Our Lord's sacrifice as we move toward Holy Week. There are so many saints to rejoice with us.

Lovingly,
Sister Wendy

Thomas Merton

---

2. Laetare Sunday—the fourth Sunday of Lent. The Latin word *Laetare*—rejoice—comes from opening words in the Gregorian chant for the Mass that day: "Rejoice O Jerusalem."

March 15, 2018

Dearest Sister Wendy,

You call to my mind the teaching of Jesus about the two servants who are instructed to do something. One says, "Will do," but doesn't. The other says no, but then does the will of the master. You say you can't produce adequate reflections on the icons but then deliver something absolutely wonderful! I can imagine that it is daunting when you think in terms of a book, but I wonder if—when you just let go and freely share some of the reflections that are suggested to you by praying on the mystery revealed in the icon, you will find that one reflection leads to four, ten, and who knows what.

What you have written is exactly what I would hope for. I found this very moving, as I had never thought before about the significance of John recognizing Jesus as the Lamb of God. A lamb sounds so meek and mild, but of course you are right—that he was pointing to his bloody sacrifice.

I liked what you said about Nouwen and Merton being "badly equipped to be holy." That gives me hope, since I am certainly ill-equipped. My hope is that I can squeeze through by clinging to the coattails of the holy people I write about. (Or write to!)

March 16, 2018

Dearest Robert,

Although I am of course happy that you liked what I said about Fr. Bill's icon of St. John the Baptist, the scenario you sketch out for further work is not realistic. You have no idea how few thoughts I have. I look at the icons and am taken into their holiness, they pray with me. But I have no ideas or insights whatever about the subject. To produce that piece on John the Baptist I had to put the icon away and force myself to do some thinking. You'll notice that in the course of our letters thoughts do occur to me, but they come naturally and are elicited by what we're talking about. No thoughts come from looking at icons. It has to be a labor. I must confess to you also it's a labor from which I shrink. Normally my mind is completely unhampered by any agenda. I am free to look at Our Blessed Lord without hindrance. But when I have to write something there is a hindrance. Ideas invade my mind and I do not want them. Yet, I have to suffer them because I am committed to this project, whatever it is.

By the way, I thought that Nouwen's letters got steadily better and in the last few years of his life were at their deepest. It still seems to me a marvel how desire for God can cut through all that seems insuperable obstacle. It will cut through it for you, as it does for me. We only have to want Him and He will do it for us.

I look forward to hearing more of what you think of the icon idea. I must admit I'm baffled as to why I ever thought of it.

With love and joy and gratitude,
Sister Wendy

———

March 22, 2018

Dearest Sister Wendy,

I sense your low energy and want to assure you, truly, that you shouldn't suffer over Fr. Bill's icons, unless you feel so inspired. This is not one of my editor's ploys of reverse psychology. I am sure it was a great reward for him just to hear from you that you were moved to consider this.

———

Sister Wendy did produce a further commentary on Fr. Bill's icon of Rutilio Grande, a Salvadoran Jesuit priest and martyr who would later be canonized. But in the end she acknowledged that she lacked the energy to continue. "I just wish I had more vigor," she wrote. "Still we love God in the state that we are in, and it's in this feebleness that I can let Him be strong." Reminders of Sister Wendy's deteriorating health were increasing in frequency.

April 5, 2018

Dearest Robert,

While you've been under such pressures I've been peacefully in my room able to receive the transformative grace of Easter. As for poor Mr. Trump, remember that you only have two options: First, you can decide actively to do something. I'm not sufficiently *au fait* with political maneuvers to know what that something could be, but clearly the whole country must be teeming with people as distressed as you are. Only in united action can this distress have any practical effect. But if you don't feel that you want, or are called, to enter into this activity, then you have no other choice but to put the whole sad business into the hands of Our Blessed Lord. You're getting the worst of it—ravaged with anger and sorrow, and so not able to receive the peace that is the mark always of His presence. One notices it often in the Easter readings: Jesus begins by saying "Peace." I don't think we can receive Him unless our souls are at peace, but there is a peace that comes from knowing we've done what we can, and a peace that comes from entrusting our anxieties to Him because we see no chance of activity. But I feel very much for you and for Sister Lesley, too, who suffers at this terrible period of American history.

The chest infection has come back with some vigor, lots of coughs and wheezing, which of course worries dear Sister Lesley. The doctor is coming tomorrow, and we'll see. My suspicion is that it is not a chest infection at all, but that the pulmonary fibrosis, which has been in remission, has started activity again; and it could be that this state is now set for what is left of my life. It's a sacred thing to have such constricted and difficult breathing, because it's at every breath that we receive Him. We couldn't forget the presence of the Holy Spirit even if we wanted to, because our very body is calling us to repeat the "Yes" He is saying to the Father within us.

Very much love to you both, and may all your books sell more and more and more,

Sister Wendy

––––––––

April 5, 2018

Dearest Sister Wendy,

I can't think of anything worse than difficulty breathing. Knowing that every breath involves a struggle, it is terribly moving to me to think that your letters are written with such a precious gift.

This letter is particularly moving to me. You are quite right that one must either do something or put everything in the hands of God. James Cone said that writing and teaching were his way of fighting against white supremacy. Fortunately, I do feel that what I do is the most effective form of action, given my particular abilities. I refer to my editorial work. I have just finished compiling a book of the pope's words about refugees and migrants, which couldn't be more timely and important.[3] I have just helped my father complete his great exposé of the nuclear madness, and Sister Helen Prejean, with her work on the death penalty, and James Cone, on completing his final book. In all these ways I have the consolation of knowing that words are also actions; they are also works of mercy, peace, and justice.

––––––––

3. Pope Francis, *A Stranger and You Welcomed Me: A Call to Mercy and Solidarity with Migrants and Refugees*, ed. Robert Ellsberg (Maryknoll, NY: Orbis Books, 2018).

My father, "a person of hope"

I described a trip to Maryland where I gathered with my sister and other family members to celebrate my father's 87th birthday.

My stepmother Patricia talked about how my father had said that he would feel his life would be incomplete if he had not finished this book, and expressed her hope that now he could rest and take satisfaction in what he has accomplished. She noted, for instance, that there are a million people alive today in Indochina because of him, and his contribution to ending the war.

She asked him to close his eyes, as she put her hand over his heart, and asked him to imagine and receive all the love of so many people around the world. It was all very moving.

Afterward, he spoke about the time he was arrested at the United Nations with a group that had been billed as "persons of faith." Mostly clergy, though he was somehow there. Someone asked him, "Are you a 'person of faith'?" He answered, "Not exactly, but I am a person of hope."

I realize that that is one of the great theological virtues. And I don't know anybody who has acted more courageously or "faithfully" in that spirit.

We got back late yesterday. I was greeted today by the wonderful new Apostolic Exhortation by Pope Francis on the call to holiness. I wrote the Vatican and secured permission to bring out a small edition as soon as we can. I will write some kind of introduction.[4]

———————

April 12, 2018

Darling Robert,

I'm not sure if I will be getting better, but it is really quite unimportant. As you know, all you laid out so beautifully in your book on happiness is something God has given me to live.

I hope you send your book to the Pope.

Not much more breath, so I'll simply rejoice with you and send my love.

Sister Wendy

———————

———————

4. Pope Francis, *Rejoice and Be Glad: On the Call to Holiness in Today's World* (Maryknoll, NY: Orbis Books, 2018).

April 13, 2018

Dearest Sister Wendy,

It concerns me to think that it may cause you great exertion to dictate replies to my letters, and I want to assure you, as I did with Bill's icons, that you should feel under no obligation to reply. It is enough for me to picture you smiling, and raising your hands as you did for us at the exchange of peace at Mass in Quidenham.

————

A concerning letter came from Sister Lesley on April 13, noting that Sister Wendy had been fighting a chest infection on and off since February. "At this point she is coming along quite well, doing all the things she normally does, reading voraciously, healthy appetite, good humor (as always), and sleeping as well as usual. So there is no cause for great worry; but she and I wanted you to know about her current condition, and ask you, her dearest friends, to keep her in your prayers, as I know you do."

There was a pause in our correspondence while Sister Lesley attended a conference outside the monastery. In the interim, I sent an introduction I had written for an edition of the Pope's exhortation on holiness as well as reports about a number of trips to speak about saints, the latest political outrages, and finally reflections on the death of my beloved author, James Cone.

May 2, 2018

Dearest Robert,

Sister Lesley will print out for me your words about James Cone, but I can see from the picture how radiant he is with the light of God. You know what you are talking about when you say that one saint sparks off another, because your life has been so full of people who really love Our Blessed Lord, and have drawn you into their ambiance. I just hope you don't overwork and overstrain because I think you are a precious element in the Kingdom of God.

Abbot John, of St. John's in Minnesota, one of the very few priests with whom I have felt a spiritual connection, feels that the present troubles with poor Mr. Trump are significant of a greater national trouble. If this is so, and bad times are ahead for your country, at least let us resolutely offer it to Our Blessed Lord and trust Him.

Love to you and to Monica,
Sister Wendy

————

On May 4, Sister Lesley sent another letter to friends to let us know that Sister Wendy had had a fall and broken her arm. With a plaster cast up to her elbow, she was "recovering well, not in too much pain, and she is her usual accepting, grateful, smiling self."

May 7, 2018

Dearest Robert,

I'm so happy the retreat went beautifully. I love the picture of you and Monica—so at home with one another.

I'm not up to writing more but I am up to praying more, so I hold you in my loving prayers.

Gratefully and affectionately,
Sister Wendy

Monica and I

I wrote Sister Wendy about watching the wedding of Prince Harry and Meghan Markle, in which the presiding Episcopal bishop, Michael Curry, who is African American, quoted from Pierre Teilhard de Chardin. I also wrote about overnight visits by my friend Jim Forest and Kate Hennessy, Dorothy Day's granddaughter, and about the funeral of James Cone, at which I was honored to serve as a pallbearer. I prayed for her recovery and her happiness.

May 21, 2018

Dearest Robert,

Indeed I am happy, very, very happy. But I'm not well, partly because of the arm, which makes it impossible to get out of bed by myself and get out of the wheelchair myself, etc., but more because of the chest problems. The cough becomes a kind of choking which makes it difficult to live through, and I've told dearest Sister Lesley that one of these times I may not live through it. She will know that that is the way I have gone to God.

James Cone's funeral sounds so beautiful, so celebratory. I must say that apart from your vocation to write about the saints, you have also lived a life that has brought you personal knowledge of contemporary saints who are your authors and even come to stay with you. So your life is blessed from many directions and at the center is beautiful Monica.

The sisters watched the wedding, so I heard a bit of it from Sister Lesley. It seems to me that Prince Harry has been very fortunate in finding a bride of such substance. Everybody seems to have enjoyed the Episcopal minister, though I think some were rather disconcerted. How lovely are the different ways in which our temperaments and our backgrounds open us up to the Holy Spirit.

May you and all your family feel the gentle brightness of His illumination.

Lovingly,
Sister Wendy

June 4, 2018

Dearest Sister Wendy,

Oh, I am so sorry to hear about your cough. That can be exhausting, not to mention the overall strain it makes on the body. It is one of the worst things to suffer. Please don't worry about offering me anything beyond your prayers.

Yesterday Monica and I went for a walk in the woods behind our house, and it must have been just the perfect day when the trail was ablaze with white wild rose bushes. The path was absolutely surrounded by them, giving off the most wonderful scent, truly an "odor of sanctity."

June 5, 2018

Dearest Robert,

Words between coughs... So not many of them, but very loving and appreciative. Sympathy is such a beautiful quality and you seem really to enter into my little ailment. I don't know whether this is the beginning of the end, or an infection that will be cleared up, or a new constant element in my life. Whichever it is, I welcome it and thank God for the privilege of having things a little rough for once.

I feel through you I have contact with such a wide, beautiful, intellectual world and the natural world, too, with all those white rose bushes.

Last evening I heard a bird singing—what a gift!

Lovingly and gratefully,
Sister Wendy

June 6, 2018

Dearest Sister Wendy,

Tomorrow we are going to the Catholic Theological Society meeting in Indianapolis.

If you could wake up in our sylvan surroundings you would hear many lovely birdsongs (and the occasional raucous crow). Our backyard is a refuge for robins. Yesterday we saw the first hummingbird of the season. And then the most surprising sight: an enormous raccoon, creeping across the porch.

For the first time Sister Wendy began signing her letters with "goodbye." And yet there would be more good days.

June 7, 2018

Dearest Robert,

Just to thank you and to say I wish I could wake up in your glade, and yet since God is here, what better place could I possibly want? I hope you find spiritual nourishment even in Indianapolis, with its suggestions of loud motor cars racing.

There is an improvement in the cough, for which I am enormously grateful. Who knows what today and tomorrow and the future will bring?

Breath is failing, though love never fails, so I am saying goodbye and God bless,

Sister Wendy

June 14, 2018

Dearest Robert,

My arm is out of plaster and I have a brace for some weeks. Strangely it is more painful now, but blessedly more useful. Did I tell you that I can now get out of bed by myself? This was an enormous gift to me because for these last weeks I've had to rely on poor, overtasked, ever generous Lesley. I must say that if I had realized the weight my illness would lay upon the community I might have considered going to a convalescent home. But oh, how I would have hated it! The cough unfortunately is not an infection, but a growing hardening of the lungs because of the fibrosis. Again, this is all God's will and I thank Him.

Goodbye, dearest Robert, and a grateful and loving kiss to beautiful Monica.

Sister Wendy

––––––––

June 14, 2018

Dearest Sister Wendy,

How glad I am to know that you have better functioning use of your arm—both for getting in and out of bed, and for reading, even though I am sure it gives Sister Lesley great joy to be of service to you.

I read today about the ingredients for a happy marriage, and it said the main problem in relationships is criticism. The ideal is a ratio of twenty to one positive to negative interactions during the day. But I could hardly assign such a ratio; it would have to be more like 1000 to one (and I would have to be very generous in scoring even one negative). We are so blessed to have found each other.

––––––––

June 15, 2018

Dearest Robert,

Thank God my reading capacity is almost back to normal, though it isn't completely normal intellectually, alas. I am exceedingly tired and sometimes anything but just resting in the Lord is beyond me. But only sometimes. There's still a great reservoir of intellectual eagerness there, which makes books a continual delight. The doctor will be coming again today, and I hope to get some insight on this cough. It is better, but it still can consume quite long periods of struggle.

Much love, dear Robert,
Sister Wendy

––––––––

I described for Sister Wendy my trip to the Oblate School of Theology in San Antonio to speak at a conference on "downward mobility"—a phrase that was widely used by Henri Nouwen. I acknowledged that it is a meaningless idea for most of the world, all those who are uncertain of their next meal. But in a culture that puts such emphasis on "winning" and "greatness," I thought that the way of Jesus and his self-emptying calls us to focus on a different goal. I cited the Gospel story of the rich young man.

I also pointed out that my talk in Texas took place against a new policy of "zero tolerance" for immigrants seeking asylum on the southern border. It was emerging that children—even toddlers—were being separated from their parents.

June 25, 2018

Dearest Robert,

So much of spiritual and emotional interest in your letter. As for the tragedies on the border, one can hardly bear to think of them—oh, so much to pray about. Your strong and beautiful lecture makes it so clear what are the desires of Jesus and how they have been consistently ignored. I suppose contemplative religious have that sorrow as one of their primary concerns. May we all be faithful.

You do so much work, dear Robert, and it's all so very worthwhile—beautiful deep topics, beautiful deep agendas. I just hope that you don't wear yourself out, but there's nothing I can do except, once again, hold it up to God.

With much love and prayer,
Sister Wendy

June 28, 2018

Dearest Robert,

I think knowing what your vocation is, what God is asking of you, and therefore what God is giving you, is so important. People flounder when they haven't clarity here. It's one of the graces I'm most grateful for, that by and large I've never had any difficulty about this. I feel ashamed that I'm not more useful; but I know that to be useless and penitent, and put all that behind me so as to concentrate wholly on God, is my blessed calling.

My cough is diminishing, which makes me feel very much better, something for which I am very thankful.

The Feast of Saints Peter and Paul is tomorrow, those two idiosyncratic individuals who followed Our Lord so resolutely and showed us that anyone can become holy.

Lovingly,
Sister Wendy

—————

July 9, 2018

Dearest Sister Wendy,

I dreamed that I received a letter from you—not by email, but handwritten. Not in your own tiny script, but still pretty difficult to read, in pencil, with lots of smudges and words scratched out. Nevertheless I could quickly discern that it was a text of extraordinary spiritual wisdom, disclosing your deepest insights about prayer and the nature of reality. I tried to read it aloud to some people but I was stumbling so much over the text, as if I were translating from another language, that I could see that nobody else could get the point. I said, "This will be clearer once I have typed it out." At this point I could see in the midst of the lines a little golden light, moving around, deeper and deeper— like a glistening figure walking toward a distant horizon. I thought, "That is her best, ideal self, which she has been pursuing throughout her life."

It seems like a lot has happened in the past week or so. I finished Sister Helen's book.[5] And I started something new. Feeling that our Spring list is a little short, our production manager said to me, in jest, "Can't you just write a new book over the summer?" And as I thought about it I began to feel that there was indeed a book lying amidst various talks and articles—sort of like the topic of my retreat at Quidenham: How to read other lives—and our own lives—as a spiritual text. So I am working on that.

Monica is well. She has been avidly following the World Cup (it always amuses me how much she knows about sports). Today is France vs. Belgium (where her mother was born).

Speaking of mothers—the other day my iPad (a cross between a cell phone and a computer) suddenly began making a dialing tone. It was sitting on a counter, and I hadn't touched it. I glanced at it and saw that it was dialing my mother (!)—her picture popped up. At that moment, a recording announced that this number was disconnected.

—————

5. Sister Helen Prejean, *River of Fire: My Spiritual Journey* (New York: Random House, 2019).

P.S. Friday was my 31st anniversary at Orbis. As I am 62, that means that I have now spent half of my life here!

———————

July 10, 2018

Dearest Robert,

That was an unusually supernatural-style letter. I cannot explain the mystery of your machine and your mother. One can only think that God must be calling her to memory for some special reason. Perhaps to thank Him for giving you such a mother and to pray that all she gave you bears fruit.

I'm afraid, however, that your letter from me was inauthentic. You can tell by the fact that there were those emendations and scratchings out, whereas all I write is in one uninterrupted line and I don't change things, *quod scripsi, scripsi.* This is not because what I've written is especially good, but because I don't want to spend any more time on it. Your writing is quite different, and I'm truly delighted that you're going to spend time on another book. You have so much to give.

I must also say about my "letter" that one of my great lacks is any kind of self-image. St. Teresa, and other saints for that matter, insist on the need to know oneself, but I've never managed this. There doesn't really seem to be a "me" of any substance, a vacancy rather; but since I want Our Lord to be my substance, this is joy. It is He whom I have sought all my life, my golden reality. But I think that the letter shows how you can draw spiritual meaning for yourself, despite there not being objective material for it. If we want Him, we will receive Him. He is potential always in all that we experience, and it is for us to look attentively and see him.

Much love and joy, and the hope that one day I will write you a beautiful letter—a real one.

Sister Wendy

———————

July 11, 2018

Dearest Sister Wendy,

In recounting my dream about "you," I deliberately reported it as it occurred in the dream, without my own interpretation. In the dream I said to myself, "That is her true, best self, which she has been following all her life." I knew on waking that, of course, you would scoff at this. It seemed more likely that the figure was actually Christ. And while of course you don't revise your writing, I think the point was more about the difficulty of reading your writing—an experience, forgive me, which I am certain many of your correspondents would validate (in the pre-Sister Lesley days!). What was striking to me in the dream was the sense that I could read deeply into what you were saying—even without making out all the words—and that this was in some ways a communication that I could not easily share with others. It filled me with consolation.

Yesterday one of my colleagues gave me a lift from the gas station and she asked if she could share a personal story. It had to do with her praying that her son would get a job, and she went to pray at Maryknoll and an un-known priest came up and gave her a statue of Mary—and soon after that her son got the job. Did I think that was just a coincidence? I said that the difference between signs and coincidences is largely a matter of perspective. But if you are open to seeing signs and graces in the things that happen to you, you are likely to see them more frequently, and to live in hope and grat-itude. As you say, "He is potential always in all that we experience, and it is for us to look attentively and see him."

The same is true with the "call" to my mother. It did make me think about her and to thank God for such a mother.

———————

July 16, 2018

Dearest Robert,

I think what you say about the dream is very true. The suggestion that I could speak about my relationship with Our Lord is obviously something quite impossible. But as you wisely intuit, the dream was about the fact that I didn't need to speak, you knew silently.

I'm glad you have Monica and the garden to comfort you. But of course most of all I'm glad you have the faith. What Jesus gives us in the Mass is sufficient to bear us through anything, however terrible, and not only to bear us through it but to enable us to use it and help to purify the world.

Much love and gratitude,
Sister Wendy

———————

July 16, 2018

Dearest Sister Wendy,

I wrote last night about a new saint (new to me), just named Venerable: Juana de la Cruz Vázquez y Gutiérrez. A Spanish mystic and abbess of the sixteenth century, she has most interesting things to say about gender issues. She believed that she was conceived as a man but was changed in utero by God to become a woman. She believed that God was Father and Mother, that Jesus was both male and female, and that the human soul is both male and fe-

Juana de la Cruz Vázquez y Gutiérrez

male. She pictured heaven as a street lined with marriage beds, each containing God and a saint, either male or female. She recorded Jesus saying to her: "For those who desire a father, I am a father; for those who desire a mother, I am a mother; a bride, a husband, a friend, a counselor. I am whatever you need me to be."

Her cause for canonization—unsurprisingly—has proceeded by fits and starts. But Pope Francis has issued a decree of her heroic virtue.

————

July 17, 2018

Dearest Robert,

I am taken aback by your Spanish venerable. She couldn't make a more timely appearance than in these days of gender confusion. How wonderful that the Pope sees through all this psychological muddle and responds to what is completely unmuddled: her relationship to God. I think it's absolutely fundamental that God is to us what we need. He answers our deepest desires, the truth of us, and if we need a mother or a comforter or a teacher or a lover, whatever—that He will be to us.

My own feeling about gender is that it doesn't really matter. It seems to me that what we love in our friends is their humor and their goodness and their intelligence. And what gender they are doesn't play any part in this. I've been told that I'm wrong, and that women and men are basically different, but I simply can't see it. There are probably superficial differences, as there are physically; but the essence of a person seems, to me, quite unrelated to what gender they are.

So I will look forward with interest to seeing what reactions there are to this new venerable, and whether an openness to sexuality might herald a beginning of a change toward women and the priesthood. I've never wanted to be a priest myself, but to say no woman can be a priest because Jesus was a man does not seem to me to be according to the mind of God.

No more for now, dearest Robert.

Much love,
Sister Wendy

Despite weakness and infirmity, Sister Wendy could still feel her heart rejoice (as Dorothy Day had said of herself) in the encounter with great minds and souls.

July 25, 2018

Dearest Robert,

Thank you so much for the biography of Joan Chittister, which has just arrived.[6] Her face is almost exactly as I would have imagined. The strong noble face of a rhetorician, delighting in her fluency and the good that her words will accomplish, and the vistas they will open up for people.

Joan Chittister

The biography opens with a talk she gave and it is based upon a remark of great wisdom: that it is not whether we believe in God, but what kind of God we believe in. She says we are absolutely formed by our vision of God. That's why I am certain that these sad decisions of the Church will eventually change, because one cannot look at God and not understand that He does not want these exclusions. However, just as Jesus had to accommodate Himself to the ethos of the first century, so the twenty-first-century Church has to deal with those ages in which it has been unquestioned, taken for granted that God is male, and that really only man is a full human being. There were all those years of fear of sex, too. The secular world is coming to grips with a

---

6. Tom Roberts, *Joan Chittister: Her Journey from Certainty to Faith* (Maryknoll, NY: Orbis Books, 2015).

right view of women, so eventually the Church will, too. Look how long it took the Church to understand that Galileo was not a heretic, or that Darwin did not contravene scripture. It always seems to move at the pace of the slowest, which is very purifying for those who see clearly what God wants.

I can imagine that in years to come it will seem incredible that the Church would not ordain women or married men. We are in the interim period, able to see clearly that this is a need, not only for those who long to be ordained but for the people without a priest.

The heat here is nothing compared to the heat in parts of the States, but it is debilitating all the same, especially for the relatively immobile, like me. I keep reminding myself of Richard Rolle, who as you know, experienced God's love physically as a burning heat. May this natural heat from which we are all suffering become that spiritual heat which is pure happiness.

Very much love,
Sister Wendy

July 25, 2018

Dear Sister Wendy,

I do hope you enjoy the biography of Sister Joan. I would locate the two of you quite far apart in the spectrum of personality types, and yet there are many connections, including monastic life, Jesus, and, least of all, your friendship with me! She is quite an indomitable force of nature. But there is always something rock-solid about her.

I am, of course, entirely in alignment with what you say about women and married priests, and the slow pace of change in the church.

July 26, 2018

Dearest Robert,

I marvel at the amount you give out: the talks, the retreats, the books, the articles, the social intercourse with so many people, which is more than just social, but a deep way of loving. No wonder you're not always well, dearest Robert. I hope dearest Monica watches you like a hawk—a loving, tender hawk, who stops you from doing too much.

I, on the contrary, feel I do too little, and indeed there's no "feel" about it; I don't do anything. But I genuinely believe I can't do more than this nothing.

At least one doesn't need physical strength for prayer. Whatever state we're in, that's the state in which He wants us to receive Him. Oh the bliss of it!

Seventy-one years ago today I received the habit, and the wonder of that day is still as fresh in my mind as when it happened. Of course it wasn't this habit (which I made up myself from a mixture of Benedictine and Ladies of Mary castaways), but I don't think that matters in the slightest. Being given the holy habit lasts for one's life, bearing the responsibility of living up to this public proclamation of belonging wholly to God. I'm not sure that priests and nuns are helped by wearing secular clothes with only minimal indications that they are consecrated, but that's not my affair.

Much dear love, Robert,
Sister Wendy

July 26, 2018

Dear Sister Wendy,

Monica is all too happy to accept her appointment as a tender hawk. She tries so hard to slow me down. Ironically, I see myself as shamefully lazy. Most of the work I do doesn't feel like work—it is my pleasure. It is all a matter of perspective, I think.

I am quite sure you are doing quite a lot with your life of prayer. Just the thought of what you consider "nothing" is absolutely exhausting to me.

I intended to send Sister Wendy a foreword I had written to a new book by Leonardo Boff, The Following of Jesus, *his rejoinder to the fifteenth-century spiritual classic,* The Imitation of Christ. *But evidently I sent the wrong text.*

July 30, 2018

Dearest Robert,

I think you must have pressed the wrong button because you sent something quite different, a long interview with you about Nouwen. He is a fascinating character whom I'm glad not to have known, but who in book form is very moving. I feel about him as I do about Thomas Merton. There is much self-deception and muddle in their lives; and yet there is an unwavering concentration on God. I think many people would find this very encouraging—

that it's the direction that matters, the desire, and not the spiritual achievements, as it were. One hears ideas of canonization of these two wafted
round; and although I certainly don't think they merit this on objective
virtue, I do think there's a point in their heroic fixation, despite their weakness, on the only thing that matters.

I admire your pleasure in writing. Joan Chittister has it too. And I feel
abashed that it's something I never want to do. I do it easily and on the
whole I think I do it well enough, though of course never excellently. But
there's hardly anything I've written that I chose to do. I have a sinking feeling that this is laziness, which is an evil that I especially deplore. It's because of this fear that I've accepted so many commissions in the past, and
only now do I feel, though not with complete security, that I can refuse offers on the grounds that I simply cannot do them.

I continue to be deeply impressed by Sister Joan. I must admit I feel
very little kinship with her; as you said, she and I are very different, but one
of the major differences is that she is a spiritual giant, which I most definitely am not. It's a deeply inspiring book, though I still have the last chapter to read. I hope it will say more about her prayer life. There's always the
implication, the unspoken certainty, that her extraordinary achievements
were fueled by the love of God, but she doesn't say much about this.

Community, as you know, is the great sanctifier, and anyone who lives
in solitude, as I do, has to put enormous trust in God's work. I don't think
solitude is possible without years of community, needed in my case especially to eliminate some of the selfishness. But then, without the abrasions
of daily living, the solitary life needs an intensity of surrender or it will become flaccid. With your wonderful friend, Helen Prejean, whose memoir
you told me you are editing, and with Sister Joan, you have high-quality
women in your life, as well as saintly and interesting friends. Your exposure
to such varieties of holiness seems a lovely consequence of your writing
about the saints, those short biographies that are so illuminating.

Love to Monica, the tender hawk, and yourself,
Sister Wendy

———————

July 30, 2018

Dearest Sister Wendy,

As for Nouwen and Merton being mentioned as possible saints—well, of
course they are "my" kind of saints (insofar as I have abrogated authority
over such things!) but of course they are certainly not going to be canonized,

nor should they, according to the present process and criteria. I do think they are much more edifying models for contemporary Christians than many of those in the martyrology—I can say, as someone who has read Butler's *Lives of the Saints* backwards and forwards. Of course I tend to think that many people's conception of saints—as perfect people residing in heaven—does as much harm as good, since it doesn't necessarily inspire them in their own pursuit of holiness. Whereas, I think that figures like Nouwen and Merton—as deeply flawed and complicated as they are—actually do have that kind of influence.

We have a certain image of the saint as someone who is spiritually complete or "finished"—as if a little bell goes off sometime in their life. Whereas, I believe their holiness is a quality expressed in the course of an entire life—in the way they confronted obstacles, in their own flaws, their own sufferings, their response to the needs of their time. And so what interests me are people who were on a spiritual quest to grow closer to God; and what matters is that they carried that on till the end. The problem is also the idea that those who are canonized are the only real saints among us, and therefore that all holy people should be canonized.

Anyway, I absolutely agree with you: "There is much self-deception and muddle in their lives, and yet there is an unwavering concentration on God. I think many people would find this very encouraging—that it's the *direction* that matters, the desire, and not the spiritual achievements, as it were."

———

Regarding the Jesuit martyr Rutilio Grande, I described a letter of complaint from a reader about my reflection on Grande, and his path to canonization. This reader complained that Grande was not a martyr; he had not died "in hatred of the faith," but because he mixed himself up in politics (which is of course the pretext used by his assassins—who no doubt considered themselves pious Catholics).

August 1, 2018

Dearest Robert,

Just as we now seem to have a new understanding of martyrdom, which can be more or less understood as the final moments of life, accepting death for God's sake, I am baffled by all this political business because obviously you are right. They were killed because they sought to serve God in the poor. And if that is the prerogative of the Left, it speaks very sadly of the Right. But the lives that these new martyrs led, and perhaps this is true for all martyrs, might not pass the real tests that Dorothy, for example, is undergoing. It's the end, the death that validates them. And nobody examines too closely how humble, obedient, poor, etc. they were in life. They must have been fairly all right or they couldn't have risen to their marvelous deaths. But the emphasis is not on outstanding virtue. I wonder if we could have a sort of subclass of saints, not formally canonized, yet officially held before the Church as flawed but persistent in their desire and search for God. As you say, such figures are far more encouraging than we are led to believe.

I've finished Sister Joan, deep in admiration, but rather hesitant as to whether she is a useful role-model. It's no criticism at all to say that her passionate search for God is expressed in ways that are special to her. What she does is of the essence of being a religious, how she does it is of the essence of being Joan Chittister. I think this shows very clearly in the matter of obedience, which is the most drastic of the vows, taking the axe to the root of the tree. What do we do when we feel something needs to be said or done, and our superiors say "No"?

We get exactly the same problem in Merton. It causes great suffering when you feel called to speak out and are not allowed. Merton accepted the veto, though I must say, not in a saintly manner. But Joan makes it clear that she will not accept a veto.[7] By God's grace she wasn't given one because she had a wonderfully insightful superior. But Joan told her immediately that whatever the decision, she was going to go ahead. For her that may well have been right; but a nun, I feel, sacrifices the freedom to do what she thinks is right. Joan would have taken the consequences, she calls herself reckless, and this is true.

But I feel that when we vow obedience, we sacrifice even this freedom. We trust that God will find some other prophet and that He's asking us to suffer rather than to speak. We accept that it will never be "up to us." We have given away that freedom. She never has given away that freedom and in a way she's more a consecrated virgin than a normal nun. Again, no criticism,

---

7. For a time in the early 1960s Thomas Merton yielded to the demand of his Trappist superiors that he cease his publications on the subject of nuclear war. (He was eventually released from this ban after the publication of Pope John XXIII's encyclical, *Pacem in Terris*.) A crisis for Sr. Joan Chittister came when the Vatican ordered her Benedictine prioress to forbid her from speaking at a conference in Ireland on the subject of women's ordination. Sister Joan felt compelled by conscience to disobey such an order. But her prioress, with support from the community, refused to convey the prohibition, and the crisis passed.

just a comment. I think, though, that our deep admiration for her courage and insight could lead us into action that for us would be infidelity. Whereas it is clearly not so for her.

This is a complex matter and it's hard to lay down rigid lines as to what is security-seeking and what is courage. But I think the more we understand the holiness of the Mystical Body, the Church, and its unavoidable incarnation in unholy humanity, the more we will see that a sacrificial obedience is an expression of our trust in God. The Church will see one day what we see now because the Holy Spirit is with her.

I see you moving forward into life with a great crowd of spiritual witnesses on either side. This is a very happy thing, dearest Robert, to know you and to share your life in some tiny extent.

Very much love and gratitude,
Sister Wendy

––––––––––

August 1, 2018

Dearest Sister Wendy,

I agree with you about martyrdom. Dorothy herself said that we tend to think of martyrdom as a heroic affair, but most of the time it is anonymous. Life is made up of so many small humiliations and defeats, and how we face up to these and carry on is a measure of heroism that has no great name.

As for Sister Joan, I think she has remained deeply rooted in her community. I was very moved in reading about the time her community offered her their blessing and acknowledged that she had a mission beyond the community, so that what she has done has been with their blessing and as a kind of ambassador in the world. She has done a lot to promote the message of Benedictine spirituality for people living in "the world." (I can't tell you how helpful and encouraging she has been to me in dark times in my life.)

You say such encouraging things. Thank you for reminding me of all the blessings in my life—particularly the blessing of knowing such good and holy people. But of course one of the greatest blessings has been your willingness to share so much of yourself with me. There is no one else who holds up such a holy mirror to my daily thoughts and experiences, and I don't often enough thank you.

––––––––––

August 1, 2018

Dearest Robert,

I am certain that the blessed one in our correspondence is instead me. You bring such riches to my little room, and I feel you widen my heart and make space for the graces I receive about the oneness of all in the Church. This is too deep a subject for me to go into this morning, but it's a very large one.

As for the question of obedience and submission, Teilhard de Chardin confronted this challenge and met it with saintly patience.[8] It so serves to establish the integrity of the religious, but I agree with you that Sister Joan has a unique vocation and her community has completely endorsed it. This is a wonderful thing. And I was so touched by your revelation of how she comforted you in your period of desolation.

I'm afraid not much more time or energy today, dearest Robert.

With love from your sedentary friend,
Sister Wendy

I wrote to Sister Wendy about the ongoing scandal of clergy sex abuse in the church, which was receiving fresh attention, following scandalous revelations about the former archbishop of Washington, DC, and the release of a grand jury report on the church in Pennsylvania, going back many decades. This led to reflections on penance. Contrary to the common negative understanding of penance, she saw it as a way to transform all the common negative things in one's life into positives.

August 23, 2018

Dearest Robert,

Obviously, since I don't read newspapers, I don't know much about this new scandal, but like you and Fr. Bill, I know that these wounds in the Church are our wounds. Have you read Pope Francis' letter of August 20th? It's based on "if one suffers, the whole Church suffers"—a beautiful, heartbroken letter. But he doesn't just grieve and strive to make amends, which

---

8. Jesuit theologian and scientist Pierre Teilhard de Chardin was ordered by the Vatican to desist from teaching, speaking, or publishing any of his writings on evolution. His influential works were published only after his death in 1955.

cannot, of course, be made; he also suggests a practical response. He asks that we heal the wounds by the only means possible, prayer and penance. This is very comforting amidst the overwhelming sorrow of such things. We are not helpless, we can pray for the victims and victimizers, and the whole culture that produced both. And we can find some penances that we can incorporate into our lives.

People tend to think of gigantic things when the word "penance" appears: a life without pleasure and a continual infliction of physical pain. No wonder they shrink. But, of course, penance is meant to be the acceptance of life's natural frustrations, an acceptance of joy and deliberate sacrifice to God. We don't get angry when things go wrong or despondent, we smile and accept the annoyance as a penance. This is within anybody's grasp. And it's such a joy to know that the depressing things in our lives, and the painful, can all become positive, little penances offered for the great needs of the Church.

You have great blessings coming from your family. At the heart of it all is lovely Monica, who nurtures you spiritually as well as physically. Please remind her that she has to curb your instinctive urge toward more work!

Very much love always,
Sister Wendy

Sister Wendy and I were continuously saddened by the currents of vilification against Pope Francis from certain sectors of the Church. This rose to a new level with the publication of an open letter by Italian archbishop Carlo Maria Viganò, the former papal nuncio to the United States, who called on the pope to resign. Eventually he would not only accuse the pope of forming an alliance with Satan but praise Donald Trump as an instrument of God for the salvation of civilization.

September 8, 2018

Dearest Robert,

Please pray because we have a sick sister and of course the illness of one is a grief to all.

The community is a small symbol of the Mystical Body, and in these times when the Church is so beleaguered one realizes one's responsibility to this body. Is there any way you can move the bishops to express their support of the Holy Father? Perhaps there are voices all over the Church speaking out, but all I have heard is the disloyal criticism of that ex-ambassador archbishop. I'm sure he feels he is acting out of the purest motives, but for those who read what he says it is very saddening.

Love and prayer, dearest Robert,
Sister Wendy

————————

September 10, 2018

Dearest Sister Wendy,

Of course I am horribly depressed about the battles going on in the church. The day when Archbishop Viganò wrote that letter I could think of nothing else. It appalls me that this kind of thing should be carried out by people who supposedly love the church. The result will be more cynicism. Meanwhile, most of the U.S. bishops are keeping their mouths shut. There are some who have immediately jumped on this to challenge the pope; a few of those closest to him have risen to his defense; but most of them are quiet.

I don't know why I am so tired. This will pass, I'm sure.

————————

September 12, 2018

Dearest Robert,

My poor dear Robert: everybody knows why you're so tired except you! But what can one do? You are driven by the Spirit to work yourself to a state of exhaustion and I can't see that exhortations to do less would have any effect. So I can only pray that that same Spirit supports you in your great work—and it is a great work, both at Orbis and in your books and in your speaking. With so few voices raised in defense of our faith, which includes a reverence for the Holy Father, you give precious witness.

Isn't it baffling, though, that there isn't an outcry from all the bishops of the Church to support him? There will always be some few muddled people, wounded men, who don't realize that they are re-enacting the role of the Pharisees and Sanhedrin. But where are all the others? The good sensible bishops? The pope must feel very alone. The wounds that the Church is suffering now are such a very loud call to greater love and prayer and sacrifice. I feel so blessed to have been given a vocation where I can respond without hindrance.

Sr. Elizabeth Johnson

I had sent Sister Wendy a new book by Sr. Elizabeth Johnson, a brilliant feminist theologian. In Creation and the Cross[9] *she offers a critical analysis of St. Anselm's famous "atonement" model of Christ's salvific sacrifice on the Cross. In a creative twist, she imitated Anselm's device of a dialogue with a fellow monk—in her case, a dialogue with a graduate student named "Clara." Her larger point was to expand the understanding of salvation to encompass all of God's creation.*

I've started Sister Elizabeth Johnson's book and I can't tell you how impressed and rejoiced I am to be in contact with such great intelligence—true intelligence, with humor and insight and spiritual wisdom at its heart. I must say I love clever people. But she's more than learned and clever; she has an exceptional depth of mind. I also think that her adoption of St. Anselm's method of question and answer works brilliantly. It's charming, quite apart from useful.

Please never feel you have to write to me or that I mind at all when you don't. I just want to know, in the context of your over-work and lack of stamina (relatively speaking), that all is well.

Very much love to you and to Monica,
Sister Wendy

———

In light of her enjoyment of Elizabeth Johnson's book, I wondered if Sister Wendy was aware of the "Kafkaesque scrutiny" Johnson had received at the hands of the Doctrinal Committee of the U.S. bishops. And now the chief theologian behind this investigation had recently accused the pope himself of heresy. I sent her a copy of my latest letter to Pope Francis.

September 14, 2018

Dearest Robert,

I am now half-way through Sister Elizabeth's book. Once again I had a question I wish Clara had put, and I was all set to expatiate on this, but

---

9. Elizabeth Johnson, *Creation and the Cross: The Mercy of God for a Planet in Peril* (Maryknoll, NY: Orbis Books, 2018).

your blood-chilling account of Sister Elizabeth's treatment by the Inquisition makes me feel I want to do nothing but love and support her. Mind you, I think my queries are supportive because I just wanted there to be more breadth and explanation in what she said. But I feel now I must support her with prayer and admiration only. It seems an incredible story, and if it were anyone else but you telling it I would think there was some exaggeration here. How can this possibly be?

One's heart aches for Pope Francis with these misguided and unintelligent men on all sides of him. I still feel very much that one would like to hear cries of support coming from his bishops, rather than, as far as I know, a silence. That he is betrayed and condemned should not really surprise us. In fact Sister Elizabeth can feel grateful that Our Lord has singled her out to share His condemnation and sentence. What a wonderful thing. She has not just danced happily along a path of flowers, with the sun shining; she has dragged her great truth painfully through the darkness. Your book has a little picture of her on the back and that large confident presence is so inviting. I am glad that my small mind can hang on to her coattails.

Your latest letter to Pope Francis is so beautiful that I hope it really does get to the pope because it will console him.

Today is the commemoration of the finding of the Holy Cross. I feel so weighted by what you have told me that I feel he has given me a tiny little finding of my own today.

With love and joy and gratitude,
Sister Wendy

September 16, 2018

Dearest Sister Wendy,

I am working hard on my "new" book on saints. In a way it is summing up much of what I have learned over the past twenty years since I first wrote *All Saints*. But it is coming hard for me. For every productive writing session I have hours and days of excruciating indolence. Much of my creative work seems to go on under the surface—even when I am sleeping. And then suddenly it all seems to come out.

Yesterday I finished a chapter on women saints: why the church so often forces them to conform to certain stereotypical definitions; how their lives are so often marked by creativity, audacity, inventiveness in charting a new path beyond the categories available in their time. The same is true for many male saints—but at least they didn't have to overcome restrictions on the proper "place of men," and God's will for their gender.

I shared with Sister Elizabeth that you are reading her book with enjoyment (she is a fan, who knows you from your BBC programs) and she was very curious to know your questions.

September 18, 2018

Dearest Robert,

I am touched and pleased that so great a woman as Sister Elizabeth should be aware of me. I finished her book, overwhelmed with its lyrical image of the whole world redeemed, with the frogs and the finches and the foxes all praising God. Only when I put it down did I think about the fleas. The fleas and the mosquitoes and the bedbugs and the lice: I am sure they do praise God, but are we not entitled to diminish their numbers when possible? I was thinking how everything created eats something else created, and one can see how nature allows for this. I have a nasty sentimental streak that makes me want to shrink from this aspect of nature, but it is real and must be accepted. So with the praise goes much cruelty, innocent cruelty.

I pray for you with your many calls to preach the Gospel and the many different outlets in which that preaching has to occur. Please remind Monica that she must prevent you from too much zeal.

  With love and gratitude,
  Sister Wendy

September 18, 2018

Dearest Sister Wendy,

I think you raise good points. Especially about the mosquitos. Monica loves to watch nature programs on television, but she always cries out, "Why do they have to show them eating each other!" We saw a nature film that brought this out very clearly—it was about a particular seal and a particular polar bear, both of them facing starvation. You so want the polar bear to live, yet you realize that means eating the adorable seal. In this case, the seal's "aunt" sacrifices herself to save her niece, but that may just mean saving her for another day. Meanwhile, you see the receding arctic ice that imperils both the polar bear and the seal....

Teilhard had a good sense of the destruction and trauma that is part of evolution and the circle of life. Life and death are always so closely connected.

———————

I mentioned how Pope Francis says that in the face of baseless accusations, one should keep silent; the accuser wants to be the center of attention and any reply just pumps him up. I also commented on the mystic, St. Catherine of Genoa, who believed that purgatory is a very hopeful idea since it refers to the ongoing purification we must undergo to be stripped of our sins, our imperfections, our selfishness, before we are capable of bearing direct exposure to the divine love.

September 20, 2018

Dearest Robert,

I must advise Monica very strongly to be careful of nature programs. It's very hard for people like her and me to gaze uninterruptedly on the kind of nature that we enjoy which is sweet and beautiful. This is because nature is actually not sweet and beautiful. It is cruel and a decent program has to show this.

I am utterly with our dear Pope in his attitude to accusations. Pope Francis never disappoints, does he? His spontaneous reaction always seems to be that of Jesus.

Incidentally, although I am absolutely with you about our need for purification before we can look into the face of God, it has always seemed to me that intense purification will take place in the moment of death. Isn't that when we do see Him? And won't we be filled with anguished contrition over our wasted chances to love? Let alone our active blockings of love. Obviously the anguish will be proportionate to the depth of our sinfulness; but I have never seen it as lasting beyond that encounter. After His purity has burnt away our impurity, we are one with the good thief, with Him today in paradise.

Love to you and Monica,
Sister Wendy

———————

On October 11, Sister Lesley wrote to "friends and family" to share the news that "Sister Wendy's health seems to be deteriorating." Doctors had determined that her difficulty with breathing was not some kind of infection. "This means that Sister Wendy is now in pain, though not intense, and feels unwell. She points out that this is inevitable, and is something to thank God for. I don't feel there's any immediate anxiety, but life is certainly more difficult for her. She has less energy and muscle control and life is a struggle, even though it is one that she accepts with all her heart as from God."

I received this message while at the Frankfurt Book Fair in Germany. Writing to Sister Lesley, I noted: "Being as relatively close as I am, let me say that if Sister Wendy wanted to see me, I would move mountains and come right away. I suspect she would not encourage that. But please let her know that I make that offer quite genuinely. PLEASE convey to her my love and concern over her sufferings. I know she welcomes whatever God sends her, but I hope it is not too hard."

Sister Lesley replied:

> *Dearest Robert,*
>
> *I read your message to Sister Wendy and she was very touched. She is best off in silence, struggling to preserve her energies, but she holds you in her heart and believes very much in your great apostolate. She says to tell you not to overwork!*
>
> *With love and prayers to both you and Monica,*
> *Sister Lesley*

I replied: "I am praying every day for Sister Wendy. Please pass along my love, and if she is in a position to appreciate this please share the cover of my new book (not out until next spring) and tell her that I am dedicating it to her and Monica."

To my surprise, I received a quick reply from Sister Wendy.

November 9, 2018

Dearest Robert,

What a beautiful book yours will be. I feel deeply honored at a gift I don't deserve, to be with Monica on the front page. I'm struggling, but I'm not as close to the Fullness as I had hoped. So don't worry about me, dearest Robert; remember I feel this life is already heaven and I live in bliss.

> Very much love and gratitude to my dearest Robert,
> Sister Wendy

———

November 9, 2018

Dearest Sister Wendy,

I realized today that it was exactly a year ago that Monica and I arrived at Quidenham. How much I treasure that memory. And it was the opportunity to lead that retreat that really gave me the outline for my new book.

Next week I am going to Denver where Fr. Bill is hosting an exhibition of his icons. I know he joins me in praying every day for your continued bliss.

With love,
Robert

————

November 10, 2018

Dearest Robert,

I can hardly wait to see your book! In fact anything you write has the warmth of the Holy Spirit in it. So you not only are close to Our Lord, but you show it and you share it. How wonderful for you and Monica.

My happy downward path continues, but I haven't the energy to describe it. Please give my love to Father Bill and say his gift of the Holy Mass is very precious to me.

Lovingly,
Sister Wendy

P.S. One of the unfortunate consequences of this decline is that I don't find it as easy to read as I used to. That's a small sacrifice to make to Our Lord who sacrificed infinitely more.

————

On November 21, 2018, Sister Lesley wrote me: "Sister Wendy continues to weaken physically, but she is still reading voraciously and lively in mind and heart. She was so moved that you dedicated your new book to Monica and her. That meant very much to her. It is a privilege to be the silent witness of correspondence between you and Sister Wendy. You have brought a new dimension and vision into our cloistered lives of prayer. Thank you for all you are doing to promote justice and compassion in the world. Your books and your work speak truth and give us all hope, joy, and courage. I wish I had time to read all you publish!"

————

My last word from Sister Wendy was a general letter addressed to all her friends.

December 1, 2018

This is not a bulletin from Sister Lesley but from me. I know you will be sad but I hope also very happy for me that I am close to death. I can't walk or manage without the help of one or two sisters or more. So this isn't right for the community. I've said this to the prioress and she has found a care home very close to the monastery. Of course, the big sacrifice is the Mass but if God wants that sacrifice I give it gladly. Because it's so close, Fr. Stephen himself or a sister will bring me Holy Communion every day, and Lesley will have her machine, though I've not got much energy or mental clarity, so you may not get answers. This will not be for lack of love because I value each of you so much for your goodness.

When the day comes I want you to turn to God with great thankfulness for all He has given me. This is the time of the deepest joy. Speaking to you myself, though there isn't much breath, gives me a chance to ask you to pray for Sister Lesley, who has been such a wonderful carer. I don't think there could be a better, so I am very grateful to her and she's a very dear friend and your prayers will make that clear, and I hope be a solace to her.

With love to all people whom I feel close to and am blessed by knowing.

Most lovingly,
Sister Wendy

P.S. How embarrassing it will be and depressing if the Lord works a miracle, and I don't die after all!

In reply, I sent my last letter to Sister Wendy.

December 2, 2018

Dearest Sister Wendy,

I am very happy for any word from you, though please don't strain yourself to reply, even if you are able.

You know that you are in my heart and my prayers, even when you don't hear from me. I have been tossed about with travel and deadlines—and finishing my book, *A Living Gospel*, which was very much inspired by my trip to Quidenham, and thus is appropriately dedicated to you.[10]

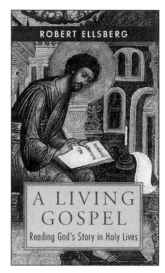

In October, when I heard that your health was declining, Monica said I should go and visit you again. But, of course, I knew that this would only be an intrusion on your peace. It was a blessing to be able to meet and embrace you, but everything we needed to say to each other has already been expressed, and what remains does not need words or physical presence.

I remember your wordless blessing, conferred from the balcony above the Chapel during Mass—it will follow me always.

I would have loved to share "your" book with you. I am attaching the first and the last chapters, which Sister Lesley can share with you if you are able, and if not, for her to share with the Sisters. The first chapter begins with a "credo" by Jorge Bergoglio (Pope Francis), written at the time of his ordination. It moves me deeply—especially when he says "I believe in my life story...." I think you would like to read that first page, if nothing else.

In the last chapter I reflect on what he has to say about a "journey faith"—how we encounter God along the path.

One of God's great gifts, through our friendship, is that you have encouraged me to reflect on the encounter with God in my "life story," as well as the path that we have shared.

Whatever comes next, I know that our hearts have touched, and thus that the small part of me that lives in you will soon accompany you to Paradise. I apologize if that is not theologically sound.

Monica and I plan to marry in January.

My children are well. Christina is thriving at the seminary; she is painting icons, and we have so much to talk about. Nicholas and his wife (and dog) are moving to California, where he has new job opportunities. Catherine is undertaking doctoral studies in Paris.

So all is well, and you needn't have any worries about me.

Here is the last paragraph of Bergoglio's "Credo":

---

10. *A Living Gospel: Reading God's Story in Holy Lives* (Maryknoll, NY: Orbis Books, 2019).

And I believe in the surprise of each day, in which will be manifest love, strength, betrayal, and sin, which will be always with me until that definitive encounter with that marvelous face which I do not know, which always escapes me, but which I wish to know and love.

If we speak again, I will be happy, but if not I know it is because you have achieved that definitive encounter with that marvelous face—which has always escaped you, but which you wish to know and love.

Peace and love, my dearest Sister,
Robert

P.S. The dedication reads:

To Monica and Sister Wendy

"It is true that those we meet can change us,
sometimes so profoundly that we are not the same afterwards,
even unto our names."
—Yann Martel, *The Life of Pi*

———————

And finally there came this message from Sister Lesley:

December 26, 2018

Dear Friends,
I was with our beloved Sister Wendy when she died peacefully early this afternoon, Wednesday, 26th December. Father Stephen anointed her on Sunday, and she was supported by your love and prayers.

With love,
Sister Lesley

EPILOGUE

Sister Wendy was happy to think that she would soon be forgotten. Her only wish was to point people toward God, and having done all that was asked of her, she was perfectly content to disappear. But that was not possible. Following her death, obituaries and tributes appeared in newspapers around the world, remembering, in the words of the *New York Times*, "a Roman Catholic nun who interrupted a cloistered life of prayer in 1991 and soared to international stardom with lyrical BBC documentaries that made her one of the most improbable art critics in television history."

That was the story that most people knew. But I wished that many others could know Sister Wendy as I had. Early in our exchange of emails she had pointed the way, encouraging the idea that our correspondence was perhaps intended for a greater purpose. This intuition bore early fruit, in the weeks after her death, when for the first time I read aloud all of this correspondence to Monica, causing her to exclaim, upon finishing: "Let's get married now!"

It was not Sister Wendy's hope that people would know *her* better. She had announced, early on, that communication "without a real purpose" was inconsistent with her vocation to solitude. One could argue that traveling around the world and starring in her own television series was also inconsistent with a life of solitude. She would not have disagreed, yet evidently that public exposure had a real purpose, and she must have concluded that the same was true of our extensive correspondence. In both cases, these were opportunities to talk about things that mattered. We began by talking about God and holiness. Gradually this expanded to talking about our lives and the way we could read God's presence in the things that happened to us and in the wider world. Ultimately, it was a conversation about the only thing that matters: learning to receive God's love and to reflect it back to the world.

As I reread our letters, following Sister Wendy's death, I thought of the conversation between St. Augustine and his mother Monica that occurred only days before her own death. The conversation had centered on the happiness of the saints in heaven. And as the "flame of love burned stronger" between them, Augustine wrote, their thoughts had "ranged over the whole compass of

material things in their various degree, up to the heavens themselves, from
which the sun and the moon and the stars shine down upon the earth."

Oblivious of the passage of time, Augustine says that they had continued their ascent, "longing and straining" for the Eternal Wisdom, until it
seemed "for one fleeting instant we reached out and touched it." Alas, such
moments melt away when we try to grasp them. So it was for Augustine and
his mother, who returned "with a sigh" to "the sound of our own speech, in
which each word has a beginning and an ending."

Well, my exchanges with Sister Wendy were not exactly like that.
Maybe it was not really like that for Augustine either, as he remembered his
last conversation with the mother who had shed so many tears over her er-
rant son. Yet in our lively and affectionate exchanges, which touched on
"the whole compass of material things," including friendships, work, books
and art, the beauty of nature, the meaning of suffering, the language of
dreams, and reasons of the heart, it often seemed as if we were reaching toward something beyond ourselves.

In the year following Sister Wendy's death, so many things occurred
that seemed to walk off the pages of our correspondence. My book, *A Living
Gospel*, so inspired by our exchanges and by my talks at Quidenham, was
published. Aside from the dedication, which I had shared with her, I included in the acknowledgments a lengthy reflection on her contribution to
the book, quoting from a striking passage from one of her last letters.
About Thomas Merton and Henri Nouwen she wrote: "There is much self
deception and muddle in their lives and yet there is an unwavering concentration on God. I think many people would find this very encouraging—
that it's the direction that matters, the desire, and not the spiritual achievements, as it were."

Later that year, I was deeply moved to receive at last a reply from Pope
Francis to one of my many missives. "Dear brother," it began, "your letter
has consoled me much for the testimony of your life and your work. I ask the
Lord to keep on accompanying you in the way of faith and of service. I am
also happy about your 'friendship' with Dorothy Day and Thomas Merton.
. . . Thanks for praying for me. I promise to do the same for you. May Jesus
bless you and the Holy Virgin care for you. Fraternally, Francisco."

How happy this letter would have made Sister Wendy, and how she
would have smiled at his mention of our "friends," Dorothy and Merton!

There are so many things I would have liked to share with her. And then
came the year of COVID, when suddenly many people were forced to become involuntary hermits. While working from home for many months, I
posted reflections on the lessons of various spiritual teachers who elected

solitude, or had it imposed on them by circumstances. What kind of wisdom could they impart to "ordinary" people entering into this unfamiliar world? I wrote about Merton and Julian of Norwich and the desert monks, but also Thoreau, Anne Frank, and Nelson Mandela in his years of solitary confinement. All of these showed that what seemed like deprivation could open us up to vast interior realms, insight, moral and spiritual adventure to those who were willing to do the work. I wrote of the poet Emily Dickinson, another natural hermit, who wrote, "Some keep the sabbath by going to church—I keep it staying at home." Her poem concludes: "So instead of getting to heaven at last—I'm going all along." All these figures brought Sister Wendy's example to mind.

In the months of working from home, I began at last to edit this correspondence. As I did so I was constantly struck anew by Sister Wendy's insights, but also with wonder at all that she was sharing about herself. It was only after several readings that I began to note with particular interest her mysterious evolution on the subject of Thomas Merton. Here was someone who prided herself on never revising a single word. *Quod scripsi, scripsi*, she liked to say: What I have written I have written. Yet here she was not simply revising a word, but revising deeply rooted attitudes and judgments. Surely there was more going on here than had initially met the eye.

I noted the theme of her isolation and sense of "oddness" and detachment from other people, going back all the way to her early childhood (with the notable exception of a childhood companion, Val, whose offer of friendship had made her feel ennobled). I noted her experience of being something of a misfit in the novitiate, and her happy submission to the rule of her superior that she not speak to any fellow students at university (a rule her fellow nuns felt was "ridiculous"). Surely she was correct in discerning her true vocation in a life of solitude and prayer; no one could have been better suited for such a life.

Yet there was evidently more work for her to accomplish in her room without a view. William Blake wrote that we are put upon this earth for a short time "that we may learn to bear the beams of love." Sister Wendy never faltered in her love for God, but perhaps she was meant to see how such a calling might allow room for love in other forms.

My friendship with Sister Wendy affected me deeply. Our conversation felt like a continuation of conversations I would have wished to pursue with Dorothy Day, or with my mother. Or with God. Happily, though in a different form, that conversation is "going all along," even after her passing.

"*You know*," she said to me as we parted after our last meeting, "*for me this is heaven*."

BIOGRAPHICAL GLOSSARY

A number of important figures appeared frequently in my correspondence with Sister Wendy. For those in need of a formal introduction, these brief notes may be helpful.

Daniel Berrigan (1921–2016) was a Jesuit priest, a poet, and courageous peacemaker. He was arrested in 1968 as part of the Catonsville 9, a group of Catholics (including his brother, Philip, also a priest) who destroyed draft files with homemade napalm as a protest against the Vietnam War. He served several years in prison for this and later acts of civil disobedience, while also working with the homeless, terminal cancer patients, and those suffering with AIDS. He was the author of many books, including a play, *The Trial of the Catonsville 9,* numerous works on the vocation of peacemaking, and commentaries on scripture. I got to know him well during my years at the Catholic Worker, and went on to publish several books by and about him.

Dorothy Day (1897–1980) spent her youth as a journalist and activist allied with radical movements on behalf of labor and social justice. The turning point in her life came with her decision in 1927, following the birth of her daughter, to become a Catholic. This involved the separation from her partner in a "common law marriage," who would not consent to be legally married. She struggled to find some way to reconcile her faith with her commitment to the poor and oppressed. The answer came following her encounter with a Frenchman, Peter Maurin, who inspired her in 1933 to start a newspaper, *The Catholic Worker,* to promote the radical social message of the gospel. This led to a movement centered in "houses of hospitality," where she and her fellow Catholic Workers embraced voluntary poverty and practiced the Works of Mercy—feeding the hungry, sheltering the homeless. Her life was rooted in prayer and the sacraments, but she constantly worked for peace and social justice, along the way facing arrest on numerous occasions. She wrote several books, most notably, a memoir, *The Long Loneliness.* I joined her community in 1975 and served for two years as managing editor of her paper. After her death in 1980 I edited her *Selected Writings,* and later her diaries and letters, and at Orbis I published other books by and about her. For many years I worked with those promoting her cause for canonization.

Daniel Ellsberg (1931–), my father, was a defense analyst who became well known for his act of copying the Pentagon Papers, a top secret history of the Vietnam War, and providing that to the *New York Times* and other newspapers in 1971. His work first in the Defense Department, and then for two years in Vietnam, and finally in reading the Pentagon Papers, convinced him that the war was not merely a problem or a mistake but a crime to be resisted. His encounter with young men going to prison for resisting the draft and his reading of texts by Gandhi, Martin Luther King Jr., and Thoreau on "civil disobedience" raised the question of what he could do to help end the war if he was willing to go to jail. After the publication of the Papers, he was arrested and charged with twelve felonies, facing 115 years in prison. The charges were eventually dropped after revelations (in connection with the Watergate scandal) of illegal government actions. He continues to spend the rest of his life working for peace, especially to awaken awareness of the dangers of nuclear war. My life was deeply affected by these events and his influence—beginning with his request, when I was 13, that I help him copy the Pentagon Papers. I worked closely with him to help him write his two volumes of memoirs, *Secrets: A Memoir of Vietnam and the Pentagon Papers* and *The Doomsday Machine: Confessions of a Nuclear War Planner.*

Jim Forest (1941–2022), a peacemaker and prolific author, was my oldest friend—dating back to our first meeting when I was sixteen. Like me, he served as a young editor of *The Catholic Worker,* and later a cofounder of the Catholic Peace Fellowship. He went to prison for his part in destroying draft files as part of the Milwaukee 14. He later moved to Alkmaar, the Netherlands, to serve as general secretary of the International Fellowship of Reconciliation, and remained there after his retirement. He played a significant role in my decision to go to the Catholic Worker, and our close friendship stretched over many decades. At Orbis, I published more than a dozen of his books, including biographies of Dorothy Day, Thomas Merton, Daniel Berrigan, and Vietnamese Zen master Thich Nhat Hanh, all of whom he knew well. His memoir, *Writing Straight with Crooked Lines,* described these encounters as well as the spiritual path that led him and his wife to the Russian Orthodox Church, a story also reflected in his bestselling *Praying with Icons.* He died in 2022 after a long period of declining health.

Julian of Norwich (1342–1416) was an English mystic, largely known from her *Shewings*, or *Revelations of Divine Love,* her meditations on a series of mystical revelations of Christ's sufferings and God's love for creation, which marked the great turning point in her life. Otherwise, we know very little about her story—even her name was taken from the Church of St. Julian in Norwich, where she was enclosed in a cell attached to the church wall and spent the rest of her life as an anchoress. Sister Wendy frequently referred to her as one of her spiritual heroes. Not only did they share a calling to solitude and prayer (and in locations in the same region of England), but they shared similar spiritual outlooks. In Christ's passion on the cross, Julian saw an image of the depth of God's love for creation—a love so great that it overshadowed any preoccupation with sin. According to the most famous line in her book, "All shall be well, and all shall be well, and all manner of things shall be well."

William Hart McNichols (1949–) is a Catholic priest and icon painter who lives in New Mexico. His work, which draws on traditional iconographic conventions, focuses both on traditional Catholic and Orthodox saints along with Jesus and Mary, as well as contemporary icons of mystics, peacemakers (like Merton, Berrigan, and Dorothy Day), and other spiritual guides. I have published several volumes of his work at Orbis and count him as one of my closest friends. Sister Wendy, who always called him "Fr. Bill," had come to know and admire his work independently. They also exchanged letters, and in her last months she contemplated the ambitious notion of writing a book of her own commentaries on some of his icons.

Thomas Merton (1915–1968) was a Trappist monk and popular spiritual writer. He became well known in 1948 with the publication of his autobiography, *The Seven Storey Mountain,* in which he described his early life as "the complete twentieth-century man," who had tasted a life of freedom, excitement, and pleasure, only to reject it all as an illusion. His book concluded with his becoming a Catholic, and then, on the eve of World War II, joining the Trappist Abbey of Gethsemani in Kentucky, where he spent the rest of his life. That was only the beginning of an ongoing spiritual journey to grow ever deeper into the heart of his vocation. Following a spiritual "epiphany" in downtown Louisville, he turned increasingly from traditional works on prayer and contemplation to engagement with the outside world. He wrote scores of books, including reflections on racism, nuclear weapons, and the Vietnam War. In 1965 he received permission to take up life as a hermit on the monastery grounds, yet continued to maintain wide contacts with intellectuals, artists, poets, and activists around the world. He also pursued serious dialogue with people of other faiths, particularly Buddhism. In 1968 he was given permission to attend a conference on monasticism in Thailand. Along the way he met the Dalai Lama and other Asian monks and spiritual teachers. On December 10, after delivering his talk at the conference, he was found dead in his room, apparently having suffered a heart attack after an accidental electric shock.

Sister Wendy was an avid reader of Merton's works, including the many posthumously published editions of his letters and journals. She had complicated feelings about Merton, and as our correspondence unfolded the evolution of her feelings seemed to track closely with her own spiritual progress. Merton played a great role in my own life, and I often had occasion to write or speak about him. He was among the figures (including Dorothy Day) cited by Pope Francis in his address to a joint session of Congress in 2015.

Henri Nouwen (1932–1996) was a Dutch-born Catholic priest and spiritual writer who spent most of his life teaching and working in North America. In his books he shared deeply his own anxious and insecure personality and his search for community and a sense of "home." After exploring life in a Trappist monastery, working in the missions in Latin America, and teaching in a number of universities, he found his deep calling when he was invited to serve as chaplain to a L'Arche community in Ontario—living among handicapped adults, while continuing a steady stream of publications. Among his books was *Return of the Prodigal Son, Life of the Beloved,* and *Our Greatest Gift.* He died suddenly of a heart attack in 1996. I knew Henri well for the last twenty years of his life, and was working with him on his last book, *Adam: God's Beloved,* when he died. After his death I served for some years as a member of his Literary Trust, and I continued to write and speak about his life and spirituality. He was deeply inspired by Merton, and they were often compared, despite their significant differences.

ACKNOWLEDGMENTS

My correspondence with Sister Wendy was initially sparked by our shared devotion to many saints and spiritual masters, and though our exchanges gradually widened to include many other subjects, this cloud of witnesses always hovered in the background. They were eventually joined by the stories of many other people—friends, family members, and fellow travelers—who crossed our paths (particularly my path). Each of them played an important role in our conversation. In one of her prescient observations, Sister Wendy wrote, "Whenever you talk about a friend, I know we're going to be talking about God."

I am grateful to all those who appear in these pages, especially my children, Nicholas, Catherine, and Christina (who, since the time of this correspondence, has chosen to be identified as Lukey). I must also express deep thanks to those who read the manuscript in earlier drafts and offered helpful suggestions: especially Michelle Jones, Roger Lipsey, Jon Sweeney, and my beloved and now-departed friend Jim Forest. Father William Hart McNichols ("Fr. Bill," as Sister Wendy referred to him), offered the most extraordinary response by painting and sending me an original portrait of Sister Wendy: "To remind you that she is watching over you."

Portrait of Sister Wendy by
Fr. William Hart McNichols

My deep thanks to those who helped bring this project to completion, particularly Celine Allen, as much for her enthusiastic dedication as for her expert design and editorial oversight; my colleagues Maria Angelini and Bernadette Price; Regina Gelfer, for her beautiful cover; and Kelly Hughes, for her support with promotion.

Two others belong in an altogether different category, having served as witnesses, audience, and occasional chorus members for this entire story of "faith and friendship." The first is my wife Monica, to whom Sister Wendy assigned the role of "tender hawk," and whom she aptly recognized as the loving heart at the center of my world. The second person, to whom this book is dedicated, is Sister Lesley Lockwood.

Sister Lesley was more than a witness and facilitator to this exchange. Literally every word was either spoken aloud or written down by her. In many ways she became a silent—and in some cases not so silent—partner. Sister Wendy frequently referred to her presence, sometimes noting her nods of agreement or occasional protests, her own empathetic response to something I had written, or her sly expression of triumph when she and I were in agreement on some point. Occasionally, exercising her prerogative as amanuensis, she would insert her own comments or words of encouragement, and I was deeply grateful for her periodic updates on Sister Wendy's condition. Since the death of our beloved friend, I have been deeply grateful for Sister Lesley's ongoing presence in our lives—yet another one of Sister Wendy's enduring gifts.

Of course my deepest thanks must go to Sister Wendy herself. In the last years of her life, for reasons that remain somewhat mysterious, this singular and solitary lover of God chose to share her wisdom and herself with me. For such a gift, there is no better way to express my gratitude than to share it with others.

INDEX